Digital Orientations

Steve Jones
General Editor

Vol. 101

The Digital Formations series is part of the Peter Lang Media and Communication list.
Every volume is peer reviewed and meets
the highest quality standards for content and production.

PETER LANG
New York • Bern • Frankfurt • Berlin
Brussels • Vienna • Oxford • Warsaw

Shaun Moores

Digital Orientations

Non-Media-Centric Media Studies and Non-Representational Theories of Practice

PETER LANG
New York • Bern • Frankfurt • Berlin
Brussels • Vienna • Oxford • Warsaw

Library of Congress Cataloging-in-Publication Data
Names: Moores, Shaun, author.
Title: Digital orientations: non-media-centric media studies and
non-representational theories of practice / Shaun Moores.
Description: New York: Peter Lang, 2018.
Series: Digital formations; Vol. 101.
Includes bibliographical references and index.
Identifiers: LCCN 2017026103 | ISBN 978-1-4331-4564-3 (pbk.: alk. paper)
ISBN 978-1-4331-4566-7 (hardback: alk. paper)
ISBN 978-1-4331-4567-4 (ebook pdf)
ISBN 9781433145681 (epub) | ISBN 9781433145698 (mobi)
Subjects: LCSH: Digital media—Social aspects.
Classification: LCC HM851.M663 | DDC 302.23/1—dc23
LC record available at https://lccn.loc.gov/2017026103

Bibliographic information published by **Die Deutsche Nationalbibliothek**.
Die Deutsche Nationalbibliothek lists this publication in the "Deutsche
Nationalbibliografie"; detailed bibliographic data are available
on the Internet at http://dnb.d-nb.de/.

To my daughters,

Eve Atkinson and Ruby Atkinson

CONTENTS

PREFACE AND ACKNOWLEDGEMENTS

Like an earlier book of mine that was published back in 2000 (*Media and Everyday Life in Modern Society*), the present one is a selection of my previously published pieces, most of them appearing here in an extensively revised form, along with a newly authored introductory chapter in which I seek to advance a distinctive position. Therefore, *Digital Orientations: Non-Media-Centric Media Studies and Non-Representational Theories of Practice* can be viewed as a second volume of collected essays, written over a period of some 10 to 15 years. Whereas the first volume brought together research that I had carried out between the mid 1980s and the late 1990s, this book assembles a range of my academic writings produced from the beginning of the 2000s through to the middle of the current decade.

Taking a retrospective look now, across the whole 30 years and more since I started out in the field of media studies, I am able to see both continuities and shifts in my work. In some ways, then, following my initial empirical research projects, which were on the arrival of early radio and satellite television in household and neighbourhood cultures, it feels as though I have been doing much the same thing all along! This is because I find myself returning, again and again, to an interest in trying to grasp the significance of media uses, usually the uses of new media technologies, in broader circumstances of day-to-day living, and in that respect the two books of collected essays have quite a lot in common. With the benefit of hindsight, I realise that I have always had a non-media-centric perspective (rather unconventional for someone in media studies), in which *everyday actions and interactions are centred* so that media, with their special characteristics and affordances, can be investigated in this quotidian context. In other ways, though, the present volume of collected essays is quite different from the first. This is because, over the past few years, I have become increasingly interested in and engaged with phenomenological and non-representational approaches drawn from fields or disciplines in the wider humanities and social sciences, where careful attention is paid to the bodily knowledges and environmental experiences of inhabitants and, crucially, where *the primacy of practice or movement is asserted*. What these approaches have increasingly led me to question are particular foundational positions in my own field, where there has been a tendency, occasionally explicit but often implicit, to make assumptions about the primacy of representation, of the cognitive and the symbolic.

If my brief opening statements here appear to be rather abstract, I want to reassure readers that I am committed to discussing the key issues in an accessible way. I want the book to be readable not only for academics but also for students in media studies and neighbouring fields, because, despite the apparent negativity of those two non- prefixes in my book's subtitle, I am putting forward *a positive case that has been developed incrementally over time*, for a change of direction or at least a change of emphasis in my field. I think it would be fair to say that the existing academic literature with which I will be dealing in the pages ahead, particularly in the areas of phenomenology and non-representational theory, is not always the most immediately accessible or readable. However, given the importance of the challenges posed by this literature to traditional ways of doing media studies, my view is that these challenges deserve to be set out as straightforwardly as possible. What I hope, then, is that readers of this book will feel sufficiently engaged with my arguments and commentaries to go on and explore for themselves many of the writings that I cite, and to carry out their own non-media-centric research on the practical and experiential dimensions of day-to-day living.

In my ordering and reworking of (by cutting from and adding to) various pieces that originally appeared as separate publications, I have sought to create a coherent, unfolding narrative or storyline, and, where at all possible, a consistent style for the book as a whole.

As indicated above, Chapter 1 is newly authored for this volume, although I have been guided there in part by my notes for an opening keynote lecture,

'Arguments for a Non-Media-Centric, Non-Representational Approach to Media and Place', which I gave at the Media and Place Conference hosted in 2014 by Leeds Metropolitan University, England. I am grateful to two of the conference organisers, Lisa Taylor and Neil Washbourne, for having invited me to deliver that keynote, providing me with an opportunity to pull together different themes in my work and to set out a statement of my current position and research trajectory. More recently, in 2016, the case that I make in my introductory chapter for non-media-centric media studies and non-representational theories of practice was aired, thanks to an invitation from Thomas Tufte, in a talk given at the New Media, Everyday Life and Social Change International Seminar at Roskilde University in Denmark.

Chapter 2 is based on a piece from which it takes its title, published in 2008 in a book that I co-edited with Andreas Hepp and others, *Connectivity, Networks and Flows: Conceptualizing Contemporary Communications*. I am grateful to Hampton Press for granting me permission to make use of that previously published material. Much earlier versions of the material in this chapter were research papers given in 2003 and 2004 at the London School of Economics and Political Science, England (thanks to Nick Couldry for the invitation, and also to the late Roger Silverstone for his feedback), University of Rome 'La Sapienza' in Italy, where I was a visiting professor in its Department of Sociology and Communication during 2003, University of Milan 'Cattolica', again in Italy (thanks to Chiara Giaccardi), and the University of Melbourne in Australia, where I was an associate professor in its Media and Communications Programme and Faculty of Arts during 2004 and 2005.

Chapter 3 is based on an article of the same title that was published in 2006 in *Participations: Journal of Audience and Reception Studies*, vol. 3, no. 2 (available at http://www.participations.org along with a lengthy response from phenomenological geographer David Seamon). I am grateful to the journal's founding editor, Martin Barker, for confirming that I am free to draw on my article for this book. Versions of the material were used as a basis for invited talks given in 2006 and 2007 at Goldsmiths, University of London and at Newcastle University, both in England (thanks to David Morley and to Rachel Woodward). Some of the issues raised by the original article were discussed in two subsequent papers, 'Understanding Media Uses in/as Place-Making Practices', presented to the Centre for Research in Socio-Cultural Change Conference held in 2006 at the University of Oxford, England, and 'Media and Senses of Place: On Situational and Phenomenological Geographies', Media@LSE Electronic Working Paper no. 12, Department of Media and Communications, London School of Economics and Political Science, published in 2007 (available at http://www.lse.uk/collections/media@lse). The latter is the text of my inaugural professorial lecture delivered in 2007 at the University of Sunderland, England.

Chapter 4 is based on an article entitled 'That Familiarity with the World Born of Habit: A Phenomenological Approach to the Study of Media Uses in Daily Living', which was published in 2009 in *Interactions: Studies in Communication and Culture*, vol. 1, no. 3, pp. 301–312. I am grateful to the publisher, Intellect, for allowing authors to make use of their own articles in later collections of their work. This piece was based, in turn, on a plenary paper given at the Transforming Audiences Conference hosted in 2009 by the University of Westminster, England, and I would also like to record my gratitude to David Gauntlett, one of the conference's organisers, who invited me to speak at that event. In part, too, I am drawing on a subsequent paper, 'Embodiment, Orientation and Habitation: On Merleau-Ponty and Everyday Media Use', which, thanks to an invitation from André Jansson, was presented to the Online Territories Colloquium at Uppsala University in Sweden in 2010.

Chapter 5 is based on two articles that I co-authored with Monika Metykova, '"I Didn't Realize How Attached I Am": On the Environmental Experiences of Trans-European Migrants', *European Journal of Cultural Studies*, vol. 13, no. 2, pp. 171–189, which was published in 2010, and 'Knowing How to Get Around: Place, Migration and Communication', *The Communication Review*, vol. 12, no. 4, pp. 313–326, published in 2009. I am grateful to Monika for granting me permission to draw on our jointly produced writings, and to Sage Publications and Routledge, respectively, for allowing authors to make use of their own articles in later collections of their work. Earlier versions of the material in these articles were first used for invited research seminar papers given in 2008 and 2009 at the University of Leeds, England (thanks to David Bell), the University of Stirling, Scotland (thanks to Stephanie Marriott), and the University of Bremen, Germany, where I was a visiting professor in its Faculty of Cultural Studies during 2009, as well as for an opening plenary paper that I gave at the Media, Communication and Cultural Studies Association 2009 Annual Conference, hosted by the University of Bradford, England, and the National Media Museum. I would like to thank Mark Goodall and Ben Roberts, the main organisers of that subject association conference, for inviting me to deliver the paper.

Chapter 6 is based on an article of the same title that was published in 2015 in *Mobilities*, vol. 10, no. 1, pp. 17–35. Again, I am grateful to Routledge for allowing authors to make use of their own articles in later collections of their work. This piece was based, in turn, on a paper given at the Association of American Geographers 2012 Annual Meeting in New York City in the United States, where I was pleased to be able to share a platform with communication geographer Paul Adams, and a version was also presented as an invited lecture at the Dutch-language Free University of Brussels in Belgium in 2013 (thanks to Kevin Smets). The chapter draws, too, on my 'Loose Ends: Lines, Media and Social Change', Media Anthropology Network e-Seminar Paper no. 40, European Association of Social Anthropologists, published in 2012 (available at http://www.media-anthropology.net with a full record of the online discussion that followed, including exchanges with Nick Couldry, Sarah Pink and others on the relevance or otherwise of non-representational theories). I would like to thank media anthropologist John Postill for the invitation to contribute to that online seminar series, and also Tim Ingold, for a much appreciated private response to the piece's critical engagement with his writings on lines, dwelling and modern living. Although I have some specific difficulties with Ingold's work, which are detailed in the chapter, in my view he is the most eloquent current advocate of non-representational theory.

Chapter 7 was originally published in 2014 as an article of the same title, co-authored with Zlatan Krajina and David Morley, in the *European Journal of Cultural Studies*, vol. 17, no. 6, pp. 682–700. The text is largely unchanged, apart from a few minor edits and a few inserted words such as the brief linking section which I have added at the end. I am grateful to Zlatan and Dave for granting me permission to include our jointly written piece, and, again, to Sage Publications for allowing authors to make use of their articles in later collections of their work. This article grew out of an academic panel discussion on non-media-centric media studies that was organised and chaired by Zlatan at the University of Zagreb in Croatia in 2013, in which Dave and I were the invited participants and our audience was made up predominantly of staff and students from the university's Department of Media and Journalism and the wider Faculty of Political Science. Some of the arguments that I contributed to the discussion had been rehearsed in an invited research seminar paper given at Karlstad University in Sweden in 2012 (thanks again to André Jansson).

Chapter 8 shares its main title, 'Digital Orientations', with that of the book as a whole and is based on an article from which the longer chapter title is taken. The piece was published in 2014 in *Mobile Media and Communication*, vol. 2, no. 2, pp. 196–208, and I acknowledge Sage Publications once more for allowing authors to make use of their own articles in later collections of their work. A first version of this material was presented as a keynote paper at the Conditions of Mediation International Communication Association Preconference held in 2013 at Birkbeck, University of London, England. I am grateful to the event's organisers, Tim Markham and Scott Rodgers, for their invitation to what was an invigorating day of discussions about phenomenology, media and contemporary social life. For me, this was also a welcome opportunity to meet up with a former lecturer from my undergraduate days in the School of Communication at the Polytechnic of Central London, England (now the University of Westminster), a leading media phenomenologist and fellow keynote panellist, Paddy Scannell, who had been working in the United States for several years. Subsequent versions of my paper were given as invited talks in 2013 and 2014 at the Centre for Advanced Academic Studies in Dubrovnik, Croatia (thanks again to Zlatan Krajina), at the University of Antwerp, Belgium (thanks again to Kevin Smets and also to Philippe Meers), and at the University of East Anglia, England (thanks to Michael Skey). A number of the issues raised were discussed in a later paper entitled 'The Finger's Journey: Piano Lessons for Media Researchers', which was an invited presentation to the Mobile Media Conference hosted by the University of Siegen in Germany in 2014. I am grateful to its principal organiser Tristan Thielmann, for inviting me to speak at that event alongside some distinguished mobilities and media researchers such as Monika Büscher, Larissa Hjorth and Christian Licoppe.

    In addition, it is important for me to offer just a few further acknowledgements. One of these is addressed generally to past and present members of the University of Sunderland's Centre for Research in Media and Cultural Studies (CRMCS), which was founded by my former colleague John Storey in 2000 and has been my academic home over the period in which the majority of the pieces that feed into this book were written. I feel fortunate to have been part of a strong community of academic colleagues and postgraduate students at CRMCS (particularly when the wider context was a challenging one). Indeed, following the submission that I led on behalf of CRMCS to the last national assessment of research quality in British universities (Research Excellence Framework 2014), a quarter of our work overall was judged by the subject panel to be in the top category of world-leading research and more than half of the rest was rated internationally excellent, and this was by some considerable distance the strongest result secured by any of the submissions from our university. I must give specific thanks to Julia Knight, CRMCS's current director, for negotiating a reduction of my teaching and marking duties during 2016 and early 2017, thereby facilitating the book's preparation, and especially to my good colleague Barbara Sadler, who took on a number of those duties. Justin Battin and Eve Forrest also deserve a special mention as two of my successful research students at CRMCS who each worked, in their own distinctive ways, with a non-media-centric perspective and with phenomenological and non-representational approaches (Justin focusing on mobile media technologies in their everyday contexts of use, and Eve researching digital photographic practice and its associated habitual movements).

On a more personal note, I would like to express my gratitude to an old friend, Mark Hammonds. Mark and I got to know each other as long ago as 1984, when he was studying for a degree in philosophy at the London School of Economics and Political Science and I was taking my rather less prestigious course in media studies at the Polytechnic of Central London. We shared a house during our final undergraduate year, at the end of which both of us gained first-class honours. Now living back in his native North East of England, Mark has recently helped me through some difficult times and that support is much appreciated.

Last but certainly not least, I am grateful to my series editor, Steve Jones from the University of Illinois at Chicago in the United States, who has provided this book project with a good publishing home. From the outset, when I initially sent him an outline proposal, Steve has shown great interest in the project, and I can only hope that what follows will live up to his high expectations.

SM
Hexham and Sunderland, 2017

· 1 ·

NON-MEDIA-CENTRIC MEDIA STUDIES AND NON-REPRESENTATIONAL THEORIES OF PRACTICE

Why is this book called *Digital Orientations*?

The main title of my book is intended to be a playful (and to some extent a provocative) one, but it has a serious purpose. Let me try to explain.

Nowadays in media studies, and in broader public discourses concerning media, *digital* is quite a commonly used word. It is not only the first term in the title of this book but also in the name of the series, 'Digital Formations', in which my book follows a large number of earlier volumes, many of them featuring the word in their titles. Media studies academics and students, along with other groups ranging from lay media practitioners to professionals in the media industry, can be heard talking about *digital media*, by which they tend to mean those new media technologies that are associated with the development of the internet and contemporary mobile communication systems. Of course, in addition, it is important to note how, in a period of rapid technological change and media convergence, the older, more established media such as newspapers, radio and television are often available in digital forms too. Indeed, some readers of the text that I am currently writing will no doubt be accessing it via an e-book format, rather than having a printed and bound copy of the more traditional sort.

In part here, I am using the word digital in that now generally accepted way, and in my role as a media studies academic I obviously take an interest in the capacities and applications of various media technologies, both new and old.[1] At the same time, however, I point in this book to what I call the *doubly digital* quality of most media today (see especially Chapter 8), partly employing that term digital in a different, less commonly articulated sense which readers will perhaps find a bit odd to begin with. This second sense of the word, for me, has to do with the seemingly mundane and insignificant observation that media technologies, including those electronic and digital media which offer virtually instantaneous communications at a distance, still tend to be operated by hand. Their uses typically involve deft, skilful movements of the human fingers or *digits*, hence my other, overlapping definition of digital media as *manual media*. Think of the hands that move at speed across a computer keyboard or the sliding and tapping of fingers on the touch-screens of contemporary smart-phones and tablets. Think also of how television viewers manipulate remote-control devices to change the channel or alter the volume, and of how readers have traditionally leafed through the pages of a book, newspaper or magazine (interestingly, the designers of some touch-screen technologies have sought to simulate this page-turning manual activity).

Why, though, am I choosing to highlight, and thereby claim significance for, such ordinary, everyday practices? Surely the field of media studies, or even the subfield of new media research, has far weightier, more important matters to consider? My answers to those questions will emerge indirectly, bit by bit, in the course of the book as a whole, but at this stage I am going to have just an initial, quick go at tackling them head on, with a view to opening up the discussion of non-media-centric media studies and non-representational theories of practice that follows in this introductory chapter.

The first thing I want to say here about the notion of the doubly digital is that it helps to resist any temptation to make new media technologies themselves, interesting as they might be, the sole or even the main focus of attention (this is the provocative or mischievous element of my case concerning the digital). My aim is for that notion to shift attention, instead, onto routine practices of media use and, further still, onto a wider range of everyday actions and interactions within which these media uses are embedded. In addition, it serves to emphasise the necessarily *embodied* character of media use and, more generally, of routine social activity. Contrary to the kind of claims that were frequently made, in the early days of internet use, about the disembodiment of self-presentations and social relations in cyberspace, my notion of the doubly digital points to bodily practices or movements as crucial for what happens online, and, broadening the argument a little, it points to the necessary interconnections between online and offline environments.[2] Moving through so-called virtual worlds is typically dependent on the skilful movement of digits, as they press on keys, screens, touch-pads or mouse devices, and such movements have to be understood, too, in the context of the larger time-space rhythms of day-to-day living. Very much following on from this, the brief examples that I have given of hand and finger movement at least begin to suggest the relevance for media studies of researching forms of tacit, practical know-how in quotidian cultures (abilities that are often difficult to put into words), and of investigating the paths along which media users and others knowledgeably feel their ways, habitually yet responsively, through everyday environments of different sorts.[3] Such knowing is especially interesting, in my view, because it is so intimately bound up with doing. It is a bodily knowledge in movement.

Continuing with my initial answers to those questions that I have posed myself, this feeling-a-way-along-and-through brings me to the next term which appears in my book's main title, *orientations*. In the pages ahead (particularly from Chapter 4 onwards), I will be proposing that matters of orientation ought to become far more central to the concerns of media studies in the future.[4] A fundamental feature of everyday environmental experience is, as social anthropologist Tim Ingold (2000, p. 219) puts it, the ability 'to know where one is' and 'the way to go', or what he calls 'skills of orientation and wayfinding'. Of course, there may be occasional, temporary experiences of disorientation, when, say, someone feels completely lost in strange surroundings, but for the most part humans (and many other animals) move through worlds which they find to be familiar and which they know how to get around with ease. According to Ingold (2000, p. 219): 'Ordinary life would be well-nigh impossible if we did not.' Again, as with my observation that media technologies tend to be manually operated, readers might regard Ingold's statements here to be rather mundane and therefore insignificant. His response to that accusation, I think, and mine too, would be that it is often the most ordinary features of everyday lives, the things that are rarely a focus of attention as people perform their routine activities, which actually turn out to be of great importance for the basic ordering and reproduction of the social. Knowing the way to go when negotiating familiar environments, or being able to apply established skills of orientation in adapting to new environmental conditions, might be understood as a key element of what sociologist Anthony Giddens

(1984, p. xxiii) refers to as 'practical consciousness', which he distinguishes from 'discursive consciousness' and which ensures that people do not have to relearn, over and over, day after day, 'how to "go on"' in the daily round.[5] Try to imagine how well-nigh impossible, and how utterly draining, it would be to have to do that.

To illustrate further the significance of finding ways about, I should say something briefly here concerning the link between orientation and habitation (and it is a link that I will return to at several stages later in the book). By *habitation*, I mean the process and experience of inhabiting a world, which certain philosophers and geographers (for example, Heidegger, 1993 [1971]; Seamon, 2015 [1979]), as well as Ingold (2000, 2011) in anthropology, have also termed 'dwelling'.[6] My argument is that skilfully moving around and negotiating environments, at different geographical scales ranging from that of a computer keyboard or smart-phone screen to that of, for instance, a complex contemporary transport system, is crucial for habitation or for constituting place by making oneself at home in everyday worlds. This is a theme that I will be exploring not just conceptually but empirically and descriptively too (see, in particular, Chapters 5 and 8).

Non-media-centric media studies: A contradiction in terms?

In my attempt, above, to explain the playfully serious main title of my book, I wrote about the importance of the notion of the doubly digital firstly in terms of its potential to shift the focus away from media themselves, so as to pay more attention to everyday social activities (including, but not limited to, routine practices of media use). My reason for wanting to re-imagine the objects of study for media studies, in this specific way, is a conviction I have that media and their uses must not be considered in isolation from a range of other quotidian technologies and activities, since their embedding in the day-to-day contributes significantly to their meaningfulness. What might this type of investigation be called, then? Following David Morley (2007, 2009; see also Moores, 2012, pp. 103–110), I want to call it a form of *non-media-centric media studies* (and see Chapter 7, in which Morley and I are involved in a fuller discussion of that label and its associated perspective).

I do accept that such a cumbersome name may appear to many readers, on the face of it, to be *a contradiction in terms*. After all, the idea of media studies certainly seems to suggest an academic field in which media are the central object of study, *so how can media studies possibly be non-media-centric?* For me, though, one of the fundamental problems with this field that I was a student in, and have subsequently taught and researched in for over 30 years now, is precisely that *its emphasis has tended to be too much on media*. I have been arguing openly for quite a while that it is necessary to challenge any idea 'that media studies are simply about "studying media"' (Moores, 2005, p. 3), insisting 'they should not be', and I therefore agree with Morley (2007, p. 200) when he states that 'we need to "de-centre" the media in our analytical framework, so as to understand better the ways in which media processes and everyday life are interwoven with each other'.[7]

Looking back, I am able to see that my own work, from the initial, historical research that I did on broadcasting's entry into the domestic sphere (Moores, 1988) right through to my recent writings on media uses as matters of orientation and as manual activities (see Chapters 6 and 8), has been centrally concerned with *everyday lives and habits*. In that work, I have always sought to de-centre media by situating media and their uses in relation to many other things and practices, from household furnishings through to the playing of musical instruments, performing handicraft tasks or going for a walk. Retrospectively, I realise that what I have been up to all along is a kind of non-media-centric media studies, even if I had not always realised that this is what I was up to whilst I was doing it and whilst I did not, at least until the last few years, have a name to give to it.

Of course, I am not claiming to be the only one in my field who has been employing a non-media-centric perspective. There are other academics in media and cultural studies whose work could also, I feel, be put into this category retrospectively. A few of them are referred to later in the book (see especially Chapter 7), and the recent work of Zlatan Krajina (2014), one of my co-authors here, can be regarded as part of a new generation of non-media-centric media studies. Still, it is Morley's research that provides the most sustained illustration of the tradition which he goes on to name. For example, his classic study of television viewing in family contexts (Morley, 1986; see also Morley, 1992, pp. 138–158), in which he spoke at length with members of selected households in London, turned out to be far less about television than it was about social relationships in families and different meanings of home, dealing with wider issues that had to do with the gendered organisation of domestic labour and leisure, and connecting with certain feminist critical approaches (see, for instance, Hobson, 1980; Radway, 1984). In a commentary on this study that I offered many years ago, I asked, in a sympathetic manner, whether television viewing was in fact 'just one of several possible ways in' (Moores, 1993, p. 54) to the analysis of domestic power and interaction. There, I drew a number of parallels between Morley's investigation and that carried out in the same period by sociologists Nickie Charles and Marion Kerr (1988), whose alternative way in was via food and eating habits in families but whose research findings were remarkably similar (although they appear to have been unaware of Morley's work in media studies). I went on to argue 'that we should welcome a blurring, or overlapping, of research on audiences with wider studies of…consumption, technology and everyday life' (Moores, 1993, p. 54).[8]

Having encouraged that blurring of research interests back in the 1990s, I would now go further and propose that where it is productive to do so, and not only with regard to the domestic sphere or to acts of consumption, it is important to blur academic boundaries between media studies and a wide spread of fields or disciplines across the humanities and social sciences which have a concern with everyday things and practices. For me, this involves making connections with, in particular, elements of phenomenological philosophy and human geography as well as work from anthropology and sociology, but I fully accept that others in media studies might prefer to forge their links elsewhere. Turning again to Morley (2011), this time to his more recent writing, there is a good indication of one potential inter-field or interdisciplinary way forward for the non-media-centric perspective, because he is committed to rethinking the concept of communications by recovering an old Marxist definition of that term as the interrelated movements of information, people and commodities, by seeking an overlap with the emerging 'new mobilities paradigm' (Sheller & Urry, 2006) in social theory and research, and by calling for the restoration of what he refers to (see Chapter 7) as a 'broken link' between media studies and transport studies.

De-centring media (and reconceptualising communications), in the manner that Morley recommends, must not result in a failure to appreciate that media have their distinctive characteristics and affordances, which mark them out as different from other technologies or instruments. The activities afforded by televisions and computers are not quite the same as those facilitated by, for instance, pianos, handsaws, shoes, ovens, fridges, cars and trains. Still, if, in Morley's words, media studies academics and students ought to be paying 'sufficient attention to the particularities of the media…without reifying their status and thus isolating them from the…contexts in which they operate' (Morley, 2007, p. 1), it is even more important for them to appreciate the intricate ways in which media use is stitched into the fabric of people's daily routines and thoroughly entangled there. To understand the everyday meaningfulness of media, it is necessary *to explore the weave of the wider quotidian fabric* rather than focusing too tightly on the study of media technologies and texts.

I should add here that I am not the first academic in media studies to employ this notion of a quotidian fabric. Roger Silverstone (1994, p. 2), writing about the position of television in everyday worlds, asks: 'How is it that such a…medium has found its way so profoundly and intimately into the fabric of our daily lives?' Non-media-centric media studies are concerned with just such questions, also posing them in relation to many other media. Crucially, as Silverstone's work, both individual and collaborative, implied (see, for example, Morley & Silverstone, 1990; Silverstone, 1990; Silverstone et al., 1992), providing answers involves the development of an outward-looking form of media studies, so as to link up with broader views of the day-to-day from beyond the field's usual limits.

I can see the case that media technologies and texts have often been overlooked in the past by academics based elsewhere in the humanities and social sciences, and that media-centred media studies have evidently played a vital role in drawing attention to these things, but the general way forward for media studies that I am recommending in this book would require joining forces with others, whichever neighbouring field or discipline they may come from, who are committed to the analysis of everyday practices or movements of various types. In the context of media studies as a field, it makes sense to conceive of such a venture as non-media-centric. However, as I argue in the course of a new cross-boundary dialogue between geographers and media studies scholars, *Communications/Media/Geographies* (Adams et al., 2017), this might eventually lead to the formation of an interdisciplinary area with a name like 'everyday-life studies' (Moores, 2017).[9]

Non-representational theories of practice: To de-centre representation?

Back in the opening section of this chapter, when I was addressing the main title of my book, I also argued that the idea of the doubly digital is important for me because it points to issues of bodily activity and knowledge, and I went on to relate these to matters of orientation (of habitation too). The *non-representational theories of practice* that I introduce in this current, lengthy section, some of which will be discussed at still greater length in later chapters, deal with precisely that range of concerns to do with embodiment, skilful movement through environments and dwelling or place-making. Nowadays, my own distinctive take on doing non-media-centric media studies is closely bound up with such non-representational theories or approaches.[10]

What is the significance, then, of this term non-representational? Given the centrality of the concept of representation in critical media studies since the 1970s, and given the influence of a broader linguistic turn across the humanities and social sciences dating from roughly the same period, *how could media studies, or even everyday-life studies, possibly be carried out in such a way as to de-centre representation?* My commitment to a non-representational theory of media use in day-to-day living might well appear to readers, at first sight, to be just as implausible and contradictory as the notion of non-media-centric media studies. After all, for many years it was common for undergraduate students in my academic field, somewhere near to the start of their degree courses, to be told that a central concern of media studies is with how cognitive perceptions of a world are shaped in particular ways by systems of representation (perhaps predominantly the ideological symbolic representations produced by media institutions), and with how meaning gets made in the interpretative, inter-discursive encounters between media texts and audiences.[11] To be sure, and to anticipate immediate objections, I am not proposing that the field should cease to deal with language, the cognitive and the symbolic. What I am insisting, though, is that this is not the most appropriate starting point for doing media studies. Again, let me try to explain.

In the humanities and social sciences today, the notion of the non-representational is typically associated with the work of geographer Nigel Thrift (1996, 2007), who has long advocated what he calls non-representational theory, or, sometimes in the plural, non-representational theories, and also with the writings of a wider group of contemporary geographers, several of whom are former colleagues or postgraduate students of Thrift's (see, for example, Anderson & Harrison, 2010). It is worth noting, however, that the term non-representational has been used in the discipline of philosophy too, without any reference to Thrift and his fellow non-representational theorists from geography. For instance, Warren Frisina (2002) looks to develop what he names a non-representational theory of knowledge, which draws on, among many other influences, the pragmatism of John Dewey and the process philosophy of Alfred North Whitehead (the latter is also of considerable interest to Thrift). Charles Taylor (2006, p. 212), meanwhile, employs the term in discussing the phenomenological philosophy of Martin Heidegger and Maurice Merleau-Ponty, writing of the importance in everyday practice or movement of a non-representational 'background', and arguing that 'what it is to act, to get around in the world…is not a matter of representations' (see also Taylor, 2005). Rather, in his words: 'To know one's way about is to be… moving around, handling things…is inseparable from our actual dealings with things…is a kind of "knowing how"' (Taylor, 2006, p. 212).

Indeed, Thrift (1999, p. 303) retrospectively claims both Heidegger and Merleau-Ponty as non-representational theorists, and one of the two related ways in which he uses that term non-representational seems to come out of the tradition of phenomenological philosophy. In this context, the word is employed by a philosopher like Taylor in explaining phenomenology's critique of rationalism.[12] For Taylor (2006, p. 204), a highly problematic element of 'the dominant rationalist view…an outlook that has to some extent colonized the common sense of our civilization' is its conceptualisation of 'an agent who in perceiving the world takes in "bits" of information from his or her surroundings…in order to emerge with the "picture" of the world he or she has', before acting 'on the basis of this picture'. As he goes on to note, such a view of cognitive or mental representation as a basis for human action fits all too neatly with modern ideas about the mind as a sort of computer, which have entered into the popular imagination over recent years. In response to the dominant rationalist view, and in opposition to 'computer models of the mind' (Taylor, 2006, p. 204), phenomenology offers an alternative, non-representational theory of perception and action, which focuses on *the engaged, embodied agency of moving around and handling things*, in a practically knowledgeable fashion, in everyday worlds.[13]

From my perspective, it is Merleau-Ponty's phenomenology of perception (see especially Merleau-Ponty, 2002 [1962]) that provides a particularly strong basis for critiquing rationalism, or what he preferred to call, back in the mid-20th Century, intellectualism, and I will be returning to his work on several occasions in the pages ahead (see, in particular, Chapter 4). Alongside Taylor, another contemporary philosopher who writes clearly and helpfully about Merleau-Ponty's approach, confirming the key features of engaged agency in day-to-day living, is Taylor Carman (2008, p. 19):

> Perception is not mental representation, according to Merleau-Ponty, but skilful bodily orientation and negotiation in given circumstances. To perceive is not to have inner mental states, but to know and find your way around an environment. More simply, to perceive is to have a body and to have a body is to inhabit a world.

In the short passage reproduced here, Carman highlights precisely those non-representational theoretical concerns which are of special interest to me in many of the chapters to follow, emphasising Merleau-Ponty's reflections on embodiment, orientation and habitation.

In the footsteps of Merleau-Ponty (2004 [1964], p. 37), who wrote of the always 'incarnate subject', Thrift (2004, p. 90) contends that 'only the smallest part of thinking is explicitly cognitive…the other thinking…lies in the body'. He adds that he is not seeking to deny the importance of cognition, which clearly is important, but rather to extend radically conceptions of what thinking might be, just as Merleau-Ponty (2002 [1962], pp. 165–167) sought to extend radically established notions of knowledge, comprehension or understanding, by writing of a 'knowledge in the hands' that is caught up with 'bodily effort' and by claiming more generally that 'it is the body which…"comprehends" movement…the body which "understands" in the acquisition of habit'. This apparently absurd phrase of Merleau-Ponty's, knowledge in the hands, which emerges from his reflections on the practice of typing, fits closely with that definition I offered earlier of doubly digital media as, in part, skilfully operated manual media, and it is to be a recurring theme of my book.

A second, overlapping way in which Thrift initially used the term non-representational came out of his critique of, or frustration with, a certain kind of then-new cultural geography that was flourishing by the 1980s and 1990s, broadly in parallel with the sort of media studies that I now have my doubts about. The frustration he felt was as a result of that geographical work focusing too much, at least in his view, on issues of language, signification and textuality, and this was seen by Thrift (1996, p. 1) to be at the expense of attending adequately to what he refers to as *the sensuousness of practice*.[14]

Ben Anderson (2009, p. 503), who is part of a younger generation of non-representational theorists in the discipline of geography, explains fairly straightforwardly in the following passage just what was at stake in the move beyond the '"new" cultural geography' of that time, and in doing so he manages to highlight the overlap between Thrift's two working definitions of the non-representational:

> Non-representational theory affirms an imperative to expand the foci of 'new' cultural geography beyond either…a sphere of representation or a human subject who relates to the world by representing aspects of the world through…interpretation…. Each mirrors the other in that they both assume that the primary relation between… subject and…world is at the level of signification. In contrast, non-representational

theories are theories of practice in that their focus is on what humans and/or non-humans do, and how the reproduction and revision of practices underpin…meaning.

In the context of this particular debate within geography, Hayden Lorimer (2005, p. 84), who also shares Thrift's interests in 'everyday routines…embodied movements…practical skills…sensuous dispositions' and so on, proposes adopting the term 'more-than-representational' rather than non-representational, fearing that the non- prefix may have 'proven an unfortunate hindrance', as a source of misunderstandings in discussions with less sympathetic fellow geographers. I imagine that the non- prefix might be a source of confusion, too, for academics and students in media studies, at least some of whom are likely to worry that a form of non- or even more-than-representational media studies would mark a departure from concerns with media texts and narratives (I will be seeking to address such worries shortly).

Overall, to sum up the contents of this section so far, the intervention that Thrift makes with his notion of the non-representational is *to call into question the centrality of representations to life*, whether that is the assumed centrality of mental picturing or, as claimed by many of those academics who took the linguistic turn, of sign-systems and texts. The approach that he is advocating, then, might best be thought of as *both anti-rationalist and anti-structuralist*.[15] On each of these counts, I am fully in agreement with Thrift that such a de-centring of representation is necessary in the humanities and social sciences (although I do sometimes feel that he could argue the case more accessibly). This is why I am committed to the development of media studies that are, in the ways suggested above, non-representational as well as non-media-centric in their theoretical or methodological orientations, especially since so much work in my academic field, even that which has paid serious attention to audience interpretations (see the opening pages of Chapter 4), has typically begun with the problematic assumption that it is only through language or systems of representation that worlds can be made to mean.[16]

Whilst Ingold (2015a), whose remarks on skills of orientation and on dwelling or habitation were mentioned earlier in the chapter (and whose name will reappear in Chapters 3, 4, 6, 7 and 8), has only very recently identified himself explicitly with the project of non-representational theory, he had previously made arguments about representation that are strikingly similar to those advanced by Thrift in geography.[17] Ingold's anthropology has its sights trained on much the same type of targets, and when writing of representation he approaches that word, as Thrift does, in different but interrelated ways.

On the one hand, Ingold (2011, p. 77), again in the footsteps of Merleau-Ponty, contests the dominant rationalist or intellectualist view that
action has to be 'preceded by' mental representation, or that there can be
'no action without forethought'. Equally, on the other hand, he is critical
of the many social and cultural anthropologists who have assumed that
humans must necessarily relate to their environments via 'systems of significant symbols' (Ingold, 2011, p. 76), a phrase lifted quite deliberately from
the work of Clifford Geertz (1973, p. 46), or that 'the raw material of experience' (Ingold, 2000, p. 160) has to be given shape by these representational
systems before it becomes meaningful. Ingold is clearly taking issue here
with any assumption of the primacy of language or the symbolic. Of course,
as I have already suggested, the anthropological view that Ingold criticises
is rather similar to the one offered by those cultural geographers whose work
frustrated Thrift, or by those in media studies who have assumed that worlds
only come to mean once they have been refracted through the prism of representation (and who have therefore tended to be suspicious of the category
of lived experience).[18]

So, if I am in agreement with Thrift and Ingold that a de-centring of representation is required, to go alongside the de-centring of media which was
proposed earlier, what do these non-representational theorists from the disciplines of geography and anthropology suggest should be centred instead? In
keeping with the emphasis on everyday lives that I have favoured throughout
my academic career, Thrift (1999, p. 308) points to 'the primacy of practice'
and Ingold (2011, p. 12) to 'the primacy of movement'.[19] Both are still interested in *meaning*, but regard it as *emerging out of habitual practices or movements*, or out of what Taylor (2006, p. 212) chooses to call 'our actual dealings
with things' while 'moving around' environments, rather than simply being
imposed upon action and experience via sign-systems. Crucially, Ingold (2011,
p. 77) writes of a potential for meanings to be made 'in the absence of symbolic representation', which reminds me of Merleau-Ponty's claim, many years
before, to have 'discovered through the study of motility…a new meaning of
the word "meaning"' (Merleau-Ponty, 2002 [1962], p. 170). Motility is a term
that this phenomenological philosopher employs when referring to skilful
bodily movement, and he regards body-world relations, which are incorporations, as meaningful in themselves prior to reflection and symbolisation. An
example of this sort of meaningfulness would be what some phenomenological geographers, writing back in the 1970s (see, for discussion, Chapter 3),
have called *senses of place* and 'at-homeness' (Seamon, 2015 [1979], p. 70).

These are constituted precisely through routine practices of the body and through everyday 'environmental experience' (Tuan, 1977, p. v; and see especially Seamon, 2015 [1979]).[20]

Attending to meanings made in the absence of symbolic representation, as Ingold puts it, does involve a departure from 'textualist' (Thrift, 1999, p. 302) perspectives in cultural analysis, but it need not prevent the study of media texts and their uses as threads in what I described above as the weave of a wider quotidian fabric. Non- or more-than-representational theories are certainly not designed to rule out the study of, for instance, utterances, sounds, images and writings, or listening, viewing and reading. Far from it. What they do insist on, however, is an approach which understands these things 'to be in and of the world of embodied practice and performance' (Wylie, 2007, p. 164), so as to challenge any lingering ideas (inherited from structuralism and semiotics) about linguistic or representational systems that are somehow 'anterior to, and determinative of, that world'.

Although there are probably very few media studies scholars who would still identify themselves directly with the structuralist tradition, I argue (see Chapter 7) that 'one of the main difficulties facing media studies today is the field's inability to leave behind entirely some of its early structuralist influences'. In my view, then, it is principally because of this inheritance that the field of media studies has hung on for so long to its own, now largely implicit, assumption of the primacy of representation. I favour those alternative approaches to language and text in media and communication studies, and in the humanities and social sciences more generally, which involve putting an emphasis on *talk as a practice or a doing*, on talk-in-interaction and genres of speech performance, in relation to other kinds of everyday action and interaction.[21]

One possible and potentially promising way forward for non-representational approaches to studying media texts and narratives, as they are embedded in or stitched into the day-to-day, is suggested by Ingold's 'idea that life is lived along lines' (Ingold, 2011, p. 4). In his writings on lines (see, most obviously, Ingold, 2007, 2015b), one of the many interesting things that he does is to draw a comparison between what he thinks of as lines of movement on foot and the lines of moving through stories (of walking and of storytelling or reading). This is a little bit like the link that I was making earlier in the chapter, when discussing my notion of the doubly digital, between the movements of hands and fingers or digits on keyboards, touch-screens and so on, and movements through media environments or worlds. Ingold (2007, p. 91) proposes, then, that reading can be understood as treading 'a trail through the text', a path or line along which readers might know as they go, and he therefore conceptualises narratives as inhabited landscapes of a sort (I should add here that his is not a view of landscape-as-text, as in textualist cultural geography, but rather of *text-as-landscape*). Readers may acquire an inhabitant knowledge (see Chapter 6, for a fuller account of that key concept of Ingold's). Such knowing-while-going, like that of the walker, 'grows along the paths they tread' (Ingold, 2015b, p. 47).[22] Of course, in the spirit of non-media-centric media studies or everyday-life studies, it is also crucial for such a take on narrative and reading practices to be set in the broader context of what Ingold (2007, p. xi) calls a 'comparative anthropology of the line', precisely so that life's multiple threads of knowledge-in-movement and of place-making might be seen to form a meshwork of entanglements (see also Hodder, 2012; Pink, 2012).[23]

Finally in this section, to bring my preliminary discussion of phenomenological and non-representational approaches to a close, I want to pose myself a couple of further questions, and, as before, to have a go at answering them directly here. If an admirable feature of what Thrift refers to as textualist perspectives in cultural analysis is that they are typically committed to the politics of representation and identity (and this would certainly apply to much work done within the critical paradigm of media studies since the 1970s), what are the political implications of a turn to concerns with embodiment, orientation and habitation, and of asserting the primacy of practice or movement? In short, *what about the politics of all this?*

I suspect that some of my peers in the field of media studies, if they have got this far into the introductory chapter, are likely to have answered these questions for themselves by now, regarding my interest in media uses as manual activities to be a retreat from any critical, political commitment. After all, a consideration of hand and finger movement (or even my wider interest in the embodied nature of routine social activity, in finding ways about and in making oneself at home) is at something of a distance from asking about, say, matters of signification, ideology and hegemony, or from the 'political economy' of communication (see, for example, Mosco, 2009). Nevertheless, I want to insist that engaging with non-representational theories of practice does not, and should not, necessarily lead to a rejection of concerns with difference, inequality and power.

It has to be admitted (indeed, I do admit this, notably in Chapter 3) that one of the limitations of phenomenology, despite its admirable commitment to dealing with the detail of daily routines and skilful, improvised conduct, is

NON-REPRESENTATIONAL THEORIES OF PRACTICE

15

a tendency towards universalism and a corresponding difficulty in accounting adequately for social differences. For instance, in phenomenological philosophy, Merleau-Ponty tends to talk of the body in the singular, rather than of a plurality of habituated bodies (see Grosz, 1994), for which he has been interrogated by feminist and queer theorists such as Iris Marion Young (2005 [1980]) and Sara Ahmed (2006), who emphasise the gendered aspects of embodiment and motility or seek to develop a phenomenology of sexual orientations. Similarly, in phenomenological geography, habitation processes and place-making practices are sometimes conceptualised in the broadest possible terms, as when David Seamon (1980, p. 148) writes of the 'essential nature of…dwelling on earth'. Even in contemporary non-representational theory, assertions of the primacy of practice or movement tend not to be related closely enough to an investigation of practices or movements in their social and historical specificity. It is for this reason that I am persuaded by Pierre Bourdieu's call for the need 'to sociologize…phenomenological analysis' (see Bourdieu & Wacquant, 1992, p. 73).

There are several features of Bourdieu's social theory of practice (see especially Bourdieu, 1977, 1990, 2000) that have a phenomenological or non-representational ring to them. Like Merleau-Ponty, his compatriot from an earlier academic generation, Bourdieu was deeply suspicious of intellectualism and, without neglecting the cognitive and symbolic dimensions of life (see, for example, Bourdieu, 1991), was concerned with people's bodily orientations in their everyday environments. Writing of bodily or corporeal knowledge, he declares his interest in forms of 'practical understanding…a practical comprehension of the world quite different from the…decoding that is normally designated by the idea of comprehension' (Bourdieu, 2000, pp. 135–136).[24] The concept of habitus, to which he returns again and again in his work, names a set of acquired, embodied dispositions that are both durable and adaptable or generative. This 'habitus' (Bourdieu, 2000, pp. 143–144) is a 'practical… intentionality…a way of bearing the body' in given circumstances. Where Bourdieu's social theory goes beyond Merleau-Ponty's philosophy, though, is in conceptualising these dispositions as 'marks of social position' (Bourdieu, 1977, p. 82), so that the strong feelings of familiarity and attachment which a human geographer like Seamon calls at-homeness can be seen as a tight fit between the habitus and a socially and historically specific habitat.[25]

It is crucial to add here that Bourdieu is not simply offering a theory of the determination of action and subjectivity by an objective social structure. He rejects such a 'social physics' (see Bourdieu & Wacquant, 1992, pp. 7–9), just as he also rejects what he refers to as an 'unreconstructed phenomenology'.

However, he does still want to be able to talk, quite rightly, about the forma-tion and reproduction of particular types of class habitus or about gendered habits of bodily comportment. A sociological term like class is very rarely used by contemporary non-representational theorists such as Thrift and Ingold, presumably because that term would be regarded as a problematic objective category, and yet Bourdieu's theory of practice helps to explain how the divi-sions and relations of social class are of course inseparable from bodily move-ments, incarnate subjects and inter-corporeal or human-thing interactions (in a manner that is similar in certain respects to Giddens' view of social structure and action as a duality). In the spirit of Bourdieu's writings, or of Elizabeth Grosz's notion of 'corporeal feminism' (Grosz, 1994), I am suggest-ing that something to be considered for the future, as ways of conducting non-media-centric, non-representational media studies are developed further, is what *the politics of orientation* (and habitation) might look like.[26]

Let me give just one indication of how what I am calling the politics of orientation and habitation could be relevant for a non-representational approach to the study of media uses. I referred above to Ingold's linking of lines of movement on foot with the lines of moving through stories, and his proposal that reading can be understood as treading a trail through the text, along which readers might know as they go and thereby inhabit a narrative. Whilst I find this proposal very interesting, work still remains to be done on precisely who knows what as they go where, and on who feels at ease or uneasy when moving through which particular media worlds. Ingold's view that skills of orientation and wayfinding are a fundamental feature of everyday lives is surely right, but it is necessary to try to extend his arguments about life lived along lines and about habitation as 'lineal' (Ingold, 2011, p. 149) by investi-gating the *socially differentiated experiences of travelling and dwelling*.

A brief link to the next chapter

In what I have written in the three sections above, there are already several pointers forward to what follows in the later chapters of my book, and for that reason it would not be productive at this stage for me to provide a preview of each of the pieces still to come, as often happens in the introduction to a volume of this kind. However, one of those pieces ahead (Chapter 2) has yet to be mentioned in this introductory chapter. As a brief link to the next chapter, then, I want to offer a few words about it here (and, to aid continuity throughout the book, I will also offer brief links onwards at the end of subsequent chapters).

It is fitting that the first of the essays included in this collection, in an extensively revised form, is 'Conceptualising Place in a World of Flows', because, in retrospect, it marks the start of some important shifts in my work. When I originally drafted that material, I was just beginning to develop my interdisciplinary interests in movement and dwelling, and also beginning to discover phenomenological analysis as a potentially valuable and distinctive take on doing non-media-centric media studies. The move towards phenomenology is made mainly near to the end of the essay, via my engagement with a pioneering book by media theorist and historian Paddy Scannell (1996), whose account of broadcasting in modern living draws on elements of Heidegger's philosophy (and see Scannell, 2014). A key interest of Scannell's is in how the uses of radio and television have contributed to what he regards as 'new possibilities of being' (Scannell, 1996, p. 91) or 'ways of being in the world' (Scannell, 1996, p. 173) for listeners and viewers.

So Chapter 2 involves an exploration of Scannell's idea that broadcasting facilitates an instantaneous 'doubling of place' (Scannell, 1996, p. 172; and see Moores, 2004), but I will consider the work of a number of other academic authors too (most notably, Manuel Castells, John Urry, Doreen Massey and Joshua Meyrowitz), all of whom have things to say about the conceptualisation of place in relation to the flows or mobilities that characterise globalising processes. Indeed, my discussion in the next chapter connects with something I was saying earlier in the current one, about Morley's reconceptualising of communications (Morley, 2011) and his call to repair the break between media and transport studies, since the mix of electronically mediated information flows with the movements of people and commodities is a crucial theme for me there.

Notes

1. It is always helpful to remember that, as Carolyn Marvin (1988, p. 3) puts it: 'New technologies is a historically relative term.' In the words of the title of her classic study, there was a time when old technologies were new. Indeed, the first empirical research that I did was concerned with the significance of early radio as a new media technology in everyday lives during the 1920s and 1930s (Moores, 1988).

2. For me, a key turning point in internet research was the ethnographic study presented by Daniel Miller and Don Slater (2000). In the opening chapter of their book, they distance their work from what they call an 'earlier generation of internet writing that was

concerned with the internet primarily through such notions as "cyberspace" or "virtual-ity"' (Miller & Slater, 2000, p. 4). Their preference, then, is to approach online spaces 'as continuous with and embedded in other social spaces...as part of everyday life, not apart from it' (Miller & Slater, 2000, pp. 5–7; and see Wellman & Haythornthwaite, 2002). For example, in their study of internet use in Trinidad, they show how the same style of informal talk can be found across online and offline environments, with some discussions moving between the internet and, say, school or street settings. Christine Hine (2015) offers a recent retrospective commentary on that ground-breaking ethnography done by Miller and Slater, in the context of her important account of the internet as 'embedded' and 'everyday' but also as 'embodied'.

3. The concept of tacit knowledge is most closely associated with the work of philosopher Michael Polanyi (2009 [1966], 2015 [1958]). He sought to 'reconsider human knowledge by starting from the fact that we know more than we can tell' (Polanyi, 2009 [1966], p. 4). As will become evident later in my discussion, his concerns with tacit knowing in 'skilful performance' (Polanyi, 2015 [1958], p. 49) are in some ways similar to those of phe-nomenological philosophers such as Martin Heidegger and Maurice Merleau-Ponty, and, although Polanyi's philosophy is not in the phenomenological tradition, it is worth noting that he did share with Merleau-Ponty certain interests in psychological theory. Sociologist of science Harry Collins (2010) provides a contemporary engagement with and extension of Polanyi's work that includes comparisons with phenomenology. There, Collins (2010, p. 11) refers to embodied, practical know-how as 'somatic tacit knowledge'.

4. I realise that with the development of the internet it became common, for new media researchers and ordinary users alike, to speak of navigation (of navigating cyberspace). How-ever, there are key differences between the concepts of orientation and navigation, and the notion of navigating spaces is too closely caught up with traditional modes of cartographic representation and with the problematic idea of cognitive maps (see Ingold, 2000, pp. 219–242). One of the few academic authors in media studies for whom matters of bodily orien-tation have been important is Vivian Sobchack (2004), although much of her writing is on cinema and film experience. I should add that I have been reading with interest a recently published book in this 'Digital Formations' series, written by communication researcher John McArthur (2016), which is on the subject of digital 'proxemics' and has some highly promising chapter titles such as 'Bodies in Motion' and 'Finding Our Way'. He and I are clearly working on similar themes, then, and I welcome this overlap. Still, McArthur's the-oretical starting points are rather different to those of my own book (for instance, he makes no reference to phenomenological approaches) and he is operating with what seems at times to be quite a limited conception of orientation. For example, at one point he defines orien-tation simply as the 'direction a person is facing' (McArthur, 2016, p. 96).

5. Geographer Nigel Thrift (2004, p. 81), in one of his several attempts at outlining non-representational theory, refers to such knowing-how-to-go-on as 'the everyday skills that get us by', and, interestingly, among the influences on Thrift's geographical work has been Anthony Giddens' social theory of 'structuration' (Giddens, 1979, 1981, 1984; and see, on structuration, Moores, 2005).

6. One of the things that Tim Ingold is known for in the discipline of anthropology is his development of a phenomenologically inspired dwelling perspective, which I will be

discussing in Chapter 6, yet over the past few years he has voiced his doubts about that concept of dwelling. For example, he writes of the term that it can have an unfortunate 'aura of snug, well-wrapped localism' (Ingold, 2011, p. 12), and goes on to say that: 'I rather regret having placed so much weight on it, and now prefer the less loaded concept of habitation.' Whilst I certainly welcome Ingold's notion of processes of habitation, it is not necessary, in my view, to ditch the concept of dwelling, as long as it is always understood in relation to orientation and movement.

7. Indeed, David Morley (2007, p. 228) refers specifically there to my book *Media/Theory: Thinking about Media and Communications* (Moores, 2005), which was published in the 'Comedia' series that he edits, as 'an interesting attempt to develop a non-media-centric theory' for media studies.

8. See the book that I co-edited at around this time with feminist sociologist Stevi Jackson, *The Politics of Domestic Consumption: Critical Readings* (Jackson & Moores, 1995), for a collection that brings together research on household social relations done by Morley, Nickie Charles and Marion Kerr, Christine Delphy, Ann Gray, Dorothy Hobson, Janice Radway and many more academic authors from media and cultural studies, sociology and other fields or disciplines.

9. Although the specific field name of everyday-life studies does not yet exist, at least as an established institutional category in the university system, there is now a considerable amount of literature across the humanities and social sciences on the subject of the everyday, from classic publications (for example, de Certeau, 1984; Goffman, 1990 [1959]; Lefebvre, 1984 [1971]) through to the many more recent, book-length discussions in this area, which could potentially form the basis for a whole interdisciplinary teaching and research programme. Rather than making a long list of those references here, I will simply point at this stage to two of my favourite books on the everyday and the ordinary over recent years (which are Ehn & Löfgren, 2010; Highmore, 2011). One of the things I particularly like about these studies is the shared commitment they have to an exploration of, as Ben Highmore (2011, p. 3) poses it: 'What's going on when nothing much is happening?' (or, more precisely, when it appears that nothing much is happening, because actually the answer is quite a lot).

10. I think it becomes clear, towards the end of the discussion in Chapter 7, that my turn to non-representational theories of practice is what now distinguishes my non-media-centric media studies from Morley's. He undoubtedly has a serious interest in several of the issues that are dealt with by these approaches, but I sense his reluctance to travel quite so far down a phenomenological or non-representational route as I have gone over recent years.

11. For many years, of course, I told students something along these lines myself, and by far the most eloquent exponent of that concern was Stuart Hall. Although I have great respect and admiration for him as a teacher and theorist in critical media and cultural studies, and whilst I was proud to be invited to work as a consultant author for the UK's Open University (OU) on a course that he chaired (see Moores, 1997), it is now my view that Hall's take on media tended to put too much emphasis on the cognitive and the symbolic, dating back to his seminal paper on the 'encoding' and 'decoding' of television discourse (Hall, 1973). A good illustration of this emphasis is an introductory, video-recorded lecture of his on representation and the media, which is available from the Media Education

Foundation (see www.mediaed.org). There, he says, for instance, that 'to become a cul-
tured subject rather than a biological individual, rather than just a blob of genetic material,
is…to internalise…the grid of one's culture…a system of representation', and he proceeds
to speak of such an internalisation as constitutive of 'the conceptual maps in our heads
which allow us to come to a sense of what is going on in the world', claiming confidently
that 'nothing meaningful exists outside of discourse'. What Hall offers, then, is effectively
an assertion of the primacy of language or representation, in which there is a clear divide
between culture (understood in representational terms) and biology or materiality, in
which the body is, in his words, just a blob (to be invested with meanings or constructed
as meaningful through discourse), and in which subjectivity and meaning only become
possible via symbolic representations. It is true that elsewhere (Hall, 1997, pp. 2–3) he
does seek to qualify this view to some extent, by admitting that subjectivities must be more
than representational systems internalised 'in the head' because they involve 'feelings,
attachments and emotions', and by acknowledging, too, that an 'emphasis on cultural
practices is important', and yet he still conceptualises feeling and bodily 'expression' as
things to be 'read', and what he thinks of as 'cultural practices' are the signifying practices of representation and interpretation. I get no sense in his writing of bodies-moving-
responsively-through-environments as the potential generators of a meaningfulness that
exceeds representation. Let me add one further observation here to what is already an
exceptionally, but necessarily, long footnote. Thrift (1997) was another of the consultant
authors who wrote for the OU course that I mentioned, on culture, media and identities,
which Hall chaired and I contributed to, and for which Morley was the external assessor.
Indeed, Thrift's is the chapter that precedes mine in the course volume on consumption
and everyday life, and Hall (1997, pp. 5–7) clearly realised the main differences between
his own take and Thrift's, since he compares the 'social constructionist approach' of critical media and cultural studies with what he refers to as a more 'performative approach to
meaning' found in that volume (see also Finnegan, 1997).

12. Alongside Heidegger and Merleau-Ponty, Charles Taylor (2006, p. 202) includes Ludwig
Wittgenstein on 'that small list of 20th-century philosophers who have helped us emerge…
from the grip of modern rationalism', and Wittgenstein's later philosophical investigations
(together with phenomenology and other approaches such as ethnomethodology and
science and technology studies) have had a significant influence on practice theory (see
especially Schatzki, 1996; Schatzki et al., 2001). In an interview, Thrift (see Thrift et al.,
2010, p. 184) refers to much of his own early work on the notion of the non-representational as 'what would now be regarded as "practice theory"', and in media anthropology
(Bräuchler & Postill, 2010) practice theory has helpfully been applied in reflections on
media use in day-to-day living. Interestingly, given my remarks above on media and food
in domestic contexts, the application of practice theory is evident, too, in the sociological
analysis of eating (Warde, 2016).

13. Like Taylor, Heideggerian scholar Hubert Dreyfus (1991, 2014) has long been opposed to
computer models of the mind and has discussed this engaged, embodied agency in terms of
what he calls skilful 'coping' (see also Dreyfus & Taylor, 2015).

14. See geographer John Wylie's book on landscape (Wylie, 2007) for a valuable comparison
between, say, cultural analyses of landscape-as-text and the landscape phenomenologies

that are associated with a non-representational approach. Summarising the circumstances of Thrift's critique of then-new cultural geography, Wylie (2007, p. 163) writes of Thrift being confronted by 'a situation in which everyday life, embodied experience and practice…were considered as the secondary effects or outworkings of a more primary realm of cultural discourse'.

15. A number of the contributors to the collection on non-representational theories and geography edited by Ben Anderson and Paul Harrison (2010) identify themselves as post-structuralists, and yet my preference is for this term anti-structuralist, because it helps to indicate more directly a break from structuralism. By structuralism, I mean, of course, that tradition of analysis which emerged out of Ferdinand de Saussure's structural linguistics and his call for a science of signs to be named semiology, more often referred to subsequently as semiotics. To be anti-structuralist, then, is to reject Saussurean perspectives on language and culture, from which there is a problematic tendency to downplay the importance of historical process, of utterance or of social action and interaction in context, and from which semioticians have tended to focus on the notion of representational systems. To avoid any possible confusion, I also need to point out that in labelling myself an anti-structuralist I am not wanting to rule out talk of social structures, including the micro-social structures of talk-in-interaction (see, for example, Sacks, 1995), although, in the spirit of Giddens' theory of structuration, I would have to insist that all structural, institutional qualities to the social must be understood in relation to practices and their recursive ordering. As Giddens (see Giddens & Pierson, 1998, p. 77) puts it, 'society only has form and that form only has effects on people in so far as structure is produced and reproduced in what people do' (and it is worth noting that his concern with 'what people do' is broadly shared by Thrift and other non-representational theorists today).

16. Dreyfus and Taylor (2015, pp. 2–3; see also Taylor, 2013) point out that such 'only through' claims have a very long history in philosophy. In response to these claims, they propose what they term 'contact theory' (see Dreyfus & Taylor, 2015, pp. 71–90), or what Taylor (2013, p. 74) has also referred to as 'immersion' theory, which draws principally on Heidegger and Merleau-Ponty in acknowledging the meaningfulness of 'preconceptual engagement' with inhabited environments (or of what those phenomenological philosophers called 'being-in-the-world').

17. Indeed, in an essay that advances a non-representational approach to the 'ecology of place', Thrift (1999, pp. 308–309) quotes at some length passages from one of Ingold's discussions of dwelling (Ingold, 1995). In the intervening years, too, Ingold (2004, 2014) has accepted invitations to contribute to books which Thrift co-edited, and so, from their respective disciplinary bases, the two of them have clearly been aware of each other's developing work.

18. It should be remembered, though, that in addition to structuralism and semiotics there was another strand of work that became known as culturalism (Hall, 1986, 2016), which influenced, while not strongly enough in my view, the formation of critical media and cultural studies. This left-culturalist tradition, which developed partly into a 'cultural materialism' (see, for example, Milner, 1993; Williams, 1977, 1980), is associated in particular with the work of writers such as literary and cultural theorist Raymond Williams and social historian Edward Thompson, who certainly took seriously matters of feeling or experience

(see Pickering, 1997). Thrift (see Thrift et al., 2010, pp. 184–185) refers specifically, and perhaps surprisingly for some, to writings by Thompson (1978, 1993 [1967]) as being especially important for him near to the start of his academic career. Thompson's historical analysis of the organisation of time in industrial capitalism has continued to be a source of critical engagement for Thrift (Glennie & Thrift, 2009), but it was seemingly Thompson's fierce, uncompromising attack on Louis Althusser's structuralist-inflected Marxism that helped to put Thrift on the road to a non-representational approach.

19. Thrift and Ingold are not the only theorists to have pointed to these particular primacies. Margaret Archer (2000, pp. 121–153), whose realist social theory draws on Merleau-Ponty's phenomenology of perception, also asserts the primacy of practice. Interestingly, she includes a discussion there of Merleau-Ponty's approach to language and speech, and especially his 'insistence upon speech as a practical activity' (Archer, 2000, p. 135), so that language acquisition is seen not as 'intellectual mastery of linguistic principles' but rather as 'of a piece with acquiring other kinds of practical conduct through habit'. In addition, philosopher (and former dancer and choreographer) Maxine Sheets-Johnstone (2011) writes at length on the primacy of movement (see also Sheets-Johnstone, 2009).

20. I get a bit irritated with contemporary non-representational theorists in geography for their failure to acknowledge, as fully as they might, this earlier strand of geographical work. Within that discipline, what is usually known as humanistic geography now tends to be treated as little more than a chapter in the discipline's history. For example, Thrift, in his main outlines of non-representational theory, does not cite David Seamon's geography of 'the lifeworld' (Seamon, 2015 [1979]), with its insights into embodiment, movement and dwelling. Indeed, later geographical work on body, sense and place (Rodaway, 1994), which was influenced by phenomenological geography, is not given the credit that I believe it deserves in the writings of the non-representational geographers. They would presumably respond by arguing that their approach can be differentiated in significant ways from the earlier perspective, claiming that, say, a concern with affect, and more specifically with 'affective spaces' (McCormack, 2013) or affective atmospheres (Anderson, 2014), is not equivalent to previous interests in emotions, feelings or moods. In my view, however, the gap between phenomenological geography and today's non-representational theories is actually not so great, and there does seem to be a case here of intra-disciplinary boundary marking.

21. In media studies, Paddy Scannell's edited collection on broadcast talk (Scannell, 1991a), including his important introduction to that book, which focuses on what he calls the relevance of talk (Scannell, 1991b), was an early pointer in this direction. Very much in keeping with what I have described as the anti-structuralist tendency of non-representational theories, he reflects on his academic field at that time and complains of how 'the encoding-decoding model of communication and a model of language based on Saussure…make it well-nigh impossible to discover talk as an object of study in relation to broadcasting' (Scannell, 1991b, p. 10). One of the several alternatives suggested by his introductory essay, precisely with a view to discovering talk as an object of study for media studies, is Erving Goffman's sociology of interaction and, in particular, this sociologist's conceptualisation of face and 'face-work' (Goffman, 1967; see also Brown & Levinson, 1987, on politeness). Taking up Scannell's suggestion, Karen Atkinson and I (Atkinson & Moores, 2003) have

explored participants' attention to 'face' in the 'troubles-talk' on a radio phone-in programme, as one element of what I have called elsewhere (referring to Goffman, 1983) a
technologically mediated 'interaction order' (Moores, 1999). Also among those who came
to sympathise with Scannell's critique of structuralist influences and his interest in the
analysis of broadcast talk is a former doctoral student of mine and Andrew Tolson's, Helen
Wood (2007a, 2007b, 2009; see also Tolson, 1991, 2001, 2006), in her detailed empirical
research on women's relationships with talk shows on daytime television. I should add
that in the discipline of sociology Archer (2003, 2007), whose phenomenological (Merleau-Pontyan) take on speech as practical activity or conduct was mentioned above, has
written of a kind of ongoing 'conversation' or dialogue with oneself, which plays some part
in finding a 'way through the world'. This provides a link back to Giddens' social theory,
too, as his writings on 'modernity' (Giddens, 1990, 1991; see also Moores, 1995, 2005)
have much to say about reflexivity in relation to the routine practices of day-to-day living.

22. Ingold's observation that readers, like walkers, know as they go along reminds me of a
particular aspect of literary critic Wolfgang Iser's phenomenology of reading (see Iser,
1978). Iser (1978, p. 16) refers to the reader of fiction as a traveller 'who has to…journey
through the novel', who has a 'moving viewpoint' and never 'a total view of that journey'.
Indeed, in her subsequent commentary on Iser's theory of literary reception, Elizabeth
Freund (1987, pp. 134–151) writes helpfully of a 'peripatetic reader', emphasising that link
between reading and travelling.

23. Sarah Pink (2012; see also Pink & Leder Mackley, 2013) is a social researcher whose
writings on the everyday are of considerable interest to me because they touch on matters
of media use and draw to an extent on Ingold's ideas about lines and meshwork. I will be
referring to some of her notes on digital media use at the end of my book (at the close
of Chapter 8). For now, though, I want to say a little about archaeologist Ian Hodder's
work because, alongside Ingold, Hodder (2012) has established himself as a contemporary
thinker on entanglement with his recent book on 'the relationships between humans and
things'. As I understand the arguments put there, he contends that while social theories
of materiality and material culture, including those which have been influenced by phenomenological philosophy, seek to take things seriously (in terms of their meaningfulness
in the context of human activities), such theories have remained too human-centred and
have therefore paid insufficient attention to the force and 'object nature' (Hodder, 2012,
p. 39) of things themselves. In this regard, his approach overlaps with Bruno Latour's
actor-network theory in sociology (see Hodder, 2012, pp. 91–94) and perhaps even with
the object-oriented philosophy developed by Graham Harman. Harman's work (see, for
example, Harman, 2002), which takes an unconventional route out of Heidegger, is for
me a particularly hard-going read, but I would recommend Ingold's critical engagement
with object-oriented ontology (Ingold, 2015b, p. 16), and also his entertaining discussion
of actor-network theory (Ingold, 2011, pp. 89–94).

24. Pierre Bourdieu's use of the word decoding is telling in this context because, of course,
as I noted earlier it was a key term in Hall's conceptual vocabulary and, more generally,
in critical media studies. Bourdieu clearly regards that practical understanding or comprehension as something more than interpretation. In the final chapter of my first book,
Interpreting Audiences: The Ethnography of Media Consumption (Moores, 1993), I discussed

Bourdieu's sociology of taste and cultural distinctions (Bourdieu, 1984), but, like others in media and cultural studies during that period, I was still struggling to integrate it into areas of study that had been shaped largely by the influences of structuralism and semiotics, and I was therefore unable to appreciate fully his concern with bodily orientations and corporeal knowledge. For instance, I wrote there of how Bourdieu's notion of distinction has to do with meaningful differentiations, 'just as the signs in Saussure's language system have their values determined negatively within structured relations of difference' (Moores, 1993, p. 120). However, the differentiations or distastes that interest Bourdieu are much more than sign-values determined negatively in a linguistic or representational system, and they go well beyond any cognitive or intellectual classifications. As he makes clear, they are profoundly embodied responses and might even be experienced, on occasion, as a sense of 'disgust…horror or visceral intolerance ("sick-making") of the tastes of others' (Bourdieu, 1984, p. 56). This is about gut feelings in specific environmental conditions.

25. Ethnographic accounts of this type of fit between habitus and habitat are provided by Simon Charlesworth (2000) and Loic Wacquant (2004), both of whom draw heavily on Bourdieu's social theory. Charlesworth's focus is on working-class experience in the northern English town where he grew up, while Wacquant's is on bodily practices at a boxing gym in a black American neighbourhood. In the case of Wacquant's remarkable study, this white French sociologist actually participates as a boxer in 'a culture that is thoroughly kinetic' (Wacquant, 2004, p. xi), immersing himself in the gym setting and learning its skilful ways 'by body…with my fists and my guts'. More recently, social theorist and researcher Will Atkinson (2016, pp. 19–24) has proposed that Bourdieu's notion of habitat can usefully be recast as a concern with lifeworld. Atkinson's fascinating discussion brings Bourdieu's sociology briefly into contact with Seamon's phenomenological geography, and also with Torsten Hägerstrand's time-geography (see Chapter 3).

26. A number of non-representational and associated theorists have sought to develop an explicitly political dimension to their work. For example, Ash Amin and Nigel Thrift (2013) reflect on the 'arts' of the political and are interested in, amongst other things, what they term affective politics. Along similar lines, philosopher and social theorist Brian Massumi (2015) has recently published a collection of his dialogues with others on the politics of affect (although I am not afraid to admit that I find this book to be a difficult one). My own preference, when searching out sources of inspiration for what I am calling the politics of orientation, would be to turn elsewhere. One crucial way would be towards Tim Cresswell's identification of differentiating factors in the significance of mobility or travel (Cresswell, 2010). This human geographer labels himself, and has been labelled by others, as an 'interested sceptic' (Cresswell, 2012; Lorimer, 2005, p. 85) when it comes to contemporary non- or more-than-representational theories of practice, but from my perspective the attention that he pays to social difference, inequality and power is particularly welcome. In addition, for some clues as to what the politics of habitation might look like, see Morley (2000, 2001) and also the work of sociologist Jan Willem Duyvendak (2011) on issues of home and belonging today.

References

Adams, P., Cupples, J., Glynn, K., Jansson, A. & Moores, S. (2017), *Communications/Media/ Geographies*, New York: Routledge.

Ahmed, S. (2006), *Queer Phenomenology: Orientations, Objects, Others*, Durham, NC: Duke University Press.

Amin, A. & Thrift, N. (2013), *Arts of the Political: New Openings for the Left*, Durham, NC: Duke University Press.

Anderson, B. (2009), 'Non-Representational Theory', in Gregory, D., Johnston, R., Pratt, G., Watts, M. & Whatmore, S. (eds.) *The Dictionary of Human Geography*, fifth edition, Malden, MA: Wiley-Blackwell.

Anderson, B. (2014), *Encountering Affect: Capacities, Apparatuses, Conditions*, Farnham: Ashgate.

Anderson, B. & Harrison, P. (eds.) (2010), *Taking-Place: Non-Representational Theories and Geography*, Farnham: Ashgate.

Archer, M. (2000), *Being Human: The Problem of Agency*, Cambridge: Cambridge University Press.

Archer, M. (2003), *Structure, Agency and the Internal Conversation*, Cambridge: Cambridge University Press.

Archer, M. (2007), *Making Our Way Through the World: Human Reflexivity and Social Mobility*, Cambridge: Cambridge University Press.

Atkinson, K. & Moores, S. (2003), '"We All Have Bad Bad Days": Attending to Face in Broadcast Troubles-Talk', *The Radio Journal: International Studies in Broadcast and Audio Media*, vol. 1, no. 2, pp. 129–146.

Atkinson, W. (2016), *Beyond Bourdieu: From Genetic Structuralism to Relational Phenomenology*, Cambridge: Polity.

Bourdieu, P. (1977), *Outline of a Theory of Practice*, Cambridge: Cambridge University Press.

Bourdieu, P. (1984), *Distinction: A Social Critique of the Judgement of Taste*, London: Routledge and Kegan Paul.

Bourdieu, P. (1990), *The Logic of Practice*, Cambridge: Polity.

Bourdieu, P. (1991), *Language and Symbolic Power*, Cambridge: Polity.

Bourdieu, P. (2000), *Pascalian Meditations*, Cambridge: Polity.

Bourdieu, P. & Wacquant, L. (1992), *An Invitation to Reflexive Sociology*, Cambridge: Polity.

Bräuchler, B. & Postill, J. (eds.) (2010), *Theorising Media and Practice*, Oxford: Berghahn.

Brown, P. & Levinson, S. (1987), *Politeness: Some Universals in Language Usage*, Cambridge: Cambridge University Press.

Carman, T. (2008), *Merleau-Ponty*, London: Routledge.

Charles, N. & Kerr, M. (1988), *Women, Food and Families*, Manchester: Manchester University Press.

Charlesworth, S. (2000), *A Phenomenology of Working Class Experience*, Cambridge: Cambridge University Press.

Collins, H. (2010), *Tacit and Explicit Knowledge*, Chicago, IL: University of Chicago Press.

Cresswell, T. (2010), 'Towards a Politics of Mobility', *Environment and Planning D: Society and Space*, vol. 28, no. 1, pp. 17–31.

Cresswell, T. (2012), 'Non-Representational Theory and Me: Notes of an Interested Sceptic', *Environment and Planning D: Society and Space*, vol. 30, no. 1, pp. 96–105.

de Certeau, M. (1984), *The Practice of Everyday Life*, Berkeley, CA: University of California Press.

Dreyfus, H. (1991), *Being-in-the-World: A Commentary on Heidegger's* Being and Time, Division I, Cambridge, MA: MIT Press.

Dreyfus, H. (2014), *Skillful Coping: Essays on the Phenomenology of Everyday Perception and Action*, New York: Oxford University Press.

Dreyfus, H. & Taylor, C. (2015), *Retrieving Realism*, Cambridge, MA: Harvard University Press.

Duyvendak, J.W. (2011), *The Politics of Home: Belonging and Nostalgia in Western Europe and the United States*, Basingstoke: Palgrave Macmillan.

Ehn, B. & Löfgren, O. (2010), *The Secret World of Doing Nothing*, Berkeley, CA: University of California Press.

Finnegan, R. (1997), 'Music, Performance and Enactment', in Mackay, H. (ed.) *Consumption and Everyday Life*, London: Sage.

Freund, E. (1987), *The Return of the Reader: Reader-Response Criticism*, London: Methuen.

Frisina, W. (2002), *The Unity of Knowledge and Action: Toward a Non-Representational Theory of Knowledge*, Albany, NY: State University of New York Press.

Geertz, C. (1973), *The Interpretation of Cultures: Selected Essays*, New York: Basic Books.

Giddens, A. (1979), *Central Problems in Social Theory: Action, Structure and Contradiction in Social Analysis*, Berkeley, CA: University of California Press.

Giddens, A. (1981), *A Contemporary Critique of Historical Materialism*, Basingstoke: Macmillan.

Giddens, A. (1984), *The Constitution of Society: Outline of the Theory of Structuration*, Cambridge: Polity.

Giddens, A. (1990), *The Consequences of Modernity*, Cambridge: Polity.

Giddens, A. (1991), *Modernity and Self-Identity: Self and Society in the Late Modern Age*, Cambridge: Polity.

Giddens, A. & Pierson, C. (1998), *Conversations with Anthony Giddens: Making Sense of Modernity*, Cambridge: Polity.

Glennie, P. & Thrift, N. (2009), *Shaping the Day: A History of Timekeeping in England and Wales, 1300–1800*, Oxford: Oxford University Press.

Goffman, E. (1967), 'On Face-Work: An Analysis of Ritual Elements in Social Interaction', in *Interaction Ritual: Essays on Face-to-Face Behavior*, New York: Pantheon Books.

Goffman, E. (1983), 'The Interaction Order', *American Sociological Review*, vol. 48, no. 1, pp. 1–17.

Goffman, E. (1990 [1959]), *The Presentation of Self in Everyday Life*, London: Penguin.

Grosz, E. (1994), *Volatile Bodies: Toward a Corporeal Feminism*, Bloomington, IN: Indiana University Press.

Hall, S. (1973), 'Encoding and Decoding in the Television Discourse', CCCS Stencilled Paper no. 7, Centre for Contemporary Cultural Studies, University of Birmingham.

Hall, S. (1986), 'Cultural Studies: Two Paradigms', in Collins, R., Curran, J., Garnham, N., Scannell, P., Schlesinger, P. & Sparks, C. (eds.) *Media, Culture and Society: A Critical Reader*, London: Sage.

Hall, S. (1997), 'Introduction', in Hall, S. (ed.) *Representation: Cultural Representations and Signifying Practices*, London: Sage.

Hall, S. (2016), *Cultural Studies 1983: A Theoretical History*, Durham, NC: Duke University Press.

Harman, G. (2002), *Tool-Being: Heidegger and the Metaphysics of Objects*, Chicago, IL: Open Court.

Heidegger, M. (1993 [1971]), 'Building Dwelling Thinking', in Krell, D. (ed.) *Martin Heidegger: Basic Writings*, London: Routledge.

Highmore, B. (2011), *Ordinary Lives: Studies in the Everyday*, London: Routledge.

Hine, C. (2015), *Ethnography for the Internet: Embedded, Embodied and Everyday*, London: Bloomsbury Academic.

Hobson, D. (1980), 'Housewives and the Mass Media', in Hall, S., Hobson, D., Lowe, A. & Willis, P. (eds.) *Culture, Media, Language: Working Papers in Cultural Studies, 1972–79*, London: Hutchinson.

Hodder, I. (2012), *Entangled: An Archaeology of the Relationships Between Humans and Things*, Malden, MA: Wiley-Blackwell.

Ingold, T. (1995), 'Building, Dwelling, Living: How Animals and People Make Themselves at Home in the World', in Strathern, M. (ed.) *Shifting Contexts: Transformations in Anthropological Knowledge*, London: Routledge.

Ingold, T. (2000), *The Perception of the Environment: Essays on Livelihood, Dwelling and Skill*, London: Routledge.

Ingold, T. (2004), 'Buildings', in Harrison, S., Pile, S. & Thrift, N. (eds.) *Patterned Ground: Entanglements of Nature and Culture*, London: Reaktion Books.

Ingold, T. (2007), *Lines: A Brief History*, London: Routledge.

Ingold, T. (2011), *Being Alive: Essays on Movement, Knowledge and Description*, London: Routledge.

Ingold, T. (2014), 'Walking', in Thrift, N., Tickell, A., Woolgar, S. & Rupp, W. (eds.) *Globalization in Practice*, Oxford: Oxford University Press.

Ingold, T. (2015a), 'Foreword', in Vannini, P. (ed.) *Non-Representational Methodologies: Envisioning Research*, New York: Routledge.

Ingold, T. (2015b), *The Life of Lines*, London: Routledge.

Iser, W. (1978), *The Act of Reading: A Theory of Aesthetic Response*, Baltimore, MD: Johns Hopkins University Press.

Jackson, S. & Moores, S. (eds.) (1995), *The Politics of Domestic Consumption: Critical Readings*, London: Prentice Hall/Harvester Wheatsheaf.

Krajina, Z. (2014), *Negotiating the Mediated City: Everyday Encounters with Public Screens*, New York: Routledge.

Lefebvre, H. (1984 [1971]), *Everyday Life in the Modern World*, New Brunswick, NJ: Transaction.

Lorimer, H. (2005), 'Cultural Geography: The Busyness of Being "More-Than-Representational"', *Progress in Human Geography*, vol. 29, no. 1, pp. 83–94.

McArthur, J. (2016), *Digital Proxemics: How Technology Shapes the Ways We Move*, New York: Peter Lang.

McCormack, D. (2013), *Refrains for Moving Bodies: Experience and Experiment in Affective Spaces*, Durham, NC: Duke University Press.

Marvin, C. (1988), *When Old Technologies Were New: Thinking about Electric Communication in the Late Nineteenth Century*, New York: Oxford University Press.

Massumi, B. (2015), *Politics of Affect*, Cambridge: Polity.

Merleau-Ponty, M. (2002 [1962]), *Phenomenology of Perception*, London: Routledge.

Merleau-Ponty, M. (2004 [1964]), 'Merleau-Ponty's Prospectus of His Work', in Baldwin, T. (ed.) *Maurice Merleau-Ponty: Basic Writings*, London: Routledge.

Miller, D. & Slater, D. (2000), *The Internet: An Ethnographic Approach*, Oxford: Berg.

Milner, A. (1993), *Cultural Materialism*, Melbourne: Melbourne University Press.

Moores, S. (1988), '"The Box on the Dresser": Memories of Early Radio and Everyday Life', *Media, Culture and Society*, vol. 10, no. 1, pp. 23–40.

Moores, S. (1993), *Interpreting Audiences: The Ethnography of Media Consumption*, London: Sage.

Moores, S. (1995), 'Media, Modernity and Lived Experience', *Journal of Communication Inquiry*, vol. 19, no. 1, pp. 5–19.

Moores, S. (1997), 'Broadcasting and Its Audiences', in Mackay, H. (ed.) *Consumption and Everyday Life*, London: Sage.

Moores, S. (1999), 'The Mediated "Interaction Order"', in Hearn, J. & Roseneil, S. (eds.) *Consuming Cultures: Power and Resistance*, Basingstoke: Macmillan.

Moores, S. (2004), 'The Doubling of Place: Electronic Media, Time-Space Arrangements and Social Relationships', in Couldry, N. & McCarthy, A. (eds.) *MediaSpace: Place, Scale and Culture in a Media Age*, London: Routledge.

Moores, S. (2005), *Media/Theory: Thinking about Media and Communications*, London: Routledge.

Moores, S. (2012), *Media, Place and Mobility*, Basingstoke: Palgrave Macmillan.

Moores, S. (2017), 'For Everyday-Life Studies', in Adams, P., Cupples, J., Glynn, K., Jansson, A. & Moores, S., *Communications/Media/Geographies*, New York: Routledge.

Morley, D. (1986), *Family Television: Cultural Power and Domestic Leisure*, London: Comedia.

Morley, D. (1992), *Television, Audiences and Cultural Studies*, London: Routledge.

Morley, D. (2000), *Home Territories: Media, Mobility and Identity*, London: Routledge.

Morley, D. (2001), 'Belongings: Place, Space and Identity in a Mediated World', *European Journal of Cultural Studies*, vol. 4, no. 4, pp. 425–448.

Morley, D. (2007), *Media, Modernity and Technology: The Geography of the New*, London: Routledge.

Morley, D. (2009), 'For a Materialist, Non-Media-Centric Media Studies', *Television and New Media*, vol. 10, no. 1, pp. 114–116.

Morley, D. (2011), 'Communications and Transport: The Mobility of Information, People and Commodities', *Media, Culture and Society*, vol. 33, no. 5, pp. 743–759.

Morley, D. & Silverstone, R. (1990), 'Domestic Communication: Technologies and Meanings', *Media, Culture and Society*, vol. 12, no. 1, pp. 31–55.

Mosco, V. (2009), *The Political Economy of Communication: Rethinking and Renewal*, London: Sage.

Pickering, M. (1997), *History, Experience and Cultural Studies*, Basingstoke: Macmillan.

Pink, S. (2012), *Situating Everyday Life: Practices and Places*, London: Sage.

Pink, S. & Leder Mackley, K. (2013), 'Saturated and Situated: Expanding the Meaning of Media in the Routines of Everyday Life', *Media, Culture and Society*, vol. 35, no. 6, pp. 677–691.

Polanyi, M. (2009 [1966]), *The Tacit Dimension*, Chicago, IL: University of Chicago Press.

Polanyi, M. (2015 [1958]), *Personal Knowledge: Towards a Post-Critical Philosophy*, Chicago, IL: University of Chicago Press.

Radway, J. (1984), *Reading the Romance: Women, Patriarchy and Popular Literature*, Chapel Hill, NC: University of North Carolina Press.

Rodaway, P. (1994), *Sensuous Geographies: Body, Sense and Place*, London: Routledge.

Sacks, H. (1995), *Lectures on Conversation*, Oxford: Blackwell.

Scannell, P. (ed.) (1991a), *Broadcast Talk*, London: Sage.

Scannell, P. (1991b), 'Introduction: The Relevance of Talk', in Scannell, P. (ed.) *Broadcast Talk*, London: Sage.

Scannell, P. (1996), *Radio, Television and Modern Life: A Phenomenological Approach*, Oxford: Blackwell.

Scannell, P. (2014), *Television and the Meaning of Live: An Enquiry into the Human Situation*, Cambridge: Polity.

Schatzki, T. (1996), *Social Practices: A Wittgensteinian Approach to Human Activity and the Social*, Cambridge: Cambridge University Press.

Schatzki, T., Knorr Cetina, K. & von Savigny, E. (eds.) (2001), *The Practice Turn in Contemporary Theory*, London: Routledge.

Seamon, D. (1980), 'Body-Subject, Time-Space Routines and Place-Ballets', in Buttimer, A. & Seamon, D. (eds.) *The Human Experience of Space and Place*, London: Croom Helm.

Seamon, D. (2015 [1979]), *A Geography of the Lifeworld: Movement, Rest and Encounter*, London: Routledge.

Sheets-Johnstone, M. (2009), *The Corporeal Turn: An Interdisciplinary Reader*, Exeter: Imprint Academic.

Sheets-Johnstone, M. (2011), *The Primacy of Movement*, second edition, Amsterdam: John Benjamins.

Sheller, M. & Urry, J. (2006), 'The New Mobilities Paradigm', *Environment and Planning A*, vol. 38, no. 2, pp. 207–226.

Silverstone, R. (1990), 'Television and Everyday Life: Towards an Anthropology of the Television Audience', in Ferguson, M. (ed.) *Public Communication: The New Imperatives – Future Directions for Media Research*, London: Sage.

Silverstone, R. (1994), *Television and Everyday Life*, London: Routledge.

Silverstone, R., Hirsch, E. & Morley, D. (1992), 'Information and Communication Technologies and the Moral Economy of the Household', in Silverstone, R. & Hirsch, E. (eds.) *Consuming Technologies: Media and Information in Domestic Spaces*, London: Routledge.

Sobchack, V. (2004), *Carnal Thoughts: Embodiment and Moving Image Culture*, Berkeley, CA: University of California Press.

Taylor, C. (2005), 'Merleau-Ponty and the Epistemological Picture', in Carman, T. & Hansen, M. (eds.) *The Cambridge Companion to Merleau-Ponty*, New York: Cambridge University Press.

Taylor, C. (2006), 'Engaged Agency and Background in Heidegger', in Guignon, C. (ed.) *The Cambridge Companion to Heidegger*, second edition, New York: Cambridge University Press.

Taylor, C. (2013), 'Retrieving Realism', in Schear, J. (ed.) *Mind, Reason and Being-in-the-World: The McDowell–Dreyfus Debate*, London: Routledge.

Thompson, E. (1978), *The Poverty of Theory and Other Essays*, London: Merlin.

Thompson, E. (1993 [1967]), 'Time, Work-Discipline and Industrial Capitalism', in *Customs in Common*, London: Penguin.

Thrift, N. (1996), *Spatial Formations*, London: Sage.

Thrift, N. (1997), '"Us" and "Them": Re-Imagining Places, Re-Imagining Identities', in Mackay, H. (ed.) *Consumption and Everyday Life*, London: Sage.

Thrift, N. (1999), 'Steps to an Ecology of Place', in Massey, D., Allen, J. & Sarre, P. (eds.) *Human Geography Today*, Cambridge: Polity.

Thrift, N. (2004), 'Summoning Life', in Cloke, P., Crang, P. & Goodwin, M. (eds.) *Envisioning Human Geographies*, London: Arnold.

Thrift, N. (2007), *Non-Representational Theory: Space/Politics/Affect*, London: Routledge.

Thrift, N., Harrison, P. & Anderson, B. (2010), '"The 27th Letter": An Interview with Nigel Thrift', in Anderson, B. & Harrison, P. (eds.) *Taking-Place: Non-Representational Theories and Geography*, Farnham: Ashgate.

Tolson, A. (1991), 'Televised Chat and the Synthetic Personality', in Scannell, P. (ed.) *Broadcast Talk*, London: Sage.

Tolson, A. (ed.) (2001), *Television Talk Shows: Discourse, Performance, Spectacle*, Mahwah, NJ: Lawrence Erlbaum.

Tolson, A. (2006), *Media Talk: Spoken Discourse on TV and Radio*, Edinburgh: Edinburgh University Press.

Tuan, Y. (1977), *Space and Place: The Perspective of Experience*, Minneapolis, MN: University of Minnesota Press.

Wacquant, L. (2004), *Body and Soul: Notebooks of an Apprentice Boxer*, New York: Oxford University Press.

Warde, A. (2016), *The Practice of Eating*, Cambridge: Polity.

Wellman, B. & Haythornthwaite, C. (eds.) (2002), *The Internet in Everyday Life*, Malden, MA: Blackwell.

Williams, R. (1977), *Marxism and Literature*, Oxford: Oxford University Press.

Williams, R. (1980), *Problems in Materialism and Culture: Selected Essays*, London: Verso.

Wood, H. (2007a), 'The Mediated Conversational Floor: An Interactive Approach to Audience Reception Analysis', *Media, Culture and Society*, vol. 29, no. 1, pp. 75–103.

Wood, H. (2007b), 'Television is Happening: Methodological Considerations for Capturing Digital Television Reception', *European Journal of Cultural Studies*, vol. 10, no. 4, pp. 485–506.

Wood, H. (2009), *Talking with Television: Women, Talk Shows and Modern Self-Reflexivity*, Urbana, IL: University of Illinois Press.

Wylie, J. (2007), *Landscape*, London: Routledge.

Young, I.M. (2005 [1980]), 'Throwing Like a Girl: A Phenomenology of Feminine Body Comportment, Motility and Spatiality', in *On Female Body Experience: Throwing Like a Girl and Other Essays*, New York: Oxford University Press.

· 2 ·

CONCEPTUALISING PLACE
IN A WORLD OF FLOWS

In the context of arguments about the rise of 'the network society' (Castells, 1996) and about the social 'as mobility' (Urry, 2000, p. 2; see also Elliott & Urry, 2010; Urry, 2007), in which contemporary social change is accounted for primarily in terms of intensified transnational flows or mobilities, I want to focus in this chapter on understandings of place. *How is it best, then, to conceptualise place in a world of flows (including, but also exceeding, those information flows that are enabled by modern media of communication)?* I will be attempting to answer that question through a critical discussion of ideas put forward by several social, spatial and communication theorists. It is appropriate for me to begin by considering aspects of the work done by Manuel Castells and John Urry, social theorists cited above in the opening sentence of my chapter, because, in the humanities and social sciences, they have been perhaps the most widely referenced thinkers on global networks and flows, and because they have each raised, in their overlapping yet different ways, important issues to do with the constitution of places in relation to various sorts of movement. I will then go on to look at some of Doreen Massey's work in geography, concentrating on her interrelated notions of 'global sense of place' (Massey, 1991, 1994), 'the openness of places' (Massey, 1995, p. 59) and 'the thrownto-getherness of place' (Massey, 2005, p. 141), before turning to consider Joshua

Meyrowitz's no-sense-of-place thesis (Meyrowitz, 1985) and 'second-generation medium theory' (Meyrowitz, 1994, p. 58), and, finally, Paddy Scannell's
phenomenological analysis of broadcasting (see especially Scannell, 1996,
2014). As I explain towards the end of the chapter, Meyrowitz and Scannell
have written, respectively and contrastingly, of place as marginalised or as
pluralised in electronic media use.

The space of flows and the space of places

In the first volume in a trilogy on matters of the information age, Castells
(1996) offers an impressively wide-ranging assessment of what he names the
network society.[1] For the specific purposes of this chapter, though, my main
concern is with the social theory of space that he advances there (in particular, Castells' distinction between the *space of flows* and the *space of places*).
I want to argue that this theorisation of space, whilst it has some interesting
and admirable features, has a significant problem or contradiction at its heart.

Space is defined by Castells (1996, p. 411), in general terms, as 'the
material support of time-sharing social practices', but he is keen to stress that
'simultaneous practices' today do not necessarily rely on the 'contiguity' of
participants in social interaction. Indeed, in his view, 'it is fundamental that
we separate the basic concept of material support of simultaneous practices
from the notion of contiguity' (Castells, 1996, p. 411).[2] This is because there
is, according to Castells, a new spatial form that is characteristic of the network society, which he calls the space of flows. His contention is that 'our
society is constructed around flows…flows of capital, flows of information…
flows of organizational interaction, flows of images…and…sounds' (Castells,
1996, pp. 411–412). He sees those flows as having been afforded by the development of certain technologies or technological systems, 'microelectronics,
telecommunications, computer processing, broadcasting systems…and high-
speed transportation' (Castells, 1996, p. 412). In a later, co-authored book
(Castells et al., 2007, p. 171), it is also noted that use of 'mobile communication technology greatly contributes to the spread of the space of flows'.[3]

It is at this stage, when Castells is introducing his concept of the space of
flows, that he first reflects on the consequences of such flows for the constitution of places in the network society. He proposes that although its overall
logic may be placeless, in fact:

The space of flows is not placeless...places do not disappear, but their logic and meaning become absorbed in the network...no place exists by itself...places are the nodes
of the network...the location of strategically important functions. (Castells, 1996,
pp. 412–413)

The example with which he proceeds to illustrate his argument is that of 'the
global...financial system' (Castells, 1996, p, 413). So in 'the network of global
financial flows' (Castells, 1996, p. 470), the 'nodes of the network' are locations such as 'stock exchange markets, and their ancillary advanced services
centres' around the world.

What is absolutely crucial to appreciate here, however, is that Castells'
references in the passage above to places as nodes (absorbed in networks)
are not references made to all places but rather to particular types of location
only, which have, as he puts it, strategically important functions in relation
to the space of flows. Castells does not even consider these node-locations
to be part of what he calls the space of places. This is, I realise, a potentially
confusing point that he is making, which requires further explanation. Let me
try to show, then, how he distinguishes the space of flows from the space of
places, and how he therefore distinguishes places as nodes from other kinds of
location that are regarded as being outside the global space of flows.

To his credit, Castells seems to draw the distinction between those two
types of space, and, correspondingly, two types of place, principally in an effort
to deal with social differences and relations of power. He associates the space
of flows with 'dominant processes and functions' (Castells, 1996, p. 412) in the
network society, whilst associating the space of places with 'subordinate functions...and people'. In his view, the subordinated live in locations that are not
only disconnected from the space of flows but also 'increasingly segregated and
disconnected from each other' (Castells, 1996, p. 476). As he puts the case
succinctly at one moment in his writing, 'people are local' (Castells, 1996,
p. 415) whereas: 'The space of power and wealth is projected throughout the
world.' Indeed, Castells (1996, p. 428) warns that 'we may be heading toward
life in parallel universes' as a result of an increasing divergence between the
space of flows and the space of places, with the latter being characterised by
locations in which, in his words, 'function and meaning are self-contained
within the boundaries of physical contiguity' (Castells, 1996, p. 423).

Undoubtedly, there are important issues to do with power and inequality
or with stasis in relation to movement, and I will be returning to these later in
discussing Massey's work. However, the basic problem or contradiction that
I see in Castells' theory of space becomes evident, I feel, when he provides a

specific example (and it is an interesting one) of life in what he is calling the space of places. The example that he chooses, of a district of Paris known as Belleville, has a particular personal relevance for him, as he indicates at the start of the following description:

> Belleville was, as for so many immigrants throughout its history, my entry point to Paris.... As a 20-year-old political exile...I was given shelter by a Spanish construction worker...who introduced me to...the place.... 30 years after our first encounter... new immigrants (Asians, Yugoslavs) have joined a long-established stream of Tunisian Jews, Maghrebian Muslims...and Southern Europeans, themselves the successors of the intra-urban exiles pushed into Belleville in the nineteenth century.... New middle-class households, generally young, have joined the neighbourhood because of its urban vitality.... Cultures and histories, in a truly plural urbanity, interact in the space. (Castells, 1996, pp. 423–424)

On the evidence presented there by Castells, this district of Paris is far from being segregated, disconnected or self-contained within boundaries. All of the things that he mentions in his description, including the circumstances of his own arrival in Paris years ago, involve movements and links across the city or the globe. He appears to be quite right in his assertion that Belleville's distinctive plural urbanity has been formed through a mixing or confluence of streams (although he is oddly reluctant to classify these population migrations as flows) or through an interaction of cultures and histories. Furthermore, I find it difficult to imagine that most of the district's contemporary residents, as they engage in their routine local activities, would not be accessing various flows, including rapid transnational flows, of information, images and sounds in their everyday lives, and in that sense it is surely misleading to characterise such lives simply as static and localised.[4] So Castells' theoretical definition of the space of places and his illustrative example of that sort of space seem to me to be, in certain crucial respects, at odds with each other.

I should add, in fairness to him, that Castells (2000, 2005; see also Castells & Ince, 2003, pp. 55–58) does go on to revise his social theory of space at a later stage in his work on what he terms the information age, and he does so in a way that appears to acknowledge, at least to some extent, the problem or contradiction to which I have been pointing. As geographer David Bell (2007, p. 74) observes, Castells comes 'to see the space of flows and the space of places as more...folded together' and 'also sees an error in his own prior articulation of the space of flows only to the techno-elites'. For instance, rather than regarding the space of flows and the space of places as diametrically opposed spatial forms leading towards life in parallel universes, Castells (2000, p. 27) subsequently concedes that 'the geography of the new history will not be made, after all, of the separation...but out of the interface between place and flows'. My preference, of course, is for this revised theorisation of space or conceptualisation of place in a world of flows, which stresses the interdependence or, as he chooses to express it, *the interface between place and flows*, and which is rather closer to the understandings of place that are offered by Urry and Massey.

The social as mobility and places understood as multiplex

As I suggested at the beginning of this chapter, there are similarities between the approaches to global networks and flows taken by Castells and Urry, but one of the key differences between them arises from Urry's wish to 'interrogate the concept of the social as society' (Urry, 2000, p. 1). So whereas Castells (1996) writes of the network society, retaining a term that has traditionally been central for the academic discipline of sociology, Urry (2000, p. 1) feels the need to challenge this largely taken-for-granted idea in setting out his 'manifesto for a sociology that examines the...mobilities of peoples, objects, images...information'. He preferred to think of *the social as mobility*, arguing that the concept of the social as society is too closely caught up with 'notions of nation-state' (Urry, 2000, pp. 5–7), 'national society' and 'the system of nations'. Personally, whilst I understand and sympathise with his desire to develop a transnational sociology that would involve studying long-distance, cross-border flows in conjunction with the 'little mobilities' (Adey, 2010, p. 6) of day-to-day living, I struggle to see why Urry was unwilling for the idea of society to be rearticulated to fit contemporary social circumstances.[5]

For me, a more valuable contribution made by Urry's theory of the social as mobility is his identification and discussion of 'five interdependent "mobilities" that produce social life organized across distance' (Urry, 2007, p. 47; see also Elliott & Urry, 2010, pp. 15–16). The first of these is what he calls the 'corporeal travel of people' (Urry, 2007, p. 47), which he regards as ranging 'from daily commuting to once-in-a-lifetime exile'. Urry's reference there to exile is interesting in relation to Castells' account of Belleville, which I touched on in the previous section, because, although Castells was reluctant to classify migration (including his own political exile in Paris many years before) as part of a space of flows, Urry is quite clear in his view that it does constitute a significant flow.[6] Indeed, he describes the scale of transnational corporeal travel, including short-term journeys for work or leisure purposes as well as migrations for a longer period of residence, as 'awesome' (Urry, 2000, p. 50). Also remarkable is the current scale of an overlapping 'physical movement of objects' (Urry, 2007, p. 47), which is the second of the five kinds of mobility that he seeks to draw attention to. I say overlapping because corporeal travellers of various sorts evidently transport things with them, like, say, the souvenirs or duty-free goods that are brought back from foreign holidays by tourists, to be displayed or consumed later in the domestic sphere (on 'tripper-objects', see Urry, 2000, p. 65).[7] Of course, in addition, the day-to-day typically involves dealings with many other commodities that have travelled vast distances without being accompanied on those journeys by their eventual users. Perhaps the best example of this would be the foods from across the world that are purchased at a local supermarket (a site at which the long-distance flow of things meets up with the smaller movements of everyday shopping and eating practices).

The remaining mobilities in Urry's list are all associated with media use, and the third, fourth and fifth categories are what he named imaginative, virtual and communicative travel. He associates imaginative travelling primarily with television viewing, conceptualising the medium of television as a means of transport (and see Larsen, 1999; Moores, 1993; Morley, 2010), although he acknowledges, too, that 'people "travel" elsewhere through…guidebooks and brochures…photos, postcards, radio and film' (Urry, 2007, p. 169), and, for Urry, the mobilities afforded by these media are also classed as imaginative. Next, he regards virtual travel as that which is afforded by networked computers. In one of his early discussions of this phenomenon, virtual travel is considered in interesting ways alongside what he calls a 'virtual proximity' (see Urry, 2002, pp. 265–267), in which internet users 'can feel proximate while still distant'. Finally, Urry (2007, p. 47; see also Elliott & Urry, 2010, p. 16) thinks of communicative travelling as having been facilitated by, for instance, 'letters, telegraph, telephone, fax and mobile', yet his focus there is on what he goes on to name, more specifically, the 'mobile communicative travel' (Urry, 2007, p. 171) that is associated with media such as 'the iPod, the laptop…and the… mobile phone'. A characteristic feature of those contemporary digital technologies is that all have been designed for use by people on the move, following earlier, portable print media such as books and newspapers. Urry's discussion of mobile communicative travel highlights a further overlap, then, between his categories of mobility. There is a significant crossover not only between the first and second (corporeal travel and the physical movement of objects) but also between these types of mobility and the last of the five on the list.

I should note here, too, that it does become increasingly difficult, in circumstances of media convergence today, to sustain the distinctions that Urry drew between imaginative, virtual and communicative travelling. For example, since broadcast programmes have been available via the internet, including via digital mobile media, or since it has been possible to interact with others online via a television screen, his media-related categories become rather less clear. However, the most important point to take from Urry's identification of the whole range of interdependent mobilities is that technologically mediated flows of information need to be considered in relation to, rather than viewed as somehow surpassing, the physical transportation of humans and things. Indeed, I want to pursue that point now with reference to his thoughts on mobility and proximity (see especially Urry, 2002), which were touched on just briefly in the preceding paragraph.

Urry's coupling of virtual travel with a virtual proximity and, more broadly, his remarks on how media uses can bring 'within range...persons and happenings' (Urry, 2000, p. 68) from far away, are certainly important, but this is only part of a much bigger story about mobilities and proximities. When I get to the work of Meyrowitz and Scannell in later sections of this chapter, I will return to matters of electronically mediated proximity, which are relevant, of course, to matters of place too. At this stage, though, it is necessary to consider what Urry (2002, p. 256) calls 'a very simple question: why do people physically travel?' So, when it is possible to move around and be close to people and events imaginatively or virtually or communicatively, why still bother with the often time-consuming corporeal travel that is required in order to be 'face-to-face' (Urry, 2002, p. 262) or 'face-the-moment'? After all, it has to be explained why there is a continuing 'compulsion of proximity' (Boden & Molotch, 1994) in contemporary living (that is, of physical proximity), despite the arrival of various new media technologies that promise to transcend large distances virtually instantaneously. Urry's own answer is that those mobilities or travellings which he associated directly with media use 'will not simply substitute for corporeal travel since intermittent co-presence appears obligatory for sustaining much social life' (Urry, 2002, p. 258). He outlines a series of obligations to, and also desires for, this intermittent bodily co-presence, including, for instance, the feelings of having 'to go to work... to see specific people "face-to-face"...to spend moments of quality time with family...or friends...to experience a particular "live" and not a "mediated" event' (Urry, 2002, p. 262). At the same time, however, he does wonder whether electronically mediated communications could, in future, 'make the compulsion to co-presence based upon social obligations less frequent' (Urry, 2002, p. 269).

Having provided an account of certain key aspects of Urry's theory of the social as mobility, let me turn to the ways in which his framework deals with the constitution of places in relation to these flows of humans, things and information. In a discussion of dwelling, he offers the following helpful definition of *places understood as multiplex* or of *place as nexus*:

> Places can be…understood…as multiplex, as…where networks and flows coalesce…. Any such place can be viewed as the particular nexus between…propinquity characterised by intensely thick co-present interaction and…networks stretched…across distances. These propinquities and extensive networks come together to enable performances in, and of, particular places. (Urry, 2000, p. 140)

What I particularly like about his definition is its emphasis on place as a coming together and entangling or enmeshing of little mobilities with long-distance movements of different sorts, and on place not simply as a location but also *as an ongoing performance*. Such an understanding of place is in keeping with, and yet goes beyond, the notion of an interface between place and flows that is found in Castells' revised social theory of space. Furthermore, in Urry's wider reflections on dwellings in the context of travellings, which included a fascinating discussion of 'inhabiting-the-car' (Urry, 2007, pp. 124–128; see also Bull, 2001; Thrift, 2004) in practices of driving, he makes some promising references to phenomenological philosophy (most notably, Heidegger, 1993 [1971]), starting to open up issues of habit and embodiment that I will be addressing in detail in later chapters.[8]

The notion of place in this age of globalisation

When he set out his understanding of place as multiplex or as nexus, Urry acknowledged a debt to Massey's thinking in the discipline of geography, and it is her work on places that I concentrate on in the current section. Like Urry, who asked why people still engage in corporeal travel today, Massey (1995, p. 46) also poses a simple question, which is similar to the one with which I framed this chapter at the outset: 'What happens to the notion of place now, in this age of globalization?' As I indicated in my introductory remarks near to the beginning of the chapter, her answers have involved the development of a series of interrelated concepts such as *global sense of place*, *the openness of places* and, more recently, *the throwntogetherness of place*.

Looking back at the emergence of her distinctive perspective on place, Massey (2005, p. 196) writes of how she wanted to 'retain an appreciation of specificity, of...the "local"...while at the same time insisting on internationalism', and she notes how: 'It was in this context that I worked towards what I would come to call "a global sense of place".' Indeed, for Massey (1994, p. 5), the 'particularity of any place' has to do, at least in part, with its mix of 'links and interconnections to..."beyond"', so that 'the global' is seen 'as part of what constitutes the local, the outside as part of the inside'. From this perspective, an appreciation of the specificity of the local is not to do with an 'internalized history' (Massey, 1994, p. 154) but rather with 'the fact that it is constructed out of a particular constellation of social relations, meeting and weaving together at a particular locus...a meeting place' (and note the similarity here between Massey's notion of place as locus or meeting place and Urry's subsequent conceptualisation of place).

Massey's global sense of place, then, involves a questioning of any idea of boundaries as 'divisions which frame simple enclosures' (Massey, 1994, p. 155) and, instead, incorporates an understanding of the openness of places or of place as 'extroverted'.[9] In later work, with her account of place's 'throwntogetherness' (Massey, 2005, pp. 140–141), she returned to the same theme, challenging a 'view of place as settled and pre-given...only to be disturbed by "external" forces' and insisting that 'the uniqueness of place' is precisely to do with the ongoing negotiation (Urry might say a performance) of a 'here-and-now', which is necessarily bound up with a multiplicity of 'theres' and 'thens'. Interestingly, in that more recent discussion, Massey (2005) also sought to extend her earlier approach to take in various non-human movements, ranging from those of other animals through to those of rocks. Things, even the seemingly most fixed of things such as hills, are never wholly stable but always shifting and in process, she asserts.

Focusing, for the purposes of this chapter, on Massey's writings about place in 'current global-local times' (Massey, 1994, p. 152), and leaving aside her interesting thoughts on slower-paced changes over many thousands of years, it would be useful for me to refer to some of the examples that she provides to illustrate her theoretical arguments. The first of these relates to London, the city that she lived in, and the second more specifically to Kilburn, which was her local district there.

Near to the start of a book-length case study of London as a world city, Massey (2007, p. 13) points out that a standard geographical question asked about this city is 'where does London end?' However, rather than trying to answer such a question, she proceeds to voice her doubts about its validity:

> Maybe places do not lend themselves to having lines drawn around them. London is an extreme example…but this is a general point…. There is a vast geography of dependencies, relations and effects that spreads out from here around the globe. This is…to argue that, in considering the politics and the practices, and the very character, of this place, it is necessary to follow…the lines of its engagement with elsewhere. Such lines of engagement are…part of what makes it what it is. (Massey, 2007, p. 13)

Here, she clearly has problems with any attempt to investigate places as entities with enclosing boundaries, and her reference to lines of engagement with elsewhere that help to constitute the character of a place (in this case, a vast geography spreading out from London around the globe) can be traced back to her earlier conceptualisation of places as open or porous. The lines that she was concerned to draw are not those of a city's outer edges but rather of what she had previously called a mix of links and interconnections to beyond.[10]

The second London-related example that I take from her work, which is an account of her local shopping street, Kilburn High Road, is concerned with just such a mix of links, or with the negotiation of a here-and-now that is caught up with a multiplicity of theres and thens. As she puts it: 'It is (or ought to be) impossible even to begin thinking about Kilburn High Road without bringing into play half the world and a considerable amount of British imperialist history' (Massey, 1994, p. 154). So her description mentions, for instance, a newspaper stand that 'sells papers from every county of what my neighbours, many of whom come from there, still often call the Irish Free State' (Massey, 1994, pp. 152–153), whilst across the road 'there's a shop which as long as I can remember has displayed saris in the window…life-sized models of Indian women…and reams of cloth'. Kilburn's throwntogetherness, for Massey, is unique. It has 'a character of its own' (Massey, 1994, p. 153) that has to do with the particular circumstances of its geographical and historical connectedness, and yet she also makes the important argument that Kilburn's distinctive character 'is absolutely not a seamless, coherent identity, a single sense of place which everyone shares'. Rather, she thinks of this area as having 'multiple identities' (Massey, 1994, p. 153), which are a consequence of people's different 'routes through the place, their favourite haunts within it…the connections they make (physically, or by phone or post, or in memory and imagination) between here and the rest of the world'.

A third helpful example moves the discussion out of London and the urban mix of Kilburn, and a few miles northwards into some small villages in rural Cambridgeshire. However, Massey (1995, pp. 59–60), in reporting the findings of empirical research that she was involved in there, retains a strong interest in the multiple identities of meeting places and in matters of social difference, identifying four groups in these country villages with varied 'activity spaces':

> There are high-tech scientists, mainly men, whose work is based in Cambridge, though they…have computers with modem links at home as well. The companies they work for operate in a highly internationalized part of the economy, and these employees spend their time in constant contact with, and physically travelling between, colleagues and customers all around the world…. At the other extreme are people who have never been to London and only rarely…made it as far as Cambridge…. These are people who…work locally…on the farms…in the village shops and services…. There are other groups, too, in a sense in-between these two in terms of…spatiality. There are people who work more or less locally…nearby or in Cambridge…maybe as cleaners or caterers…for firms which are multinational…. There are women who are the partners of the high-tech men, some of them presently at home with small children…often being the heart and soul of local meetings and charities. For shopping, they are more likely to drive into Cambridge…and they may have family in other parts of the country, whom they visit regularly and who visit them.

She is interested in the divisions of class and gender which become evident when investigating what she calls the spatiality of these different groups (that is, the uneven reach of their social activities). Indeed, Massey's discussion of those Cambridgeshire villages and her general commitment to a politics of place and space (see Featherstone & Painter, 2013) do invite comparisons with elements of Castells' work on the network society. So, for Castells, the high-tech scientists in this account would presumably be regarded as part of a larger grouping of techno-elites, moving extensively within the space of flows, while the group of villagers at the other extreme, as Massey puts it, would be seen as living a disconnected existence in a space of places. Still, her conceptualisation of place in a world of flows manages to take on board issues of inequality and power in a way that is rather more nuanced and complex than his.

For instance, Massey (1995, p. 60) observes that: 'Even the most "local" of the local people here have their lives touched by wider events…are linked into a broader geographical field…farms where they work may be affected by European legislation passed in Brussels.' Also for the cleaners and caterers who, in her words, work more or less locally, decisions taken thousands of miles away on another continent, in the head offices of a multinational firm, could significantly touch their lives, and of course there is the more routine 'intrusion' (Giddens, 1991, p. 27) of information flowing into their everyday worlds, which is brought by broadcasting, the press and, these days most likely, the internet too. A further nuanced point made by Massey (1995, p. 60) is that the people in these four groups, 'with their contrasting activity spaces', have lives which nevertheless 'touch each other…intersect': 'They…sometimes interact.' This intersecting and interacting is partly friendly and co-operative but can involve major frictions, for example over the rising property prices that are associated with an influx of relatively well-off newcomers. Those lives may be very different, then, but they are not quite operating in what Castells once referred to as parallel universes.[11]

No sense of place?

As I turn now to consider work done by Meyrowitz and Scannell, in this section and the one that follows it, my focus will be more fully on media uses and information flows. It should be evident, given the ground covered so far, that I favour a non-media-centric perspective from which flows of information are seen in the context of a wider range of mobilities (including the physical transportation of humans and things). My preference, then, is for social change in current global-local times to be 'understood as a multifaceted…phenomenon' (Held et al., 1999, p. 27). Still, the particularities of media deserve careful attention when thinking about matters of place and about 'the spatial reorganisation of social relations' (Massey, 1994, p. 121), and both Meyrowitz and Scannell present interesting (though ultimately differing) analyses of the consequences of electronic media use for a transformation in 'the "situational geography" of social life' (Meyrowitz, 1985, p. 6). So whereas Meyrowitz (1985) arrives at his influential *no-sense-of-place thesis*, Scannell (1996; see also Moores, 2004) chooses to conceptualise place as doubled or as pluralised in modern living.

Meyrowitz's book on electronic media and place (Meyrowitz, 1985), in which he developed an innovative model of social situations that is the result of a bold theoretical synthesis, can justifiably be thought of as a classic in media studies. In my view, it remains relevant for discussions in this academic field over 30 years after its publication. The theoretical synthesis that I refer to here is of 'two seemingly incompatible perspectives' (Meyrowitz, 1985, p. 7).

On the one hand, then, Meyrowitz (1985, p. 16, 1994) draws on a tradition of analysis that he calls medium theory, which he associates in particular with Marshall McLuhan's writings (see especially McLuhan, 1994 [1964]; McLuhan & Zingrone, 1997; and see Meyrowitz, 1994, 2003) but which has a longer history in the study of communications (for example, see Innis, 1951). Whereas much mainstream media analysis has emphasised in some way the importance of 'message content' (Meyrowitz, 1985, p. 20), medium theory, as its name is designed to indicate, pays greater attention to the medium of communication itself. As McLuhan (1994 [1964], p. 7) famously declared, 'the medium is the message' for medium theorists, and what they take to be crucial is any medium's capacity to alter 'the scale and form of human association and action' (McLuhan, 1994 [1964], p. 9). For example, in the case of television, McLuhan was among the first to see that the medium's affordance for live transmissions of images and sounds across potentially vast distances introduced a distinctive kind of simultaneity into contemporary social life (he coined the now widely used phrase the global village), and this can clearly be related to Castells' later insistence that in the network society simultaneous practices no longer rely on the contiguity of participants.

However, on the other hand, Meyrowitz (1985, p. 28) draws on an apparently unrelated tradition in the social sciences that he names 'situationism', which he discusses with particular reference to Erving Goffman's sociological writings (see especially Goffman, 1990 [1959]; Lemert & Branaman, 1997; and see Meyrowitz, 1986). In situationism, there is a firmly established concern with face-to-face interactions in circumstances of physical proximity, and a tendency to assume some necessary connection between social situations and physical locations. Goffman (1990 [1959], p. 246) was attempting to explore the organisation of 'social encounters…that come into being whenever persons enter one another's immediate physical presence', and, as Meyrowitz (1985, p. 28) notes, this sociologist is probably best known for 'using the metaphor of drama' in that exploration (employing terms such as 'actors', 'performances' and 'settings', most notably in his early work on presentations of self in everyday lives).

Could there be a way, asked Meyrowitz, of bringing together these different perspectives and traditions? Given the apparent theoretical distance between them, how might the ideas of McLuhan and Goffman be productively combined? Having been fascinated by both authors when he first read them as a student, these are the questions that came to occupy his work and which eventually formed the basis for his new model of *situations as information-systems*. With this model, which Meyrowitz (1994) thinks of as an instance of second-generation medium theory but which may equally be thought of as next-generation situationism, he was trying to take account of the 'complementary strengths and weaknesses' (Meyrowitz, 1985, p. 4) of those two perspectives. McLuhan had offered insights into the characteristics of specific media technologies, especially electronic media, reflecting on their consequences for modes of social organisation yet showing little interest in the dynamics of interaction. Goffman, meanwhile, had a valuable focus on the details of interpersonal encounters in conditions of physical co-presence, but with little regard for the significance of technologically mediated communication at a distance.[12]

The answer, for Meyrowitz (1985, p. 37), was to dismantle the taken-for-granted connection that situationist sociology had made between social situations and physical locations, thereby developing a 'more inclusive notion of "patterns of access to information"' (it is important to note that when he writes of access to information, Meyrowitz is thinking principally about a witnessing of 'social performances'). This inclusive notion by no means rules out investigations of face-to-face communication, of the sort that Goffman was well known for, and yet, crucially, it involves a sufficiently broad definition of a social situation to allow also for the analysis of technologically 'mediated encounters' (Meyrowitz, 1985, p. 37), in which there is access to the performances of others who are physically absent or distant.[13] I very much welcome that notion with its extended understanding of situations, because it enables physical locations and what Meyrowitz (1985, p. 38) helpfully terms 'media "settings"' to be seen as overlapping environments or as 'part of a continuum rather than a dichotomy'.

Indeed, this new model of situations as information-systems, or of situations defined in terms of access to electronically proximate as well as physically immediate performances, is closely related to Meyrowitz's argument about a shifting *situational geography of social life*:

> Now…information is able to flow through walls and rush across great distances…the social spheres defined by walls and gates are…only one type of interactional environment…electronic media affect social behavior…by reorganizing the social settings in which people interact. (Meyrowitz, 1985, pp. viii–ix)

With his reference in the passage above to information flowing through walls, there is something of a parallel with Massey's conceptualisation of places as open or porous. Rather like her, Meyrowitz has certain problems with the idea of social spheres being defined by enclosing boundaries.

Up to this point in my discussion of Meyrowitz's work, I am generally in agreement with him (although I do have worries about the technological determinism of medium theory, including its second-generation form, and its rather too media-centred account of social change). Where I depart from Meyrowitz (1985, p. 8) is over the assertion evident in his book's title that electronic media are giving rise to 'a "placeless" culture', and I come now to my critique of his reflections on media, place and placelessness.[14]

When Meyrowitz states that people today increasingly have no sense of place, he means this in different but interrelated ways, which depend on the two meanings that the word place has in his work. As should be implicit in the discussion so far, one of those meanings involves an understanding of place as physical location, and, now that people are potentially 'in touch' (Meyrowitz, 1985, p. 308) with others and 'tuned in' to a wider world virtually instantaneously, via electronic media of communication, so it is the case that, at least according to Meyrowitz, physical location ceases to have the significance that it once had when social spheres were defined by walls and gates. The other meaning of place, for him, has to do with people's positioning in social roles and hierarchies, or with issues of 'social "place"' (Meyrowitz, 1985, p. 308), and, following on directly from his proposal that the importance of physical location is diminished as information flows through walls and rushes across great distances, he claims that these roles and hierarchies are shifting:

> Evolution in media…has changed the logic of the social order…. Many…no longer seem to 'know their place'…the changing relationship between physical and social place has affected almost every social role. Our world…for the first time in modern history…is relatively placeless.

Whilst arguing that almost every social role is affected when patterns of proximity to performances are altered, Meyrowitz (1985, p. 308) does emphasise what he regards as the special impact 'on social groups that were once defined in terms of their physical isolation in specific locations…kitchens, playgrounds…and so forth', and I need to explain a little more about this because some of his claims are controversial in the context of media studies.

For example, unusually for a communication theorist, Meyrowitz (1985, p. 224) claims that the arrival of television and other electronic media 'liberates' many women from their previous 'informational confines' in the household, and also that these technologies 'foster a "situational androgyny"' (which is certainly a distinctive take on the politics of gender and media).

Similarly, when he turns to consider generational divisions, his claim is that there is a 'blurring of childhood and adulthood' (Meyrowitz, 1985, p. 226) in modern living, with the old hierarchy between children and their parents or teachers dissolving as a consequence of electronic media use. 'Children may still be sheltered at home', observes Meyrowitz (1994, p. 67), 'but television now takes them across the globe before parents give them permission to cross the street.' They are, in Urry's terms, imaginative travellers from an early age. In addition, Meyrowitz (1985, p. 163) remarks that at school the teachers are often in a position of having to respond to 'information available directly to children through television'. He therefore believes that evolution in media has served as a challenge to authority or as a democratising force.

In response to Meyrowitz's no-sense-of-place thesis, there are several objections that I could make but I will restrict myself to a short statement of three key criticisms here. The first and perhaps the most obvious difficulty with this thesis, for me, is its tendency to overestimate the degree to which social roles and hierarchies are actually shifting. As I have already indicated, I have no trouble at all with the argument that there has been a transformation in the situational geography of social life, with physical settings for interaction being joined and overlaid by media settings or new interactional environments, but that does not necessarily lead to a flattening out of differences and a dissolving of power relations in the social order (see also Leyshon, 1995). Neither does it necessarily mean (and this is the second of the criticisms I am putting to Meyrowitz) that physical location, including the physical isolation of some social groups, has lost its significance.[15] At one stage in his classic book, Meyrowitz (1985, pp. 117–118) argues that there has been 'a redefinition of the nature of "imprisonment"', since those prisoners who use electronic media are no longer in circumstances of 'informational isolation'. Even so, to pose the obvious question, who would want to live behind bars? The fact of incarceration surely remains the most crucial feature of the experience of being imprisoned, and this is certainly still one case in which, as Massey put it, boundaries matter. A third criticism, which points forward to the next section of my chapter, has to do with Meyrowitz's reluctance to employ the word place when referring to what he calls a media setting or environment. Just occasionally he does, as when he writes in his book's introduction that an electronic medium can simultaneously bring 'many different types of people to the same "place"' (Meyrowitz, 1985, p. 6; and see Adams, 1992). However, Meyrowitz more typically considers the uses of television and other electronic media to be caught up with a marginalisation of place, understood in this context primarily as physical setting. As I will show, Scannell (1996) offers an alternative, preferable view of contemporary situational geography with his notion of *a doubling of place*.

A doubling of place

There are some interesting similarities between the perspectives of Meyrowitz and Scannell. For instance, while Scannell's two major contributions to the phenomenology of broadcasting (Scannell, 1996, 2014) feature no references to McLuhan (but see Scannell, 2007, pp. 129–136), he nevertheless shares the general concern with media and time-space relations that Meyrowitz had inherited from first-generation medium theory. Furthermore, Scannell's theoretical reference points do include Goffman's sociology, as well as other sociologies of interaction and micro-social order such as ethnomethodology and conversation analysis, where Scannell (1996, p. 4) finds there to be a helpful focus on 'the social practices of everyday existence'. Another overlap between Meyrowitz and Scannell is their implicit agreement that media have an environmental quality. In Scannell's work, this is less explicitly stated, and yet it is clearly there in his observation that listeners and viewers find their 'way about in' (Scannell, 1996, p. 8) broadcasting's programme output (an observation to which I return later in the book, when considering matters of orientation).

At the same time, though, there are some significant differences too. The most notable of these, as I have suggested, is the distinction between Meyrowitz's thoughts on a marginalisation of place and Scannell's doubling-of-place idea, which I will explain shortly, but it is relevant to note that this grows out of a larger difference in perspectives which has to do with Scannell's development of *a phenomenological approach* to radio and television. When writing about the tradition of situationism in the social sciences, Meyrowitz refers in passing to particular sociologists, such as Alfred Schutz (1967) and Peter Berger and Thomas Luckmann (1991 [1966]), who have been influenced by aspects of phenomenological philosophy. For Scannell (1996, 2014), however, phenomenology (see especially Heidegger, 1962) is far more central, with this theorist and social historian of broadcasting reflecting at length on the implications of radio and television use for what he regards as *new ways of being in the world*.[16]

Scannell (1996, p. 91) initially airs the idea of doubling as he discusses broadcasting's occasional eventfulness, proposing that listeners and viewers who engage with media events (coverage of major sports occasions is an example of this eventfulness) have the 'magical' possibility of 'being in two places at once'. Eventful happenings that would once have been experienced as 'far away' (Scannell, 1996, p. 90) are transformed by broadcasting, becoming 'close at hand and graspable' (notice Scannell's metaphorical reference there to manual activity), and the liveness of the broadcast coverage is crucial for the experiences of audience members, 'since it offers the real sense of access to an event in its moment-by-moment unfolding' (Scannell, 1996, p. 84). In such circumstances, argues Scannell (1996, p. 76): 'Public events now occur, simultaneously, in two different places…the place of the event itself and that in which it is watched and heard.'

More recently, in his latest book on broadcasting and liveness, Scannell (2014, p. 63) has returned to the theme of doubling, expanding on his earlier reflections in the context of asking a basic question about 'what happens… when I turn on the television set':

> Before I turn on the television I am in the room…I am in my place and my time. After turning it on…I am in two worlds at one and the same time…my world and the world of broadcast television…. In turning on the television, I enter a doubled spatiality and a doubled temporality…the 'here' of where I am (in the room) and the 'there' of television wherever it may be (Afghanistan…the football stadium)…. The room does not disappear when I turn on the television…I have my cup of tea at home in the living room and I watch the match taking place…. I am now…in a here-and-there…I am now in…my time (in the room, watching television) and the now of the time of television (as it tells me the news, shows me the match). Broadcasting… creates a spanned spatiality and temporality.

Although he still makes reference here to the eventfulness of live sports coverage, as well as to what he has called the typically more routinised eventfulness of broadcast news (see Scannell, 1996, p. 160), his interest in what happens whenever television gets turned on is an indication that he understands the medium's pluralised or *spanned spatiality and temporality* to be a general characteristic of broadcasting, a feature of its 'dailiness' (Scannell, 1996, pp. 144–178) rather than just an occasional occurrence. Indeed, the liveness or 'phenomenal now of broadcasting' (Scannell, 1996, p. 172) can be experienced even when a programme has been recorded prior to the moment of transmission, and, according to Scannell (2014, p. 97), even when a recording is played back at a later time by an audience member: 'Whenever I hit the replay button, the living moment comes to life once more…recording redeems the living moment from death.'[17]

While the focus of Scannell's phenomenological analysis is very much on broadcasting, I want to expand further now on his notion of a doubling of place, by suggesting that it might be applied more widely in thinking about the uses of electronic and digital media. Without doubt broadcast radio and television have their distinctive features (their own particularities), but something they have in common with, say, the telephone as a medium, including the mobile or cell phone, is precisely that affordance of liveness and the capacity to '"double" reality' (Scannell, 1996, p. 173) virtually instantaneously.[18]

In fact, there is a remarkable echo of Scannell's idea of doubling in some work that conversation analyst Emanuel Schegloff (2002) has done on telephone use, even though I assume that Schegloff would not have been aware of Scannell's phenomenology of broadcasting.[19] This conversation analyst offers the following story, which is set on a train carriage in New York and also, to be exact, in a media environment of talk-in-interaction:

> A young woman is talking on the cell phone, apparently to her boyfriend, with whom she is in something of a crisis. Her voice projects in far-from-dulcet tones. Most of the passengers take up a physical and postural stance of busying themselves with other foci of attention (their reading matter, the scene passing by the train's windows, etc.), busy doing 'not overhearing this conversation'…except for one passenger. And when the protagonist of this tale has her eyes intersect this fellow-passenger's gaze, she calls out in outraged protest, 'Do you mind?! This is a private conversation!' (Schegloff, 2002, pp. 285–286)

The young woman in that story is, as Schegloff (2002, p. 286) puts it, 'in two places at the same time…and the railroad car is only one of them'. The other 'place that she is' (Schegloff, 2002, pp. 286–287), he continues, 'is "on the telephone"…there are two "theres" there', and this pluralisation of place clearly involves what Urry might have thought of as the mixing of mobile communicative travel with a physical transportation of humans and things.

This tale that Schegloff tells is one in which there is intended humour, which relates, of course, to the woman's insistence that she is having a private conversation when at least her contributions to the talk-in-interaction on the telephone are audible to fellow passengers in the carriage. Nevertheless, Schegloff (2002, p. 286) goes on to identify reasons for her claim to be upheld, as she is, after all, 'talking to her boyfriend, about intimate matters, in…argumentative mode, and this…makes it a private conversation'. Indeed, her definition of the circumstances is supported in a way by those passengers who are, in Schegloff's ethnomethodological terms, doing not overhearing. However, in the moment at which the woman on her mobile phone notices the single passenger who has refused to participate in this collaboratively performed

pretence, perhaps as a result of being irritated by the intrusion of argumenta-
tive talk into public space, what Schegloff calls the *two theres there* come into
conflict with one another.

A brief link to the next chapter

In the current chapter, I have reviewed critically a range of approaches to the
conceptualisation of place today. Rejecting arguments about a separation of
the spaces of flows and places or about the growing placelessness of contemporary social life, I favour perspectives on place as constituted at an interface
with flows or mobilities of various sorts, and on places in current global-local times as multiplex, open or pluralised (as opposed to being marginalised).
There is far more to say about place, though, and in the next chapter I want to
take my discussion further by pursuing an interest in phenomenology, which
I have only just begun to develop here with reference to Scannell's pioneering account of the experiences of radio and television use. In particular, I
will be considering some work in the field of human geography that mostly
predates Massey's reflections on the global sense and throwntogetherness of
place, and which foreshadows many aspects of the non- or more-than-representational geographies that are now associated with Nigel Thrift and others
in his discipline. This work has the potential, in my view, to extend Meyrowitz's important insights into electronic media and situational geography, by
paying detailed attention to the phenomenological geography of day-to-day
living and, especially, to everyday environmental experiences and place-making practices.[20]

Notes

1. For Manuel Castells' general definition of a network (and for some concrete examples
   of networks including what he calls the global network of the new media), see Castells
   (1996, pp. 470–471). In subsequent work too (see especially Castells, 2001), he develops
   his ideas about the network society in a worthwhile way, pursuing an interest in new media
   technologies and pointing to an emergent form of networked individualism.
2. There are parallels here with how sociologist John Thompson (1995, p. 32), in advancing
   his theory of media and modernity, writes of a changed 'experience of simultaneity' or
   'sense of "now"' in contemporary social life.
3. Given the attention that Castells (1996, 2001; Castells et al., 2007) pays to new media
   associated with the internet and mobile communication (to digital media), it is worth
   noting that there are others (Mattelart, 2000; Standage, 1998) who would have their

doubts about the newness of the social transformations he identifies, arguing that the 'networking' principle has a long history or writing of telegraphy as a 'Victorian internet'.

4. See also social theorist John Tomlinson (1999, p. 9), who helpfully observes that although 'the paradigmatic experience of global modernity for most people' may still be one of 'local life', this is a distinctive sort of local living in which globalisation has brought a range of things 'to them'. Indeed, Tomlinson's argument echoes one made earlier by Anthony Giddens (1990, p. 19, 1991, p. 27) concerning the 'phantasmagoric' character of places in modern social conditions or the 'intrusion of distant events' into everyday worlds.

5. The kind of sociology that John Urry advocated has much in common with Arjun Appadurai's earlier call for a 'transnational anthropology' (Appadurai, 1996, p. 48), since Appadurai shows a strong interest in the relations between ethnoscapes of moving people and mediascapes of moving images and sounds, and also connects with the case made by anthropologist Ulf Hannerz (1996, pp. 3–4) for 'new understandings of...transnational connections' in a world where 'boundaries...are not what they used to be'.

6. Castells (2000, p. 20), in keeping with his initial association of the space of flows only with dominant processes and functions, continues to limit his own understanding of corporeal-travel-as-flow to the high-speed and typically cosseted mobilities of those powerful 'social actors who operate the networks', who move along their 'global corridors'.

7. Before he became known primarily as a social theorist of mobilities, Urry (1990) had established a reputation for himself partly as a sociologist of tourism.

8. In fact, there are some interesting areas of overlap between Urry's theory of the social as mobility and Nigel Thrift's non-representational theory. For example, in discussing the corporeal travel of people, Urry (2007, p. 47) writes of how 'bodies encounter...the physical world...sensuously' and more specifically of the touch 'of the feet on the pavement or the...hands on...the steering wheel', while Thrift (1996, p. 259), in one of his early discussions of a non-representational approach, writes of a contemporary 'structure of feeling which I call mobility', going on to refer to 'a massive increase in the volume of travel... with the general democratisation of the automobile and the aircraft' (Thrift, 1996, pp. 279–280) and also to new developments in 'telecommunications'. Although they are from different disciplinary backgrounds (in sociology and geography respectively), Urry and Thrift have long been involved in interdisciplinary debates concerning the social and the spatial (see, for example, Gregory & Urry, 1985).

9. A clarification and an observation can usefully be added here. The clarification has to do with Doreen Massey's position on boundaries, because it is important to note that while she is indeed opposed to understanding places as bounded entities Massey (1995, p. 68) nevertheless accepts that there are significant social acts of boundary-marking and that 'boundaries matter' as a consequence: 'Where you live in relation to them determines the level of your...taxes and the services you receive.' My observation, meanwhile, is that her idea of an extroverted global sense of place or of the openness of places is not only caught up with a geographical analysis of place and space but is also intended to name a progressive political stance, a commitment to '"outwardlookingness"...a positivity and aliveness to the world beyond one's own turf' (Massey, 2005, p. 15). On occasion, then, she chose to speak of a 'progressive sense of place' (Massey, 1993).

10. Despite Massey's talk of the notion of place *in this age of globalisation* or in current global-local times, she does not regard globalising processes as a wholly new phenomenon and realises that places have always had a degree of openness and throwntogetherness. For instance, she takes the example of Liverpool as an old port city with a highly distinctive character that has been shaped largely by its lines of engagement with elsewhere (through trade and migration) over several centuries (see Massey, 1995, p. 61). So 'what we are currently experiencing' (Massey, 1995, p. 63), she contends, is not the beginning of transnational connections but rather their 'intensification'.

11. More broadly, Massey's interest in matters of social difference leads her to write of 'the power geometry of it all' (Massey, 1994, p. 149), by which she means how 'different social groups…are placed in very different ways in relation to…flows and interconnections'. In this context, she adds another level of complexity to debates about inequality and power with her insistence that such a geometry involves far more than just a division between those who are physically on the move and those who have to stay put. There is also the crucial issue of 'differentiated mobility' (Massey, 1994, p. 149), evident in a contrast that she makes between 'the jet-setters' and 'groups who are doing a lot of physical moving, but are not "in charge" of the process in the same way…refugees…undocumented migrant workers' and so on (see also Cresswell, 2010).

12. Late in his academic career, Erving Goffman (1981) did publish an essay on radio talk, although, as Joshua Meyrowitz (1985, p. 345) notes, no serious consideration is given there to issues of media and social change.

13. Although I have described Meyrowitz's model of social situations as innovative (and I stand by this judgement), two social scientists who were writing three decades before him, Donald Horton and Richard Wohl (1986 [1956]), can be credited with the development of an approach that anticipates elements of Meyrowitz's work, as he acknowledges (Meyrowitz, 1985, pp. 119–121). Horton and Wohl (1986 [1956]) are particularly interested in the 'para-social interaction', involving non-reciprocal relations of 'intimacy at a distance', between early television presenters and physically absent audience members, and their analysis focuses on the resemblance between this interaction-at-a-distance and certain features of face-to-face communication. For example, they refer to the mode of direct address and the simulation of conversational-give-and-take that is to be found in the talk of television show hosts (see also Thompson, 1995).

14. Meyrowitz is not alone in associating the development of media and communications with ideas about a growing placelessness in modern living. Over recent years, in the humanities and social sciences more generally, perhaps the most widely cited author to write on this theme is anthropologist Marc Augé (2009 [1995]), who offers an analysis of what he terms non-places. In human geography, too, Edward Relph (2008 [1976]) has written on mass communications and placelessness. Like Meyrowitz, Augé and Relph undeniably have valuable things to say. For example, I welcome the way in which both Augé and Relph make connections between media and transport technologies, whilst also bringing in questions of architecture and urban design. Still, I believe that all three of these theorists are wrong in their assumptions that contemporary media use necessarily leads to or contributes to a placeless existence.

15. Indeed, there have been some recent developments in media studies (more specifically, in mobile media research) that go against this aspect of Meyrowitz's no-sense-of-place thesis, with arguments being made for the continuing importance of localities in media use. I am thinking here of work done by Adriana de Souza e Silva and her collaborators, Eric Gordon and Jordan Frith (de Souza e Silva & Frith, 2012; Gordon & de Souza e Silva, 2011). So Gordon and de Souza e Silva (2011, p. 173) say that they find 'less and less convincing' the case that media technologies 'disconnect us from physical spaces', while de Souza e Silva and Frith (2012, p. 169) contend that 'predictions of the decreasing importance of place have not come true'. Their interest is in the emergence of what they call net locality (de Souza e Silva & Frith, 2012, p. 74; Gordon & de Souza e Silva, 2011), and they point out that through the uses of 'mobile, location-aware technologies… locations acquire increased relevance' (de Souza e Silva & Frith, 2012, p. 169) as physical settings are now augmented by a digital network of information that is organised according to the user's location. Still, it does strike me that in certain respects this recent work on new, location-aware mobile media actually reproduces some other, problematic aspects of Meyrowitz's thesis. For instance, despite their occasional protestations to the contrary, de Souza e Silva and her co-authors seem to be presenting a fairly media-centred account that is focused on particular technological developments in media hardware and software.

16. Interestingly, although he was a philosopher writing his landmark study on being and time around 90 years ago, in the very early years of broadcasting, Martin Heidegger (1962, pp. 138–140) himself includes some brief comments on radio in the context of a wider discussion of the 'spatiality of being-in-the-world', regarding that new medium as part of a 'push…towards the conquest of remoteness' in contemporary social life.

17. I sense the influence here of what Paddy Scannell (2014, p. 31) calls Roland Barthes' 'beautiful essay on photography' (Barthes, 1984). Indeed, one vivid memory that I have of being a final-year undergraduate student of Scannell's is of his announcement, on arrival at a regular Monday morning session, that instead of the scheduled topic for that week (the course as a whole was supposed to be about theories of ideology and discourse) the focus of the class would be on what was then this newly published book of Barthes', which Scannell had been reading over the weekend. He proceeded to give a fascinating, unscripted lecture linking Barthes' reflections on photography with, amongst other things, the fictional writings of Marcel Proust. For me now, as well as for Scannell, Barthes is an intriguing academic figure because despite being strongly influenced by structuralism in the early part of his career (for example, Barthes, 1968) he arrived at a position, certainly by the time of his late work on responses to photographic images, which has more of a phenomenological feel to it (see, for my commentary, Moores, 2005, pp. 133–137).

18. Of course, they have also had this in common, for a while now, with computer-mediated communications. Sociologist Lori Kendall (2002, p. 8; and see Miller & Slater, 2000; Wellman & Haythornthwaite, 2002) was among the first to write of a pluralisation of place (without employing Scannell's word doubling) in everyday internet use, when she noted that no one occupies 'only cyberspace' and that an online somewhere always 'in some sense overlays…physical place'.

19. Alongside Harvey Sacks, Emanuel Schegloff was one of the founding figures of conversation analysis in the discipline of sociology, and has long worked on the topic of telephone

talk (see, for example, Sacks et al., 1974; Schegloff, 1986). He is also the author of a
lengthy introduction to Sacks' collected lectures on conversation, which were posthu-
mously published following Sacks' untimely death (see Sacks, 1995).

20. In a newly published piece, Meyrowitz (2015) acknowledges the potential for his insights
to be extended in this way, responding directly to another, longer version of my sympathetic critique of his work (see Moores, 2012). He states there that his new piece on
electronic media and place might 'be thought of as part of a "conversation" with Moores'
(Meyrowitz, 2015, p. 124).

References

Adams, P. (1992), 'Television as Gathering Place', *Annals of the Association of American Geographers*, vol. 82, no. 1, pp. 117–135.

Adey, P. (2010), *Mobility*, London: Routledge.

Appadurai, A. (1996), *Modernity at Large: Cultural Dimensions of Globalization*, Minneapolis,
MN: University of Minnesota Press.

Augé, M. (2009 [1995]), *Non-Places*, London: Verso.

Barthes, R. (1968), *Elements of Semiology*, New York: Hill and Wang.

Barthes, R. (1984), *Camera Lucida: Reflections on Photography*, London: Fontana.

Bell, D. (2007), *Cyberculture Theorists: Manuel Castells and Donna Haraway*, London: Routledge.

Berger, P. & Luckmann, T. (1991 [1966]), *The Social Construction of Reality: A Treatise in the
Sociology of Knowledge*, London: Penguin.

Boden, D. & Molotch, H. (1994), 'The Compulsion of Proximity', in Friedland, R. & Boden, D.
(eds.) *NowHere: Space, Time and Modernity*, Berkeley, CA: University of California Press.

Bull, M. (2001), 'Soundscapes of the Car: A Critical Study of Automobile Habitation', in
Miller, D. (ed.) *Car Cultures*, Oxford: Berg.

Castells, M. (1996), *The Rise of the Network Society*, Malden, MA: Blackwell.

Castells, M. (2000), 'Grassrooting the Space of Flows', in Wheeler, J., Aoyama, Y. & Warf,
B. (eds.) *Cities in the Telecommunications Age: The Fracturing of Geographies*, New York:
Routledge.

Castells, M. (2001), *The Internet Galaxy: Reflections on the Internet, Business and Society*, Oxford:
Oxford University Press.

Castells, M. (2005), 'Space of Flows, Space of Places: Materials for a Theory of Urbanism in the
Information Age', in Sanyal, B. (ed.) *Comparative Planning Cultures*, New York: Routledge.

Castells, M., Fernández-Ardèvol, M., Qui, J. & Sey, A. (2007), *Mobile Communication and
Society: A Global Perspective*, Cambridge, MA: MIT Press.

Castells, M. & Ince, M. (2003), *Conversations with Manuel Castells*, Cambridge: Polity.

Cresswell, T. (2010), 'Towards a Politics of Mobility', *Environment and Planning D: Society and
Space*, vol. 28, no. 1, pp. 17–31.

de Souza e Silva, A. & Frith, J. (2012), *Mobile Interfaces in Public Spaces: Locational Privacy,
Control and Urban Sociability*, New York: Routledge.

Elliott, A. & Urry, J. (2010), *Mobile Lives*, London: Routledge.

Featherstone, D. & Painter, J. (eds.) (2013), *Spatial Politics: Essays for Doreen Massey*, Oxford: Wiley-Blackwell.

Giddens, A. (1990), *The Consequences of Modernity*, Cambridge: Polity.

Giddens, A. (1991), *Modernity and Self-Identity: Self and Society in the Late Modern Age*, Cambridge: Polity.

Goffman, E. (1981), 'Radio Talk: A Study of the Ways of Our Errors', in *Forms of Talk*, Philadelphia, PA: University of Pennsylvania Press.

Goffman, E. (1990 [1959]), *The Presentation of Self in Everyday Life*, London: Penguin.

Gordon, E. & de Souza e Silva, A. (2011), *Net Locality: Why Location Matters in a Networked World*, Malden, MA: Wiley-Blackwell.

Gregory, D. & Urry, J. (eds.) (1985), *Social Relations and Spatial Structures*, Basingstoke: Macmillan.

Hannerz, U. (1996), *Transnational Connections: Culture, People, Places*, London: Routledge.

Heidegger, M. (1962), *Being and Time*, Oxford: Blackwell.

Heidegger, M. (1993 [1971]), 'Building Dwelling Thinking', in Krell, D. (ed.) *Martin Heidegger: Basic Writings*, London: Routledge.

Held, D., McGrew, A., Goldblatt, D. & Perraton, J. (1999), *Global Transformations: Politics, Economics and Culture*, Cambridge: Polity.

Horton, D. & Wohl, R. (1986 [1956]), 'Mass Communication and Para-Social Interaction: Observations on Intimacy at a Distance', in Gumpert, G. & Cathcart, R. (eds.) *Inter/Media: Interpersonal Communication in a Media World*, third edition, New York: Oxford University Press.

Innis, H. (1951), *The Bias of Communication*, Toronto: University of Toronto Press.

Kendall, L. (2002), *Hanging Out in the Virtual Pub: Masculinities and Relationships Online*, Berkeley, CA: University of California Press.

Larsen, P. (1999), 'Imaginary Spaces: Television, Technology and Everyday Consciousness', in Gripsrud, J. (ed.) *Television and Common Knowledge*, London: Routledge.

Lemert, C. & Braneman, A. (eds.) (1997), *The Goffman Reader*, Malden, MA: Blackwell.

Leyshon, A. (1995), 'Annihilating Space? The Speed-Up of Communications', in Allen, J. & Hamnett, C. (eds.) *A Shrinking World? Global Unevenness and Inequality*, Oxford: Oxford University Press.

Massey, D. (1991), 'A Global Sense of Place', *Marxism Today*, June issue, pp. 24–29.

Massey, D. (1993), 'Power-Geometry and a Progressive Sense of Place', in Bird, J., Curtis, B., Putnam, T., Robertson, G. & Tickner, L. (eds.) *Mapping the Futures: Local Cultures, Global Change*, London: Routledge.

Massey, D. (1994), *Space, Place and Gender*, Cambridge: Polity.

Massey, D. (1995), 'The Conceptualization of Place', in Massey, D. & Jess, P. (eds.) *A Place in the World? Places, Cultures and Globalization*, Oxford: Oxford University Press.

Massey, D. (2005), *For Space*, London: Sage.

Massey, D. (2007), *World City*, Cambridge: Polity.

Mattelart, A. (2000), *Networking the World, 1794–2000*, Minneapolis, MN: University of Minnesota Press.

McLuhan, E. & Zingrone, F. (eds.) (1997), *Essential McLuhan*, London: Routledge.

McLuhan, M. (1994 [1964]), *Understanding Media: The Extensions of Man*, Cambridge, MA: MIT Press.

Meyrowitz, J. (1985), *No Sense of Place: The Impact of Electronic Media on Social Behavior*, New York: Oxford University Press.

Meyrowitz, J. (1986), 'Television and Interpersonal Behavior: Codes of Perception and Response', in Gumpert, G. & Cathcart, R. (eds.) *Inter/Media: Interpersonal Communication in a Media World*, third edition, New York: Oxford University Press.

Meyrowitz, J. (1994), 'Medium Theory', in Crowley, D. & Mitchell, D. (eds.) *Communication Theory Today*, Cambridge: Polity.

Meyrowitz, J. (2003), 'Canonic Anti-Text: Marshall McLuhan's *Understanding Media*', in Katz, E., Peters, J., Liebes, T. & Orloff, A. (eds.) *Canonic Texts in Media Research: Are There Any? Should There Be? How about These?*, Cambridge: Polity.

Meyrowitz, J. (2015), 'Place and Its Mediated Re-Placements', in Malpas, J. (ed.) *The Intelligence of Place: Topographies and Poetics*, London: Bloomsbury Academic.

Miller, D. & Slater, D. (2000), *The Internet: An Ethnographic Approach*, Oxford: Berg.

Moores, S. (1993), 'Television, Geography and "Mobile Privatization"', *European Journal of Communication*, vol. 8, no. 3, pp. 365–379.

Moores, S. (2004), 'The Doubling of Place: Electronic Media, Time-Space Arrangements and Social Relationships', in Couldry, N. & McCarthy, A. (eds.) *MediaSpace: Place, Scale and Culture in a Media Age*, London: Routledge.

Moores, S. (2005), *Media/Theory: Thinking about Media and Communications*, London: Routledge.

Moores, S. (2012), *Media, Place and Mobility*, Basingstoke: Palgrave Macmillan.

Morley, D. (2010), 'Television as a Means of Transport: Digital Teletechnologies and Transmodal Systems', in Gripsrud, J. (ed.) *Relocating Television: Television in the Digital Context*, London: Routledge.

Relph, E. (2008 [1976]), *Place and Placelessness*, London: Pion.

Sacks, H. (1995), *Lectures on Conversation*, Oxford: Blackwell.

Sacks, H., Schegloff, E. & Jefferson, G. (1974), 'A Simplest Systematics for the Organization of Turn-Taking for Conversation', *Language*, vol. 50, no. 4, pp. 696–735.

Scannell, P. (1996), *Radio, Television and Modern Life: A Phenomenological Approach*, Oxford: Blackwell.

Scannell, P. (2007), *Media and Communication*, London: Sage.

Scannell, P. (2014), *Television and the Meaning of Live: An Enquiry into the Human Situation*, Cambridge: Polity.

Schegloff, E. (1986), 'The Routine as Achievement', *Human Studies*, vol. 9, nos. 2/3, pp. 111–151.

Schegloff, E. (2002), 'Beginnings in the Telephone', in Katz, J. & Aakhus, M. (eds.) *Perpetual Contact: Mobile Communication, Private Talk, Public Performance*, Cambridge: Cambridge University Press.

Schutz, A. (1967), *The Phenomenology of the Social World*, Evanston, IL: Northwestern University Press.

Standage, T. (1998), *The Victorian Internet: The Remarkable Story of the Telegraph and the Nineteenth Century's Online Pioneers*, London: Weidenfeld and Nicolson.

Thompson, J. (1995), *The Media and Modernity: A Social Theory of the Media*, Cambridge: Polity.

Thrift, N. (1996), *Spatial Formations*, London: Sage.

Thrift, N. (2004), 'Driving in the City', *Theory, Culture and Society*, vol. 21, nos. 4/5, pp. 41–59.

Tomlinson, J. (1999), *Globalization and Culture*, Cambridge: Polity.

Urry, J. (1990), *The Tourist Gaze: Leisure and Travel in Contemporary Societies*, London: Sage.

Urry, J. (2000), *Sociology Beyond Societies: Mobilities for the Twenty-First Century*, London: Routledge.

Urry, J. (2002), 'Mobility and Proximity', *Sociology*, vol. 36, no. 2, pp. 255–274.

Urry, J. (2007), *Mobilities*, Cambridge: Polity.

Wellman, B. & Haythornthwaite, C. (eds.) (2002), *The Internet in Everyday Life*, Malden, MA: Blackwell.

· 3 ·

MEDIA USES AND EVERYDAY ENVIRONMENTAL EXPERIENCES

A Positive Critique of Phenomenological Geography

Lifeworld, time-space routines and media uses

I will begin by reproducing a small fragment of what is, for me, some fascinating empirical material on *everyday environmental experiences* that appears in a book originally published back in the late 1970s, written by geographer David Seamon (2015 [1979], pp. 55–56):

> Waking at 7.30, making the bed, bathing, dressing, walking out of the house at eight…so one group member described a morning routine that he followed every day but Sunday. From home he walked to a nearby cafe, picked up a newspaper (which had to be *The New York Times*), ordered his usual fare (one scrambled egg and coffee) and stayed there until nine when he walked to his office…. 'I like this routine and I've noticed how I'm bothered a bit when a part of it is upset…if the *Times* is sold out, or if the booths are taken and I have to sit at a counter.'

The group member whose actions are referred to (and whose words are quoted) in this extract was a participant in one of the 'environmental experience groups' (Seamon, 2015 [1979], p. 20) which the author had set up in the American city where he was carrying out his research, and the main purpose of these groups was 'to make the lifeworld…the taken-for-granted pattern and context of everyday life…a focus of attention'.[1]

Of course, it is precisely because of the taken-for-grantedness of the every-day that what Seamon calls the *lifeworld* is typically not a focus of attention. Rather, it has to do primarily with habitual movement and pre-reflective knowledge or, as Seamon's mentor Anne Buttimer (1976, p. 281; see also Buttimer & Seamon, 1980) put it, with 'precognitive "givens"'. As the group member featured in the passage above says of his own patterned routine: 'It's not that I figure out this schedule each day…it simply unfolds' (Seamon, 2015 [1979], p. 171). What helped him to reflect on the habitual and the pre-reflective, in addition to the process of group inquiry, were those rare occa-sions when a part of this unfolding series of activities was upset or disturbed in some way, giving rise to noticing: 'A change in the world as known brings itself to attention' (Seamon, 2015 [1979], p. 117). Such changes were experi-enced as a source of mild irritation, of feeling bothered a bit.[2]

As an academic from the field of media studies, I am interested in the reference to a newspaper as an integral element of the research participant's lifeworld (and, as Seamon reports, it had to be this particular one). Reading that newspaper, much like making the bed, walking out of the house, eating scrambled egg and drinking coffee, was an utterly normal, ordinary feature of his morning routine. Indeed, the account reminds me of Hermann Bausing-er's observation that the daily paper may serve a ritual function as 'a mark of confirmation' (Bausinger, 1984, p. 344), so that 'reading it proves…the break-fast-time world is still in order', and, in his classic essay on media in everyday lives, Bausinger even comments on how regular readers can feel a disruption in the flow or rhythm of day-to-day living when, for one reason or another, their preferred daily paper is unavailable (see also Peterson, 2010).

Still, having begun by declaring that I find the data presented in Seamon's book to be fascinating (which I certainly do), I must add that I am surprised by just how few mentions there are of media in the accounts of people's *time-space routines* (Seamon, 2015 [1979], p. 54; and see Seamon, 1980) and, more generally, their everyday environmental experiences.[3] After all, the research participants were living in what Seamon describes as an industrial city in the USA, well into the second half of the 20th Century, and they would pre-sumably have had access to various modern media of communication. Along with the passage that I reproduced at the start of this chapter, there are some other interesting fragments of material in the study that point to media as part of people's everyday lives. For example, in an early evening routine that he followed after returning from work, the brother of a group member is reported to have regularly eaten a meal 'in front of the seven o'clock news on televi-sion' (Seamon, 2015 [1979], p. 56). Elsewhere, somebody remarked on the pleasurable ritual of reading a book in a particular chair before going to bed each night (see Seamon, 2015 [1979], p. 178). A further, rather different example involves the technology of the telephone: 'A few times when using the phone, I've found myself dialling my home number rather than the one I want...I guess because that number is the one I call the most often' (Seamon, 2015 [1979], pp. 164–165). However, beyond a handful of instances like these, *media uses* do not figure in the research as a significant aspect of the everyday. As should be clear from my previous advocacy of a non-media-centric perspective, I have no problem at all with a centring of what I called, earlier in my book, the quotidian fabric (so that the meanings of media and their uses are understood in that wider context), and yet, to repeat the case I am making in slightly different words, it does seem odd to me that there is quite so little discussion of media in Seamon's geography of the lifeworld.

A possible explanation for the low profile that media and their uses have in this study is that Seamon, who guided the environmental experience groups in reflecting on day-to-day living, was openly suspicious of developments in what he referred to elsewhere in his book, following the work of fellow human geographer Edward Relph (2008 [1976]), as mass communications. At one point, then, Seamon (2015 [1979], p. 91) contends that 'technology and mass culture destroy the uniqueness of places'. His argument here is borrowed directly from Relph's, and, in the following section of my chapter and beyond, I present a critique of their broadly shared position on *place-making practices and placelessness*, also reviewing the work of another pioneer of place studies, Yi-Fu Tuan (1977, 1996a [1974], 2004). Although I disagree with the overall line that Seamon and Relph (similarly, see Buttimer, 1980) take on media and social change, and while this strand of geographical work has further limitations too, which I will come to in due course, my critique is not wholly damning. On the contrary, it is intended to be, in the sense that Anthony Giddens (1993) gives the term, 'a positive critique', because I believe that many of the key concepts of *phenomenological geography* have a valuable contribution to make to investigations of everyday media use.

Phenomenological geography, place-making practices and placelessness

Phenomenological geography, which is Seamon's own (and, in my view, the most appropriate) name for this approach (see Seamon, 1980, p. 148), but which is more usually known and discussed in the discipline's secondary literature as a form of humanistic geography (see Cloke et al., 1991; Cress-well, 2004, 2013; Holloway & Hubbard, 2001; Hubbard et al., 2002; Nayak & Jeffrey, 2013; Peet, 1998), emerged partly in response to other kinds of geography that were regarded as being 'without human agency' (Ley, 1996 [1980]), such as the abstractions of positivist spatial science and of structur-alist-Marxist spatial theory. In addition, Seamon's geography of the lifeworld was an attempt to get beyond the rationalist 'theories of spatial cognition' (Seamon, 2015 [1979], p. 34) which, he notes, a number of human geog-raphers at the time had 'come to accept', and which asserted that 'spatial behaviour' is shaped by 'cognitive maps' (see, for example, Downs & Stea, 1977). 'In contrast to the view of the cognitive theorists', writes Seamon (2015 [1979], p. 35), 'I argue that cognition plays only a partial role in every-day spatial behaviour…that a sizeable portion of our everyday movements… is precognitive and involves a pre-reflective knowledge.'⁴ Seamon, along with Buttimer, Relph and Tuan, were developing their distinctive geographical approach in North America, but they drew either directly or indirectly on the insights of European phenomenological philosophers such as Edmund Husserl (who used the term lifeworld long before Seamon did), Martin Heidegger and Maurice Merleau-Ponty.

An important concept in Seamon's consideration of everyday movements is the notion of *body-subject* (see Seamon, 2015 [1979], pp. 40–41). He is clearly influenced there by Merleau-Ponty's argument, which I touched on in my opening chapter and which I return to in the next, that 'the body…is on the side of the subject' (Merleau-Ponty, 2004 [1964], pp. 35–36) or, to turn it the other way round, that subjectivity is 'incarnate' (Merleau-Ponty, 2004 [1964], p. 37). In drawing on Merleau-Ponty's philosophy and employing this notion of body-subject, Seamon (2015 [1979], p. 40) shows his interest in the 'habitual nature of movement' and he understands time-space routines to be integrations and repetitions of such habitual movement. As a twin concept to that of body-subject, he also employs the interrelated notion of *feeling-sub-ject* (see Seamon, 2015 [1979], p. 76) in an attempt to address the associated emotional or affective dimension of bodily movements through everyday environments.

Furthermore, Seamon (2015 [1979], pp. 70–71) states that 'forces of body and emotion…intertwined' can give rise to circumstances of *at-homeness*, 'the usually unnoticed, taken-for-granted situation of being comfortable in and familiar with the everyday world in which one lives', and, where there is the 'profound at-homeness' (Seamon, 2015 [1979], p. 90) of 'unselfconscious immersion' in environments, this is a condition that Relph (2008 [1976], p. 55) names *existential insideness* (see also Seamon & Sowers, 2008). Such an insideness is 'experienced without deliberate...reflection' (Relph, 2008 [1976], p. 55) and yet it is 'full with significances'. If Seamon's concepts of body-subject and feeling-subject have a Merleau-Pontyan flavour, these ideas of at-homeness and, in Relph's work, existential insideness are more closely related to the Heideggerian notion of dwelling (see Heidegger, 1993 [1971]; Relph, 2008 [1976], pp. 17–18; Seamon, 2015 [1979], p. 92) or to the concept of habitation (see especially Ingold, 2011).

That series of terms from phenomenological geography is designed to deal with the dynamics of place-making practices and with the formation of senses of place, and 'the making of place' (Holloway & Hubbard, 2001, p. 67) is perhaps the fundamental concern in this area of phenomenological-geographical inquiry. Crucially, for these geographers: 'Place...is more than location' (Tuan, 1996a [1974], p. 445).[5] So, for Tuan (1996a [1974], pp. 451–452), it is by 'following established paths' in 'daily routines' that 'a sense of place' gets constituted over time, as a *habit field* is gradually formed and as 'people are emotionally bound to their material environment' (note the similarities here with Seamon's arguments about time-space routines, body-subject, feeling-subject and at-homeness). Location is made familiar and meaningful, and only then becomes place, through habitual practice or movement, and through an associated *affective attachment*. More examples might be helpful at this stage in order to illustrate the phenomenological geographers' conceptualisations of place, and, from Tuan (1977) and Seamon (2015 [1979]), I will take three.

The first of these connects with Tuan's general observation that place is made by following established paths in daily routines, and this specific example is of the integration and repetition of bodily movements (and of relationships with material things) in domestic times and spaces:

> Pieces of furniture such as a desk, an armchair, the kitchen sink...are points along a complex path of movement that is followed day after day.... As a result of habitual use the path...acquires a density of meaning.... The path and the pauses along it constitute a...place. (Tuan, 1977, pp. 180–182)

A second example of Tuan's that I have chosen to highlight involves a broadening of scale from the domestic setting to the urban neighbourhood. He discusses a process in which 'a strange part of town...unknown space' (Tuan, 1977, p. 199) can gradually become 'familiar place...filled with meaning', as 'we...find our way' there by moving around the environment and establishing known 'routes'. Interestingly, elsewhere in his book on space and place, Tuan (1977, p. 68) comments that such knowing-the-path-in-practice does not necessarily translate easily into language or symbolic representation: 'People who are good at finding their way in the city may be poor at giving street directions to the lost, and hopeless in their attempts to draw maps.' Of course, the difficulty with putting this practical know-how into words or pictures is precisely because it is a bodily knowledge in movement, intimately bound up with doing.

For a third illustration of the making of place, I return to the urban-neighbourhood cafe that Seamon's group member (the research participant featured in the passage reproduced at the beginning of my current chapter) frequented each working day at breakfast time. In the following extract, this group member describes some of the cafe's routine social interactions 'between eight o'clock and nine' (Seamon, 2015 [1979], p. 171) and its consequent, characteristic atmosphere:

> Several 'regulars' come in during that period…the telephone repair man and several elderly people, including one woman named Claire, whom I know and say 'Good morning' to each day…. Many of these people know each other. The owner…knows every one of the regulars and what they will usually order. The situation of…recognising faces…somehow makes the place warmer.

Although the social relations of this cafe setting appear to have been ones of acquaintanceship (see Morgan, 2009), rather than of close friendship, the day-after-day, again-and-again quality of the interactions (and, therefore, the situation of recognising faces) served to create a sociable mood of warmth.

An important aspect of this third example is its emphasis on the collaborative dimension of place-making practices. The cafe-made-familiar-and-meaningful, or the cafe that is constituted as place through the habitual practices or movements of its breakfast-time regulars, as well as of its owner, is a particular instance of what Seamon (2015 [1979], pp. 54–56; see also Seamon, 1980) calls 'place ballets' or *place choreographies*. The metaphor of dance is maybe a little too romantic in this context, suggesting a view of ordinary life as art. However, there is undoubtedly a performance of a sort going on here, which is repetitive and ordered yet also skilfully improvised in interaction, as the different time-space routines or established paths of several people become enmeshed for a while in a certain social setting. Seamon (2015 [1979], p. 56) proposes that such collaborative performances of place can be found not just in cafes but also, involving much larger numbers of people, in other public settings like city streets and market squares.[6]

I broadly welcome this approach to place-making practices that the phenomenological geographers have to offer, but there are shortcomings, too, in the story that they tell about place in modern living. For me, the most serious of these shortcomings has to do with problematic assertions about placelessness (and in that regard there are some obvious parallels with Joshua Meyrowitz's work, which was discussed in my preceding chapter). Relph (2008 [1976]) is the main narrator of this side of their story. At the root of his arguments about place and placelessness is an evaluative distinction that he draws between authentic place-making, which has the potential for existential insideness, and what is seen as the inauthentic character of a new 'placeless geography' (Relph, 2008 [1976], p. 117).

Given the phenomenological geographers' definition of place in human-experiential terms, it must be possible, in principle, for there to be placeless space, since not all spaces are routinely inhabited by humans. For instance, David Ley (1996 [1980], p. 193), a geographer who was largely sympathetic to those from within his discipline who had developed insights from phenomenological philosophy, considered the surface of the moon as a limit case. Still, for Relph the sites of placelessness are not moonscapes or even earthly wildernesses. Instead, he focuses his critical attention on what he thinks of as a proliferation of 'anonymous spaces and exchangeable environments' (Relph, 2008 [1976], p. 143), which he associates with particular directions in architecture, planning and technology. The main targets of Relph's criticism in the areas of architecture or planning are modernist 'International Style' (Relph, 2008 [1976], pp. 92–93) buildings constructed from concrete, steel and glass, along with locations that 'declare themselves unequivocally to be "Vacationland" or "Consumerland"', and suburban residential estates with their seemingly 'endless subdivisions of identical houses' (Relph, 2008 [1976], p. 105). Above all, though, Relph regards the emergence of placeless geography to be a result of the technologies of mass communication.

Interestingly, Relph (2008 [1976], pp. 90–92) understands 'mass communications' to include, in addition to the print media and broadcasting that have, in his view, 'reduced...the significance of place-based communities', a range of transportation sites and systems: 'Roads, railways, airports, cutting across or imposed on the landscape rather than developing with it, are not only features of placelessness in their own right, but...have encouraged the spread of placelessness well beyond...immediate impacts.' This is that line of argument which, as I mentioned earlier, Seamon came to adopt, and which is also evident in some of Buttimer's reflections on place from that period.

So, in her case, she compares favourably 'the feeling of grass on bare feet' (Buttimer, 1980, p. 172) and 'the smells and sounds of various seasons' from her Irish childhood with 'the skyscrapers, airports, freeways and other stereo-typical components' of contemporary social life that she witnessed on arrival in North America. In her judgement, such modern design has 'derided home' (Buttimer, 1980, p. 174). Indeed, Relph (2008 [1976], p. 51) associates what he evaluates as these anonymous spaces with a condition of *existential outside-ness*, 'a sense of…alienation…of not belonging'.[7]

For two main reasons, I am not at all persuaded by this particular aspect of phenomenological-geographical analysis. The argument is flawed, and I feel that it is possible to identify certain contradictions in the position on place and placelessness taken by Relph and adopted by Seamon. Let me try to explain those reasons and contradictions.

Firstly, while the design of environments does obviously have an import-ant bearing on their use, both Relph and Seamon end up giving too much weight to architecture, planning and technology (I would go so far as to say that at times their argument is a form of technological determinism). The skyscraper, the holiday complex or shopping mall, the housing estate and modern spaces of communication, including those of transportation, are all regarded by these geographers as being innately, necessarily placeless, anon-ymous and exchangeable. My initial problem with this perspective, then, is that it appears to me to run contrary to phenomenological geography's most significant insight, which is that place (or, by implication, placelessness) has to do with more than location, because places are constituted through the habitual practices or movements of inhabitants, wherever this making of place might happen. As Relph (2008 [1976], p. 123) himself puts it, it is 'the intentionality of experience' that gives environments a lived-in quality, and surely what follows from his statement is that it is not possible for in-authen-ticity and existential outsideness to be read-off automatically from locational characteristics, from the features of urban and suburban design or from con-temporary sites and systems of communication.[8] To do so would be premature, without having investigated seriously the various personal and collaborative uses of spaces or technologies in people's everyday lives.

Secondly, following on directly from that point about the need for investi-gation, it is evident that in Seamon's own empirical material there are at least some examples, identified in the opening section of this chapter, in which media were appropriated and became meaningful for research participants as part of a lifeworld. Similarly, Seamon (2015 [1979], p. 73), with reference to his fascinating data, acknowledges that on journeys away from people's usual home territories a car and even a public 'transportation terminal' may serve as potential 'centres' of activity, 'places around which we orient our world'. Such findings quite clearly contradict the more general conclusion reached by Relph and Seamon that place is somehow destroyed by so-called mass communications.

Some further examples: Media uses understood as place-making practices

Taking a lead from Seamon's research findings rather than from his argument (echoing Relph) about media and social change, *might it be possible to understand media uses as place-making practices, alongside other such practices in day-to-day living?* I firmly believe that it is, and to do so would be to retain the key principles and much of the conceptual vocabulary of phenomenological geography whilst also, in being faithful to those principles, moving on from unwarranted claims concerning a new placeless geography. This question and answer lie right at the heart of my *positive critique*.

Further to the fragments of material on everyday media use that I have already identified in Seamon's geography of the lifeworld, there are, in fact, other helpful leads to be found in Tuan's later work (see Tuan, 2004). In an essay that pursues his long-standing interest in the formation of senses of place, he includes some examples of emotional bindings to what can be called, following Meyrowitz (1985), media settings or environments. Although Tuan's writings make no mention of the term *media environment*, and while the classic text that he wrote in the 1970s on space and place (Tuan, 1977) contains no references to media uses, these examples from his later work effectively approach media in relation to matters of environmental experience. I want, therefore, to outline them here, before going on to give yet more examples in the same spirit. However, it is crucial, first of all, for me to be clear about the advance that I see this phenomenological-geographical approach making on Meyrowitz's ideas about media use and situational geography.

As I stated in the preceding chapter, I approve of Meyrowitz's extended understanding of social situations because it enables physical locations and media settings to be viewed as overlapping environments or, as he put it, as part of a continuum rather than as a dichotomy. Indeed, I regard his model of situations as information-systems (as distinct from the problematic no-sense-of-place thesis) as being broadly compatible with Paddy Scannell's notion of a doubling of place (Scannell, 1996), which I have also previously discussed. Still, it is necessary to go beyond the observation that media facilitate a simultaneous occupation of different yet continuous spaces. What phenomenological geography provides, then, with its emphasis on place-making practices, is an approach which highlights not only the occupation but also, more importantly, *the inhabiting of environments.*[9]

Tuan's concern with repetitive movements along established paths was evident in the illustrations that he gave of domestic and neighbourhood dwelling processes (Tuan, 1977), and the theme of repeated use arises again, many years on (Tuan, 2004), in his media-related examples of habitation, which I turn to address now. Two of his examples have to do with images, another is concerned with oral or print fictions, and a final one has to do with recordings of music.

To begin with, writing on the uses of photographs, Tuan (2004, p. 50) notes that it is possible to 'develop the habit of dwelling imaginatively' in and with certain images, which 'we can visit and revisit'. For instance, photographic images of loved ones (perhaps especially the physically distant or the dear departed) have often been used in this way. After all, as Roland Barthes (1984, pp. 88–89) rightly observes, 'the important thing' in such uses is that 'the photograph possesses an evidential force...the power of authentication', and Tuan (2004, p. 49) makes a similar point when he writes that a photograph 'is not just a representation': 'When we look at the smile of a child in a faded photograph and smile back, we know that we are responding...to a... child...who once stood five feet from the camera.' Helpful as this example of photography is, though, I want to add a word of caution in response to Tuan's notion of the habit of dwelling imaginatively, so as to guard against any assumption that the uses of photographs are purely a matter of imagination or, indeed, of vision. Photographic images have traditionally been things that are handled and physically displayed, and today, when they are viewed in a digital form, it is typically by means of pressing a button, double-clicking a mouse device or touching a pad or screen with the fingers. It is therefore important to stress that whilst engagements with these images are imaginative, this dwelling imaginatively is very much part and parcel of perception as bodily orientation. In Seamon's terms, it involves an intertwining of body and emotion, of body-subject and feeling-subject.

The next media-related example that I draw from Tuan (2004, p. 51) is of visiting and revisiting a particular film (incorporating sounds as well as images), and he makes the following personal 'confession' about his cinema-going habits:

I have seen the movie *Gone with the Wind* at least a dozen times, the first time…when I was a child…. I returned to the movie again and again…. For, after several viewings, *Gone with the Wind* became a place for me.

The last few words of that extract are pivotal, because Tuan is considering how a specific media setting has become, over the course of his lifetime, far more than location. This film is transformed, by repeated viewing, into a familiar and meaningful place in and with which he feels at home and comfortable, and through which he knows his way. Furthermore, with the availability to contemporary film fans of digital recordings and playback facilities, repeat viewings are now increasingly common, and it is even possible to select favourite scenes from a movie to watch over and over, again and again.

Attending to oral or print fictions, Tuan (2004, p. 52) remarks on how 'young children…like to hear the same story over and over', and also on how 'as adults we revisit our favorite novels as we would our…hometown'. Although the narrative paths of those stories are already well trodden, so to speak, their hearers or readers return to them 'for the evocation of smells, sights…and sounds' (Tuan, 2004, p. 52) in familiar fictional worlds. Borrowing Tuan's words from another context (see Tuan, 1977, p. 182), which I discussed earlier in this chapter, such paths acquire a density of meaning over time.[10] In a similar vein, Tuan goes on to consider the intriguing question of why some people return, across their lifetimes, to listen to a favourite piece of music repeatedly. Could it be in the hope of hearing something new on each occasion of listening? He thinks not. On the contrary, suggests Tuan (2004, p. 53), it is done in order 'to be in the midst of a magical place that provides…inspiration…to be exposed to a presence…the listener…enters the music as…a place'.

Unfortunately, what detracts from Tuan's otherwise insightful comments here on media and environmental experience is his decision to rank what he sees as different types of place, with media-settings-made-familiar-and-meaningful being relegated to the status of 'surrogate place' (Tuan, 2004, p. 49) or regarded as mere 'cousins to place' (Tuan, 2004, p. 52) in relation to 'real' (Tuan, 2004, p. 49) places. While people will inevitably make value judgements for themselves about the relative significances that various environments have in their everyday lives, I wonder why a universal hierarchy of place types, especially one which devalues media uses as place-making practices, is required at all. For my part, I believe that Tuan's is an unnecessary, arbitrary and unjustified ranking. Having said this, I also want to argue that the few examples of media use discussed by Tuan, and before him by Seamon, are still potentially fruitful for those, like me, who are working in the field of media studies. In what remains of this section, then, I seek to extend their discussion with an illustration of my own and, subsequently, with an example that I draw from sociologist and ethnographic researcher Lori Kendall (2002).

For my illustration, I return to the old medium of the newspaper, a particular case of which featured in Seamon's example of the cafe-goer. In doing so, I want to think further about the characteristics of daily papers and the habits of their regular readers. It is reasonable to assume that readers are expecting to find something new each time they buy a paper, since they do so for the explicit purpose of obtaining news. However, a possibly more significant aspect of their engagement with the paper is that of finding the same things over and over. Any paper's layout tends to be fairly constant, so that readers are able to get around the media setting with ease, turning the pages with their fingers, once they have become accustomed to its established format. Pauses may be taken at the entertainment section, the sports pages, the leader column and so on, and over time readers get to know the communicative styles of specific journalists who write for the paper on a regular basis. If Tuan was to develop his analysis in the direction I am taking here, he might conclude that the newspaper is transformed into a place (there is nothing surrogate or less-than-real about it) through habitual practices or movements, as a habit field is gradually formed.

A last example, which will also lead helpfully into some of my concerns in the next section, is of the routine uses of a newer medium. It comes from Kendall's ethnographic study of social interactions and relationships in (and beyond) an online forum that she characterises as a 'virtual pub' (Kendall, 2002).[11] Her book begins with a description of the internet bar setting:

> As usual around lunchtime, the bar is crowded. A few people sit singly at tables, but most sit in small groups, often milling around from table to table to chat with others. As in many such local bars…most of the regulars here are male. Many of them work for a handful of computer companies in a nearby hi-tech industry enclave. The atmosphere is loud, casual…even raucous. Everybody knows each other. (Kendall, 2002, pp. 1–2)

This media environment might usefully be compared with the urban-neighbourhood cafe that was visited each working-day morning by Seamon's research participant, because it evidently has its own sociable mood of warmth. The 'bar' (Kendall, 2002, p. 1) was a public space inhabited at lunchtime by its regulars, who were similarly known and recognisable to one another. These were mainly men employed in the computer industry in California, hence the shared lunchtime

period on 'Pacific standard time' (Kendall, 2002, p. 23), and so the social positions of the customers there were not the same as those of the regulars who
frequented the cafe at breakfast time. As a consequence, the bar's atmosphere
was somewhat noisier. In both cases, though, there was the meshing of time-
space routines and the kind of collaborative, creative, improvised performance
that Seamon calls a place ballet or place choreography, and Kendall (2002,
p. 6) herself argues that the online forum provided its users with 'a particularly
vivid sense of "place"...of gathering together with other people'.[12]

However, something that marks out Kendall's approach from Seamon's is
the critical attention that she pays, when considering place-making practices
and processes, to issues of *difference* and power. Having observed in her opening description that most of the regulars in the bar are male, she goes on to
analyse the gendered character of the setting, asking how particular masculinities, which she regards as being broadly consistent with the regulars' offline
gender identities, get done in this making or performance of place. For example, Kendall (2002, p. 72) points to specific forms of sociable talk-in-interaction: 'Patterns of speech, persistent topics...a particular style of references
to women.' The topics of insider conversation included 'discussions of new
software...and technical advice' (Kendall, 2002, p. 73) associated with work,
and the more general mood or social atmosphere of the bar was one that in her
view positioned women 'as outsiders' (Kendall, 2002, p. 100). Interestingly,
as a female researcher doing ethnography in these specific circumstances of
social *exclusion*, she reports that she had to try 'to become one of the boys'
(Kendall, 2002, p. 98) in order to maintain access to the field.

Some further limitations:
Issues of difference, exclusion and openness

So far, my positive critique of phenomenological geography has been mainly
positive (since I like its emphasis on everyday environmental experiences
and place-making practices, which I feel can be productively appropriated
for media studies). The more critical element of my discussion has focused on
the difficulties that I have with its assertions about placelessness and modern
communications. In this section, pursuing those points about difference and
exclusion that I set out above in my brief summary of Kendall's approach, I
now want to highlight what I see as some further limitations or shortcomings
of phenomenological-geographical inquiry.

There is undoubtedly a tendency in phenomenological geography, and also in the phenomenological philosophy from which it drew, towards universalism or towards an essentialist view of a sort. At one moment, then, Seamon (1980, p. 149) writes boldly of the project of phenomenology as an attempt to identify 'the essential human condition', which, he says, may only be revealed 'when all "non-essentials"', such as 'culture' and 'history', are 'stripped' back to leave behind 'the irreducible crux of people's life-situations'. Hence his problematic general definition of phenomenological geography as an area of investigation that 'directs its attention to the essential nature of...dwelling on earth' (Seamon, 1980, p. 148). He seems to be in danger of taking (and mistaking) the words of his environmental experience group members, who were living in an American city in the 1970s and whose experiences were inevitably shot through with culture and history, as being representative of some universal state of humanity or common human-geographical condition. Indeed, Seamon (2015 [1979], p. 23) goes so far as to claim that: 'Their... descriptions reflect human experience in its typicality.' Whilst I would certainly accept that it is possible to point to features of day-to-day living that are broadly shared across different social groups, including the establishment of time-space routines and the making of places, I do not believe that it is either possible or desirable, as Seamon thinks it is, to peel away the cultural and historical specificities of movement and dwelling to discover beneath them an essential core of human existence. Routines and place-making practices will always, from the very start, take particular forms in particular social circumstances, and for this reason it is best, I am proposing, to consider *lifeworlds in the plural*.

Earlier in the chapter, I referred to Ley's critique of geographies without human agency, which helped to open up the ground within his discipline for phenomenological and related approaches to take root, but it is important to note that in the same piece he also warns against the 'uninhibited hegemony of...subjectivity' (Ley, 1996 [1980], p. 209), by which he appears to mean, at least implicitly, geography without social structure. At times, especially when Seamon refers to the essential human condition or the essential nature of dwelling, phenomenological geography is at risk of becoming just such an approach, by not having a proper appreciation of social difference and power.

Coming from a feminist-geographical perspective, Gillian Rose (1993, p. 56) takes serious issue with phenomenological geography for what she regards as its idealised conception of 'place as home', which fails to acknowledge gender differences in everyday environmental experience: 'Its home/place is not one that many feminists would recognize…it is conflict-free…and almost mystically venerated.' I should make it clear that Rose's critique of the work of Seamon, Tuan and others is, rather like mine, not a wholly damning one. So she rightly praises them for putting on the discipline's theoretical agenda matters of 'the everyday…the bodily…the emotional' (Rose, 1993, p. 53). Her main frustration, though, has to do with the way in which a geographer such as Seamon seems reluctant to go beyond statements about the body and incarnate subjectivity 'to consider differently embodied subjectivities…gender differences in senses of belonging' (Rose, 1993, p. 48). Seamon, she laments, does not fully 'specify "the" body of his place ballet' (Rose, 1993, p. 48).

Following up that argument of Rose's about the need to specify more adequately, in cultural and historical terms, the social bodies that perform particular places (as those bodies are simultaneously shaped by the environments they inhabit), I want to turn next to a study carried out in the 1990s by Simon Charlesworth (2000). His ethnography focuses on the northern English town where he grew up and it provides an interesting point of comparison with Seamon's empirical investigation in the USA from two decades before. Whereas Rose's primary critical and political concern was with gender, Charlesworth's is with social class and especially with specific formations of working-class experience. Writing as a sociologist, he does not refer to the literature of phenomenological geography, but he does look to account for what phenomenological geographers would call unselfconscious senses of place and he is influenced by Merleau-Ponty's phenomenological philosophy. Charlesworth's relation to Merleau-Ponty is rather different to Seamon's, however, because his connection to the work of that philosopher is made via Pierre Bourdieu's social theory of practice.

As I explained towards the end of my introductory chapter, Bourdieu (see Bourdieu & Wacquant, 1992, p. 73) sought to sociologise phenomenological analysis precisely by challenging its tendency towards universalism, insisting on the close link between people's embodied dispositions and their social positions. In Bourdieu's footsteps, Charlesworth (2000, p. 92) regards the research that he did in his hometown as an attempt at 'understanding the habituated manner of comportment through which the place exists', and, crucially, he realises too 'that bodily experience cannot be studied apart from the cultures in which we become…agents endowed with a form of corporeal generative knowing' (Charlesworth, 2000, p. 23). He therefore seeks to comprehend the 'particularity' (Charlesworth, 2000, p. 11) of the place-making practices, highlighting the material conditions of 'economic necessity and dispossession' in that habitat, which help to determine the distinctive being-in-the-world of the town's inhabitants. Such social conditions are obviously not confined solely to that town during the 1990s, yet Charlesworth's ethnography has an admirably strong local-historical dimension.

I ought to stress that I am not holding up this research as some sort of ideal model for future work in place studies. Another contemporary sociologist of class who is similarly inspired by Bourdieu, Mike Savage (2000; see also Bennett et al., 2009; Savage et al., 2015), has advanced legitimate criticisms of Charlesworth's writing (whilst at the same time declaring a sympathy for the overall project). What I am arguing, though, is that it is empirical work which serves as a valuable supplement to Seamon's geography, because of Charlesworth's commitment to a sociologised phenomenology and non-representational theory of the everyday, the bodily and the emotional.

Alongside these issues of difference (of specification or particularity), it is important to consider intimately related matters of social exclusion. My critical argument here is that while the phenomenological geographers had much to say about feelings of inclusion or belonging (of at-homeness and insideness), they were rather less vocal when it came to *processes of social and spatial division* or to what a fellow member of their academic discipline, David Sibley (1995), has usefully named geographies of exclusion. It is true, as I acknowledged at an earlier stage in my discussion, that Relph (2008 [1976], p. 51) writes of experiences of 'outsideness', although, at least in the context of his work, the notion of existential outsideness is too much caught up with his problematic ideas on placelessness.

Places and place-based communities may indeed, on occasion, have a homely atmosphere for their insiders, as was seen in the examples of cafe and virtual-pub settings offered by Seamon and Kendall, but it must not be forgotten that senses of place and community also tend to rely on the existence of an outside and groups of outsiders. Geographers Lewis Holloway and Phil Hubbard (2001, p. 77) remark on how, at different scales, '"home" is…a place within which only certain people and things belong', and, in a similar vein, Tim Cresswell (2004, p. 26) asserts that places are to some extent dependent on 'acts of exclusion'. Returning to the theme of social class, an extreme example of spatial divisions would be the emergence over recent years of those urban, middle-class residential enclaves known as gated communities, yet even where there are not such obvious boundaries, the spatial inequalities of class are still evident within and between modern cities, regions and nations.[13]

Approaching from the opposite direction, having just criticised phenomenological geography for its lack of attention to exclusions and boundaries, both formal and informal, the third issue that I raise as a last twist in this section has to do with its limited appreciation of the openness of places (Massey, 1995, p. 59).[14] In my previous chapter, then, the emphasis was on ways of conceptualising place in a world of flows, and there was discussion of place's *openness* or porous quality in relation to the various movements of information, people and commodities in contemporary social life (or of place as an interface with flows). The phenomenological geographers possess an undoubted strength in detailing the little mobilities of habitual bodily movement in day-to-day living. However, probably as a result of the suspicions that some of them have about modern spaces of communication, including spaces of transportation, they are somewhat weaker when it comes to theorising the entanglements of those little mobilities with the long-distance movements of humans and things.

From my perspective, this is exactly where there is now the potential for *a new theoretical synthesis* between the phenomenological geography of Seamon, Tuan and others and the key aspects of work done by Manuel Castells, John Urry and Doreen Massey (a synthesis that would retain the respective strengths and insights of each strand of analysis whilst overcoming their areas of relative weakness). So, for instance, Massey (2005, p. 183) rejects a phenomenological conception of place because she regards it as being 'too rooted, too little open to the externally relational', but equally, despite her declared sympathy for Nigel Thrift's development of 'non-representational theory in geography' (Massey, 2005, p. 75; see also Amin & Thrift, 2013), I believe that Massey's own notion of place-as-open-and-extroverted could be criticised for its failure to account fully enough for matters of dwelling or habitation. Personally, I can see no reason, in principle, why phenomenological-geographical concerns with the corporeal and affective making or performance of place need to be at odds with an interest in place's openness and in transnational flows or mobilities. It is not a case of having to opt for one or the other.

Phenomenological geography, media and migration

To repeat, then, my intention in this chapter has been to present a positive critique of phenomenological geography. I have identified what in my view are its principal limitations. However, this is in the context of having made very clear my enthusiasm for its contributions to the conceptualisation of place (which, in crucial ways, go beyond those offered by Castells, Urry, Massey, Meyrowitz and Scannell, but which can potentially complement the insights of these social, spatial and communication theorists, whose ideas on places and flows I had previously engaged with). In particular, I want to bring into my non-media-centric media studies Seamon's rich vocabulary of environmental experience, time-space routines, body-subject, feeling-subject and at-homeness, along with Tuan's key ideas about paths, pauses and habit fields, Buttimer's valuable concept of precognitive givens and Relph's important notion of existential insideness (as well as the notion of existential outsideness, once it has been separated from his and Seamon's unfounded conclusions about placeless geographies). As I hope to have shown, inter-esting analytical possibilities are opened up by approaching media uses as place-making practices amongst a range of other such practices in day-to-day living, even if those possibilities were never wholly realised by the phenome-nological geographers themselves.

In the current section of the chapter, I look to develop a point that was made much earlier when I was introducing Seamon's empirical research. Recalling how the members of his environmental experience groups were helped to reflect on the pre-reflective when their routines got disrupted, even momentarily and in minor ways, I am proposing that it is worth *investigating experiences of transnational physical migration*, since migrants, particularly in the process of and in the period soon after a physical relocation, are likely to have gone through more prolonged and profound *disturbances of routine that might throw into relief the taken-for-grantedness of lifeworlds*, giving rise to what Seamon has called noticing. The study of migrant experiences also has the potential to raise related issues, which have to do with the ways in which habitual movements and senses of place can be gradually reconstituted in new circumstances, and today this may involve the inhabiting of media environ-ments as well as place-making practices in physical settings.[15]

Indeed, in the chapter after next, I will be presenting the findings of an empirical investigation of transnational migration that Monika Metykova and I carried out, which focused on the environmental experiences of 20 young people who had travelled to live and work in Britain, during the mid 2000s, from newly joined European Union member states in Eastern Europe. For now, though, I am going to spend a little time reporting on some of my own expe-riences of migration several years ago, and I do this because it was these expe-riences, following a move to Australia and in conjunction with my reading of

Seamon's geography of the lifeworld, that initially got me thinking about the kind of research project which I set up later on returning to England. The specific examples selected for discussion below are quite deliberately *media-related cases*, with a view to supporting my wider argument that phenomenological geography has much to offer in the study of media uses, but of course I remain firmly committed to understanding media use here in the context of other practices or movements.

I should preface my personal reflections by emphasising that I do not regard them as being representative of any universal, typical experience of transnational migration. So when I went to take up an academic position at the University of Melbourne accompanied by my then partner and our two-year-old daughter (our second daughter was to be born there), we were a white, middle-class family with English as our first language, moving voluntarily from one predominantly Anglophone culture to another. It is significant, too, that while the position in Melbourne was a permanent one there was the opportunity for me to make a return to my university in England within two years, and, after a lengthy series of considerations about the relative merits of each living situation, this was an option that we eventually decided to make use of. Such a choice is clearly not open to all migrants (although, interestingly, one of the distinctive features of the trans-European migrations discussed later in the book is that there was the realistic option of returning to resettle in the country that had been left). Nevertheless, on and after our arrival in Australia, we did experience a disruption or disturbance of routine that I suspect is felt in some way by most migrants, even if the social specificities of migration and the different degrees of disturbance will be highly varied.

For example, whereas Scannell (1996) has rightly highlighted the dailiness of broadcasting and its normally routine, familiar feel for audiences, my first experiences of watching television in Melbourne, as I sat on somebody else's sofa in a rented house, were mainly ones of strangeness and outsideness. Whilst a few of the programmes were known to me, usually because they were American dramas or Australian children's shows that had also been screened in Britain, the channels and schedules, along with most of the television personalities, were unknown. Still, after several months of viewing, in which I gradually found my way about in the broadcast output and came to feel more at home and comfortable on the borrowed sofa, my fingers were moving apparently effortlessly around the buttons on the remote-control device and I was no longer searching constantly through the programme listings in order to discover what was on. In fact, over the whole time that I spent in Melbourne, I became enough of an insider to feel the odd absence of Australian television on my subsequent return to England.

To take another example of media use, my relationship to radio, in the period immediately following the move to Melbourne, was rather different. During the early months there, I very much appreciated many of the environmental changes that I was experiencing, not least of which was the welcoming warmth of late summer and autumn in Australia in comparison with the cold of midwinter in northern England that I had left behind. I can recall the pleasurable journeys that I took into work on weekday mornings, cycling across parkland, often with my daughter in a child-seat on the back of the bike on our way to the university nursery, with the city's sunlit skyscrapers rising up ahead as I rode. Even so, on occasion, I found myself thinking back to a previous, less exhilarating commute along busy roads in the car, and realised that what I missed from that drive were the familiar voices on my preferred British radio station, which I could access via the car radio (and also on the set in the kitchen, at either end of the working day). Missing those voices surprised me somewhat, particularly given the pleasures on offer in my new surroundings. From Australia, I was able to listen to my favourite station live via the internet, and yet the listening experience was increasingly detached, perhaps as a result of an evident mismatch between the British time-checks and weather reports and the contrasting conditions in Melbourne. The strong emotional tie or affective attachment that I had developed with this media environment, partly through the ritual activity of listening-while-driving which helped to make it a taken-for-granted feature of my everyday life, only became apparent to me as that tie was later unravelling.

In addition, as the family was meeting new people and as we were finding our feet more generally in a new city and a new country, we valued, alongside our individual or collective television viewing, the regular email, webcam and telephone contact that we had with physically distant friends and family members in Britain. For instance, on most mornings in Melbourne the home computer was turned on to read messages from across the globe that had been deposited for us in the inbox overnight (and note that this was before the widespread use of smart-phones and social-media sites). There was also an occasional exchange of cards, gifts and home videos via the international postal system, as well as a very occasional visit in person from a friend or relative who had flown over to see us. This period of settlement in Australia therefore involved quite a complex 'interaction mix' (Thompson, 1995, p. 87) of local, physically co-present encounters and stretched-out, technologically mediated communications at a distance, in which a range of settings was inhabited, at different scales, as other connections, such as the attachment that I had to a British radio station, were being lost. In other words, it was a period marked by what Urry (2000, p. 140) might think of as a coming together of 'propinquities and extensive networks…to enable performances in, and of, particular places'.

A brief link to the next chapter

If the preceding discussion of *media and migration* was the start of a link to the empirically focused chapter after next, the chapter to come is a continuation of my efforts to set out a theoretical framework for non-media-centric, non-representational media studies. Having already written at considerable length about what I regard as relevant work in human geography and in social and communication theory, I want to foreground phenomenological philosophy in the discussion that follows and, in particular, Merleau-Ponty's phenomenology of perception (see especially Merleau-Ponty, 2002 [1962]). As I indicated in my introductory chapter, Merleau-Ponty's philosophy, which deals with matters of embodiment, orientation and habitation, is crucially important for a critique of rationalism or intellectualism in the humanities and social sciences, and, as I have suggested here in my positive critique of phenomenological geography, Merleau-Ponty had a significant influence on Seamon's geography of the lifeworld through his ideas about bodily knowledge and subjectivity. Indeed, Merleau-Ponty has also been a key point of reference for Thrift's more recent development of non-representational theory in geography. Given his degree of influence, then, I need to offer a more detailed account than I have done so far of Merleau-Ponty's work, although the next chapter is to be rather shorter than those which have appeared up to this stage in my book.

Notes

1. For David Seamon's explanation and justification of this process of group inquiry, in which there was a shared exploration of the details of day-to-day living, see Seamon (2015 [1979], pp. 21–28).
2. I can see something of a parallel here with the breaching experiments set up by sociologist Harold Garfinkel (1984 [1967], pp. 35–75), who was the founder of the approach known as ethnomethodology and who, like Seamon (but from a different angle), was interested in studying 'the routine grounds of everyday activities'. In each case, an unsettling of the

taken-for-grantedness of the everyday served to demonstrate its usually unnoticed existence, although, in Garfinkel's experiments, which involved student volunteers in questioning the common-sense assumptions made in ordinary conversations, the resulting irritation was more strongly felt.

3. Seamon's concern with time-space routines is to some extent related to his interest in Torsten Hägerstrand's innovative 'time-geography' (see, for discussion, Pred, 1996 [1977]), with its notions of life paths and stations in time-space. Coincidentally, time-geography was also an early interest of Nigel Thrift's (see, for example, Carlstein et al., 1978) and elements of it were incorporated by Anthony Giddens into his social theory of structuration (see especially Giddens, 1984, pp. 110–119). It is worth noting, too, that after Seamon had published his geography of the lifeworld he spent a period researching at Hägerstrand's university in Sweden.

4. Back in my introductory chapter, I expressed a frustration with the way in which contemporary non-representational theorists fail to acknowledge, as fully as they might, the ground-breaking nature of the work done many years ago by Seamon and other phenomenological geographers. So those words of Seamon's that I have just quoted can be compared with Thrift's much later assertion that 'only the smallest part of thinking is explicitly cognitive' (Thrift, 2004, p. 90). Similarly, Seamon's critique of the notion of cognitive maps is echoed (unknowingly, I assume) in Tim Ingold's later development of non-representational theory in the discipline of anthropology (see Ingold, 2000, pp. 219–223). To his credit, Tim Cresswell is one of the very few contemporary human geographers to have noted that Seamon's geography of the lifeworld 'was an important precursor to' (Cresswell, 2006, p. 31) subsequent non-representational theories, and I agree with Cresswell (2012, p. 99) when he states that phenomenological geography has been 'criminally undervalued' in the humanities and social sciences. Interestingly, Cresswell's career path took him from being a postgraduate research student of Yi-Fu Tuan's through to, amongst other things, his sympathetic yet critical engagement with Thrift and other non-representational theorists (see Cresswell, 2012, 2013, pp. 227–235), which puts him in a particularly good position to appreciate the close links between these older and newer geographies.

5. Tuan (1996a [1974], p. 445) adds that it is also more than 'one's position in society', which is important with regard to Joshua Meyrowitz's dual definition of place as physical location and social position (Meyrowitz, 1985), discussed earlier in my book. Phenomenological geography points to something more about place that has to do precisely with matters of dwelling or habitation.

6. Seamon's ideas about place choreographies are another specific instance of how his work prefigured contemporary non-representational theorising. Thrift (2009, p. 92), then, goes on to write of the body 'as a link in a larger spatial dance with other…bodies and things', remarking on the way in which place is bound up with people's 'daily rhythms of being'. Tellingly, though, Thrift's point of reference there is not Seamon's dance metaphor (or this phenomenological geographer's research on time-space routines) but rather the more fashionable rhythmanalysis that has been advocated by social and spatial theorist Henri Lefebvre (2004).

7. As will become clear later in the book, I find Edward Relph's category of existential outsideness (see again Seamon & Sowers, 2008) to be helpfully applicable in certain

circumstances, even though I reject his automatic use of it in this context (that is, in the argument he is making about placelessness and modern communications).

8. Given Relph's use of the term intentionality here, I feel the need to explain just briefly, to avoid any possible confusion, that in phenomenology this concept does not equate with cognitive intent. Rather, as Taylor Carman (2008, p. 32) writes with reference to Maurice Merleau-Ponty's philosophy, the 'intentionality' of experience has to do more broadly with 'our bodily orientation and the directedness of our actions in the world'.

9. Although, as I have acknowledged, Paddy Scannell's pioneering account of broadcasting in modern living (Scannell, 1996), with its doubling-of-place idea, was important for me in my move towards phenomenology, and while Scannell's work has continued to engage with (indeed, it became an ambitious attempt to rethink) Martin Heidegger's 'question of being-in-the-world' (Scannell, 2014, p. xiii), I feel that his phenomenological media studies are still missing a fully articulated theory of dwelling or habitation. Such a theory is implicit in Scannell's writings, but it requires a more explicit appreciation of the inhabiting of media environments.

10. This theme of meaningful narrative paths or trails through a text is developed most interestingly in the work of Ingold (2007). It is a theme that I have already touched on towards the end of my introductory chapter, and I will return to it later in the book when discussing Ingold's anthropology in much greater detail.

11. What made Lori Kendall's field research particularly interesting was her insistence on doing not just an online ethnography but also participant observation of forum members at 'informal offline gatherings…in the San Francisco Bay Area and elsewhere' (Kendall, 2002, p. 19).

12. Of course, at the time that Kendall was conducting her study of this online forum, the idea of a virtual place was becoming quite common in the emerging academic literature on internet use. A good example would be William Mitchell's discussion of 'virtual places' (Mitchell, 1995, p. 22) that 'serve as shared access, multiuser locations'. Still, Kendall's understanding of place here has the advantage of stressing the routinely lived-in character of the internet bar setting, and it therefore goes beyond any notion of virtual place as location (getting closer to the phenomenological geographers' view of place as an ongoing practical accomplishment involving the formation of emotional ties or bindings).

13. For empirical data and an illuminating discussion of these inequalities in the British context, see Mike Savage et al. (2015, pp. 261–297).

14. I realise that readers may sense a potential contradiction in my criticism of phenomenological geography both for its lack of attention to boundaries and its limited appreciation of place as open or extroverted, and yet, as I explained in the preceding chapter, Doreen Massey (1995) was able to hang on coherently to each of these dimensions of place in her work (even though she clearly chose to foreground place's openness and throwntogetherness). In fairness, I should also point out that the phenomenological geographers have not been entirely quiet about what Massey (2005, p. 15) refers to as 'outwardlookingness'. For example, Anne Buttimer's reflections on the notion of 'reach' (Buttimer, 1980) are relevant here, as is Tuan's intriguing concept of 'cosmopolitan hearth' (see Tuan, 1996b, pp. 182–188).

15. Seamon (1989) himself has written on matters of migrant experience, in a piece in which he analyses a series of historical novels about trans-Atlantic migration from Northern Europe to North America in the 19th Century, and, in this piece, he raises at least some of those issues I am thinking of. His focus there is on the 'relationship between dwelling and journey...the dwelling-journey process...of leaving a place, journeying and settling in a new place' (Seamon, 1989, pp. 227–228).

References

Amin, A. & Thrift, N. (2013), 'Doreen Massey: The Light Dances on the Water', in Featherstone, D. & Painter, J. (eds.) *Spatial Politics: Essays for Doreen Massey*, Oxford: Wiley-Blackwell.

Barthes, R. (1984), *Camera Lucida: Reflections on Photography*, London: Fontana.

Bausinger, H. (1984), 'Media, Technology and Daily Life', *Media, Culture and Society*, vol. 6, no. 4, pp. 343–351.

Bennett, T., Savage, M., Silva, E., Warde, A., Gayo-Cal, M. & Wright, D. (2009), *Culture, Class, Distinction*, London: Routledge.

Bourdieu, P. & Wacquant, L. (1992), *An Invitation to Reflexive Sociology*, Cambridge: Polity.

Buttimer, A. (1976), 'Grasping the Dynamism of Lifeworld', *Annals of the Association of American Geographers*, vol. 66, no. 2, pp. 277–292.

Buttimer, A. (1980), 'Home, Reach and the Sense of Place', in Buttimer, A. & Seamon, D. (eds.) *The Human Experience of Space and Place*, London: Croom Helm.

Buttimer, A. & Seamon, D. (eds.) (1980), *The Human Experience of Space and Place*, London: Croom Helm.

Carlstein, T., Parkes, D. & Thrift, N. (eds.) (1978), *Timing Space and Spacing Time* (three volumes), London: Edward Arnold.

Carman, T. (2008), *Merleau-Ponty*, London: Routledge.

Charlesworth, S. (2000), *A Phenomenology of Working Class Experience*, Cambridge: Cambridge University Press.

Cloke, P., Philo, C. & Sadler, D. (1991), *Approaching Human Geography: An Introduction to Contemporary Theoretical Debates*, London: Paul Chapman Publishing.

Cresswell, T. (2004), *Place: A Short Introduction*, Malden, MA: Blackwell.

Cresswell, T. (2006), *On the Move: Mobility in the Modern Western World*, New York: Routledge.

Cresswell, T. (2012), 'Non-Representational Theory and Me: Notes of an Interested Sceptic', *Environment and Planning D: Society and Space*, vol. 30, no. 1, pp. 96–105.

Cresswell, T. (2013), *Geographic Thought: A Critical Introduction*, Malden, MA: Wiley-Blackwell.

Downs, R. & Stea, D. (1977), *Maps in Minds: Reflections on Cognitive Mapping*, New York: Harper and Row.

Garfinkel, H. (1984 [1967]), *Studies in Ethnomethodology*, Cambridge: Polity.

Giddens, A. (1984), *The Constitution of Society: Outline of the Theory of Structuration*, Cambridge: Polity.

Giddens, A. (1993), *New Rules of Sociological Method: A Positive Critique of Interpretative Sociologies*, second edition, Cambridge: Polity.

Heidegger, M. (1993 [1971]), 'Building Dwelling Thinking', in Krell, D. (ed.) *Martin Heidegger: Basic Writings*, London: Routledge.

Holloway, L. & Hubbard, P. (2001), *People and Place: The Extraordinary Geographies of Everyday Life*, Harlow: Pearson Education.

Hubbard, P., Kitchin, R., Bartley, B. & Fuller, D. (2002), *Thinking Geographically: Space, Theory and Contemporary Human Geography*, London: Continuum.

Ingold, T. (2000), *The Perception of the Environment: Essays on Livelihood, Dwelling and Skill*, London: Routledge.

Ingold, T. (2007), *Lines: A Brief History*, London: Routledge.

Ingold, T. (2011), *Being Alive: Essays on Movement, Knowledge and Description*, London: Routledge.

Kendall, L. (2002), *Hanging Out in the Virtual Pub: Masculinities and Relationships Online*, Berkeley, CA: University of California Press.

Lefebvre, H. (2004), *Rhythmanalysis: Space, Time and Everyday Life*, London: Continuum.

Ley, D. (1996 [1980]), 'Geography without Human Agency: A Humanistic Critique', in Agnew, J., Livingstone, D. & Rogers, A. (eds.) *Human Geography: An Essential Anthology*, Malden, MA: Blackwell.

Massey, D. (1995), 'The Conceptualization of Place', in Massey, D. & Jess, P. (eds.) *A Place in the World? Places, Cultures and Globalization*, Oxford: Oxford University Press.

Massey, D. (2005), *For Space*, London: Sage.

Merleau-Ponty, M. (2002 [1962]), *Phenomenology of Perception*, London: Routledge.

Merleau-Ponty, M. (2004 [1964]), 'Merleau-Ponty's Prospectus of His Work', in Baldwin, T. (ed.) *Maurice Merleau-Ponty: Basic Writings*, London: Routledge.

Meyrowitz, J. (1985), *No Sense of Place: The Impact of Electronic Media on Social Behavior*, New York: Oxford University Press.

Mitchell, W. (1995), *City of Bits: Space, Place and the Infobahn*, Cambridge, MA: MIT Press.

Morgan, D. (2009), *Acquaintances: The Space Between Intimates and Strangers*, Maidenhead: Open University Press.

Nayak, A. & Jeffrey, A. (2013), *Geographical Thought: An Introduction to Ideas in Human Geography*, London: Routledge.

Peet, R. (1998), *Modern Geographical Thought*, Malden, MA: Blackwell.

Peterson, M. (2010), '"But It is My Habit to Read the *Times*": Metaculture and Practice in the Reading of Indian Newspapers', in Bräuchler, B. & Postill, J. (eds.) *Theorising Media and Practice*, Oxford: Berghahn.

Pred, A. (1996 [1977]), 'The Choreography of Existence: Comments on Hägerstrand's Time-Geography and Its Usefulness', in Agnew, J., Livingstone, D. & Rogers, A. (eds.) *Human Geography: An Essential Anthology*, Malden, MA: Blackwell.

Relph, E. (2008 [1976]), *Place and Placelessness*, London: Pion.

Rose, G. (1993), *Feminism and Geography: The Limits of Geographical Knowledge*, Cambridge: Polity.

Savage, M. (2000), 'Review of Simon Charlesworth's *A Phenomenology of Working Class Experience*', *Sociological Research Online*, vol. 5, no. 3 (available at http://www.socresonline.org.uk).

Savage, M., Cunningham, N., Devine, F., Friedman, S., Laurison, D., McKenzie, L., Miles, A., Snee, H. & Wakeling, P. (2015), *Social Class in the 21st Century*, London: Pelican.

Scannell, P. (1996), *Radio, Television and Modern Life: A Phenomenological Approach*, Oxford: Blackwell.

Scannell, P. (2014), *Television and the Meaning of Live: An Enquiry into the Human Situation*, Cambridge: Polity.

Seamon, D. (1980), 'Body-Subject, Time-Space Routines and Place-Ballets', in Buttimer, A. & Seamon, D. (eds.) *The Human Experience of Space and Place*, London: Croom Helm.

Seamon, D. (1989), 'Reconciling Old and New Worlds: The Dwelling-Journey Relationship as Portrayed in Vilhelm Moberg's "Emigrant" Novels', in Seamon, D. & Mugerauer, R. (eds.) *Dwelling, Place and Environment: Towards a Phenomenology of Person and World*, New York: Columbia University Press.

Seamon, D. (2015 [1979]), *A Geography of the Lifeworld: Movement, Rest and Encounter*, London: Routledge.

Seamon, D. & Sowers, J. (2008), 'Place and Placelessness (1976): Edward Relph', in Hubbard, P., Kitchin, R. & Valentine, G. (eds.) *Key Texts in Human Geography*, London: Sage.

Sibley, D. (1995), *Geographies of Exclusion: Society and Difference in the West*, London: Routledge.

Thompson, J. (1995), *The Media and Modernity: A Social Theory of the Media*, Cambridge: Polity.

Thrift, N. (2004), 'Summoning Life', in Cloke, P., Crang, P. & Goodwin, M. (eds.) *Envisioning Human Geographies*, London: Arnold.

Thrift, N. (2009), 'Space: The Fundamental Stuff of Geography', in Clifford, N., Holloway, S., Rice, S. & Valentine, G. (eds.) *Key Concepts in Geography*, second edition, London: Sage.

Tuan, Y. (1977), *Space and Place: The Perspective of Experience*, Minneapolis, MN: University of Minnesota Press.

Tuan, Y. (1996a [1974]), 'Space and Place: Humanistic Perspective', in Agnew, J., Livingstone, D. & Rogers, A. (eds.) *Human Geography: An Essential Anthology*, Malden, MA: Blackwell.

Tuan, Y. (1996b), *Cosmos and Hearth: A Cosmopolite's Viewpoint*, Minneapolis, MN: University of Minnesota Press.

Tuan, Y. (2004), 'Sense of Place: Its Relationship to Self and Time', in Mels, T. (ed.) *Reanimating Places: A Geography of Rhythms*, Aldershot: Ashgate.

Urry, J. (2000), *Sociology Beyond Societies: Mobilities for the Twenty-First Century*, London: Routledge.

THAT FAMILIARITY WITH THE WORLD BORN OF HABIT

On Merleau-Ponty and Everyday Media Use

Interpreting audiences?

In this chapter, I advocate a particular sort of phenomenological-philosophical approach to the study of everyday media use, which picks up some of the themes from my discussion of phenomenological geography, exploring what Maurice Merleau-Ponty (2002 [1962], p. 277) has called *that familiarity with the world born of habit*.[1] To begin with, though, in order to provide a context for those who are more familiar with the literature of media studies (especially that on media audiences) than they are with phenomenological philosophy, I want to set out the main ways in which my thinking has shifted since I was writing my first book, *Interpreting Audiences: The Ethnography of Media Consumption* (Moores, 1993a), around a quarter of a century ago.[2] How has my perspective changed, then, over the years between that publication and my work on the current volume?

Perhaps the most obvious shift is that the term *audiences* is no longer central to my conceptual vocabulary, as it was back then, when I was still starting out as an academic in the field of media studies and when I would have described myself primarily as a qualitative audience researcher. There are two principal reasons for this de-centring of audiences in my work, which I will attempt to explain succinctly.

One of these reasons has to do with the range of media that are tradition-ally investigated under the banner of media studies, and with a related prob-lem that I detect in the general analytical framework that is usually employed within my field. The standard focus of media research has been on so-called mass communications (typically on communications that are associated with broadcasting and print media), and, with regard to that focus, there has also been the establishment of an overall model for investigation which empha-sises the communicative relationships between moments of production, repre-sentation and consumption or between industries, texts and audiences. Ideas about audiences have therefore tended to be bound up with a settled way of organising the field of media studies, including the teaching of this subject in universities, which in my view needs to be unsettled.[3]

A much wider definition of the object of study is required, partly so as to bring in other media and types of communication, and a revised framework and vocabulary are required too, allowing those other media and communi-cations to be seen as something more than just a supplement that leaves the field's established core untouched. Of course, I am thinking here about the need for media studies, as a whole academic area, to give greater weight to the technologically mediated interpersonal communications that are afforded today by various kinds of new media, and, crucially, I would suggest that it makes little sense to try to come at such interpersonal communications with a model of production, representation and consumption that has been inher-ited from the study of traditional media, at least not as an initial point of departure for investigating new media technologies and their uses.[4] Let me be clear, though. My argument is not only about new technology and I am not making a case for the rebranding of media studies as research into new media. After all, the telephone, in its landline mode, is an older media tech-nology for interpersonal interaction that has long been a wrongly 'neglected medium' (Fielding & Hartley, 1987; but see, for exceptions, Hopper, 1992; Moyal, 1992; Rakow, 1992) in media studies, even if uses of the mobile phone have more recently become a niche area of inquiry for several media and com-munications researchers (see, for example, Goggin, 2006, 2008; Katz, 2006; Katz & Aakhus, 2002; Ling, 2004; Ling & Donner, 2009).

What I am arguing for is an analytical framework that can facilitate the integrated study of new and old media, and the integrated study of what have usually been referred to and investigated separately as mass and interpersonal communications.[5] In my Media/Theory: Thinking about Media and Communi-cations (Moores, 2005), I employed a series of organising terms such as time, space, interactions and experiences, designed to serve as a basis for precisely this sort of media studies. Subsequently, in *Media, Place and Mobility* (Moores, 2012), I have extended that list of key terms to include others like dwelling or place-making, environments and mobilities, which could also help to facil-itate a rejuvenated media studies with a far broader scope. Indeed, the book I am now writing seeks to extend this vocabulary still further, most obviously, given its title, by foregrounding questions of bodily orientation. This list is not intended to be exhaustive (I realise that my key terms do not connect with the interests of everybody in the field) but what I hope is that it can contrib-ute to an unsettling and revision of media-studies-as-they-have-been-done-in-the-past. I should add that I now prefer to talk of media uses rather than of media consumption or, for that matter, media production, because I find it to be a more widely applicable concept.[6]

The second, closely related reason for my de-centring of audiences is one that was implicit in the empirical research which I had previously been carry-ing out on everyday media use (see Moores, 1988, 1993b), and I was already anticipating it, to some extent, as I wrote my first book all those years ago. There, I began to welcome what I called a blurring of the boundaries between audience research and broader investigations of the everyday (see Moores, 1993a, p. 54). Like a small number among my fellow researchers in media and cultural studies who were interested in audiences and media consump-tion during that period, I came to realise that in order to understand more fully the significance of media uses it is vitally important to ask how they are embedded, alongside other routine practices, in contexts of day-to-day living. Having developed that principle in my subsequent work, including in the research monograph that was my second authored book, *Satellite Television and Everyday Life: Articulating Technology* (Moores, 1996), I would characterise what I do today as a distinctive version of non-media-centric media studies (Morley, 2007, 2009).[7] David Morley (2007, p. 200), who originally employed this label, which features in the subtitle of the current volume and with which I have come to associate my work, freely acknowledges that the idea of non-media-centric media studies appears 'paradoxical'. However, the crucial purpose of Morley's label is to insist on situating media technologies and their uses within the larger 'contexts in which they operate' (Morley, 2007, p. 1). From his non-media-centric perspective (mine too), it is everyday lives and habits, not audiences or media, that must take centre stage, expanding the field's scope considerably by going beyond even the sort of integrative analyt-ical framework for media studies that I have just proposed.

Let me turn next to the other, accompanying word, *interpreting*, which was positioned in front of the term audiences in the title of my first book (Moores, 1993a). Back then, I was concerned to tell a story about advances in qualitative audience research that took as its main starting point Stuart Hall's seminal notes on the encoding and decoding of television's ideological messages (Hall, 1973). I detailed the emergence and development of a social-semiotic perspective on, to borrow the jargon of the time, signification or meaning construction in text-reader relations (see also Moores, 1990). In this type of analysis, media uses were thought of as matters of decoding or interpretation, as readings of what media theorist Roger Silverstone (1990, p. 189) once referred to, with an interesting allusion to the language of computing, as 'the texts of both hardware and software'.

While there is a specific, marginal strand of semiotic analysis for which I retain a good deal of sympathy, since it takes its lead from Valentin Volosinov's anti-structuralist theory of utterances in social intercourse (Volosinov, 1986 [1973]; see also Hall, 1982, pp. 77–80), I am doubtful these days as to whether everyday media use (or daily activity more generally) should be understood as having a primarily interpretative character, at least in the way that many audience researchers, myself included, conceptualised interpretation.[8] Semiotics, with its emphasis on linguistic and cultural codes, systems of representation and acts of interpretation, involves conceiving of meaning construction as a predominantly cognitive (if partly unconscious) and symbolic process. What I am suggesting, though, is that the significance of media and their uses involves much more than this. The phenomenological approach that I advocate in this chapter is able to point to a meaningfulness which exceeds encodings and decodings, and which might also be considered more basic.[9]

Philosopher Taylor Carman (2008, p. 106), in a valuable commentary on Merleau-Ponty's work, refers to such meaningfulness as 'our precognitive familiarity with…the world we inhabit'. Given Merleau-Ponty's strong focus on matters of *embodiment* or on body-world relations (see especially Merleau-Ponty, 2002 [1962]; but also Todes, 2001), it is his phenomenology of perception which, in my view, offers the most interesting take on this precognitive familiarity and leads his phenomenological philosophy to be regarded as a forerunner of contemporary non-representational theories, where notions of the precognitive or 'non-cognitive' (Thrift, 2004, p. 85) and of 'embodied dispositions' (Thrift, 2007, p. 58) are important. In the following section, in discussing Merleau-Ponty's approach to embodied-being-in-the-world, I will pay particular attention to his fascinating account of *the acquisition of habit* (see Merleau-Ponty, 2002 [1962], pp. 164–170), since, as he puts it, familiarity with the world is born of habit, but I will also be citing some of the earlier work of Martin Heidegger (1962) where it is directly relevant to my discussion. Like Merleau-Ponty, Heidegger provided a 'phenomenology of this familiarity' (Blattner, 2006, p. 12), argued that 'familiarity is more basic than cognition' (Blattner, 2006, p. 46) and even reflected on 'engaged dealings with the world…in which bodily abilities play a central role' (Blattner, 2006, p. 170), and yet it was left to Merleau-Ponty to fashion more fully a philosophy of the knowledgeable body 'without which Heidegger's phenomenology is…compromised' (Blattner, 2006, p. 171).

Before getting into that exploration of familiarity and habit, however, I want to conclude this opening section of the chapter by noting that there are certain things which have not changed for me since I was writing my first book. I am choosing to highlight the shifts in my thinking, but there have also been some continuities that are worthy of comment and I will briefly outline a couple of them here (these go beyond the implicit commitment, retrospectively evident from early on in my academic career, to what I now think of as a non-media-centric perspective). One is my ongoing commitment to the value of qualitative research. So whilst I no longer consider myself to be narrowly an audience researcher, and while my work no longer has the guiding aim of interpreting audiences (Moores, 1993a) or of reading the readings made by media users, I retain a keen interest in *empirical investigation and description*, as the next chapter of my book helps to show. Secondly, I have a continuing interest, too, in the social theories of practice that I was just beginning to see the importance of towards the end of my monograph on media audiences, where I referred to work done by, amongst others, Pierre Bourdieu (1977, 1984), Michel de Certeau (1984) and Anthony Giddens (1979, 1984). Indeed, my later engagements with phenomenology and non-representational theory have allowed me to appreciate the ideas of those authors rather more than I was able to at that time, because, as contemporary philosopher of technology Don Ihde (1990, p. 27) has asserted, phenomenology can best be understood as part of a 'family of' *practice theories or philosophies*, and it is to certain key aspects of phenomenological philosophy that I turn now.[10]

On the acquisition of habit and knowledge in the hands

In some explanatory remarks on his phenomenology of perception, Merleau-Ponty (2004 [1964], pp. 34–37) states that he was seeking 'to re-establish the roots of the mind in its body', writing of an *incarnate subjectivity*:

> In my work...the body is no longer merely an object in the world.... It is on the side of the subject...it inhabits...space. It applies itself to space like a hand to an instrument.... We grasp...space...our bodily situation gives us at every moment a... practical and implicit notion of the relation between...body and things, of our hold on them.

For me, what is especially interesting here, beyond Merleau-Ponty's important critique of the mind-body dualism found in forms of rationalism or intellectualism, is his use of the terms grasp and hold, and his reference to the way in which bodies inhabit environments by applying themselves like a hand to an instrument. In this case, he is clearly employing these terms metaphorically in order to make a general point about the character of an incarnate subject's immersion 'in its world' (Merleau-Ponty, 2004 [1964], p. 34), but elsewhere, in the account of the acquisition of habit that he offers, Merleau-Ponty includes more literal references to the skilful movements of human hands in body-thing relations.[11] In this section, I will be covering much of what he has to say there about embodiment, habitual practice and *knowledge in the hands* (Merleau-Ponty, 2002 [1962], p. 166), whilst also linking those ideas to some contemporary instances of media use.

Perhaps the example from Merleau-Ponty's account that is mentioned most often in commentaries on his work by later philosophers, and one which does involve the hand applying itself to an instrument of a sort, is that of the 'blind man's stick' (Merleau-Ponty, 2002 [1962], p. 165). Once the stick's user gets accustomed to finding ways about with it, having it 'well in hand' (Merleau-Ponty, 2002 [1962], pp. 165–166), its tip 'has become an area of sensitivity, extending the scope and active radius of touch...providing a parallel to sight'. As Merleau-Ponty (2002 [1962], pp. 175–176) goes on to say, in a development of this argument about an extension of the sense of touch, 'the stick has become a familiar instrument...a bodily auxiliary...the world of feelable things...now begins...not at the outer skin of the hand, but at the end of the stick'. Through skilful manipulation, then, the stick or cane used by a blind person is incorporated, and, in the process, it 'withdraws'

(Ihde, 1990, p. 40) as an object: 'The...stick is no longer an object perceived by the blind man, but an instrument with which he perceives' (Merleau-Ponty, 2002 [1962], p. 176).

Ihde (1990, pp. 72–73), in a discussion of what he terms 'embodiment relations' involving the incorporation of technologies in human perception, draws a parallel between the stick as a familiar instrument in Merleau-Ponty's example and the spectacles that he wears to sharpen his own vision. 'My glasses become part of the way I ordinarily experience my surroundings...they "withdraw" and are barely noticed, if at all', writes Ihde (1990, p. 73). He adds that: 'Embodiment relations...may occur for any sensory...dimension...the hearing aid...does this for hearing, and the blind man's cane for tactile motility' (Ihde, 1990, p. 73; see also, on hearing aids, Ihde, 2007, pp. 243–250). Indeed, he also connects Merleau-Ponty's reflections on the stick used by a blind person with Heidegger's earlier, rather different example of 'hammering with a hammer' (Heidegger, 1962, p. 98) in manual labour, and it is from Heidegger that Ihde takes the notion of withdrawal.[12] So I want to consider briefly the case of 'Heidegger's hammer' (Ihde, 1990, p. 31), which comes up in the context of this phenomenological philosopher's wider notes on 'our concernful dealings' (Heidegger, 1962, pp. 96–97) with 'equipment'.

Heidegger (1962, p. 95) insists that: 'The kind of dealing which is closest to us is...not a...perceptual cognition, but rather that kind of concern which manipulates things and puts them to use...and this has its own kind of "knowledge".' Already here, he was anticipating elements of Merleau-Ponty's phenomenology of perception, which would come almost two decades after, by seeking to go beyond the cognitive to emphasise practical, skilful uses of things (and the notion of *manipulating things* does suggest movements of the hands in particular), even if Heidegger did not specifically identify the practical know-how involved as a bodily or corporeal knowledge. His name for the things that are manipulated in concernful dealings (such as pens used for writing, needles for sewing and hammers for hammering) is equipment, defined as 'something in-order-to' (Heidegger, 1962, p. 97).

Taking the case of the hammer, it is a work tool (part of a larger range of equipment including, for instance, nails and a workbench) that has what Heidegger (1962, p. 98) calls manipulability or *readiness-to-hand*. Importantly for him, though, the ready-to-hand quality of hammers cannot be uncovered simply by inspecting their physical appearance. Rather, readiness-to-hand is uncovered in 'the hammering itself...when we deal with them by using them and manipulating them' (Heidegger, 1962, p. 98). It requires a grasping or holding of the tools and is very much bound up with '"practical" behaviour' (Heidegger, 1962, p. 99), with action in a work task rather than just with observation, and yet, in the practice or act of hammering, the tools withdraw as objects:

> The peculiarity of what is proximally ready-to-hand is that, in its readiness-to-hand, it must, as it were, withdraw.... That with which our everyday dealings proximally dwell is not the tools themselves. On the contrary, that with which we concern ourselves primarily is the work...that which is to be produced at the time.

Like the stick in Merleau-Ponty's example, the hammer becomes a bodily auxiliary and is *incorporated in the flow of action*, even if the in-order-to of the stick is wayfinding rather than the performance of certain types of productive manual labour.

The next example that I want to consider is the now-outmoded technology of the typewriter, bringing me back to Merleau-Ponty's account of the acquisition of habit, in the course of which he reflects at some length on the practice of typing. For instance, he writes there of how regular typewriter users would cultivate, over time, in their relations with the machine, 'knowledge in the hands, which is forthcoming only when bodily effort is made' (Merleau-Ponty, 2002 [1962], p. 166), so that it might be 'possible to know how to type without being able to say where the letters...are to be found on the banks of keys'.[13] Merleau-Ponty (2002 [1962], p. 167) stresses the point that this manual, practical know-how is part of a much broader bodily knowledge in movement, and he asserts that 'it is the body which "understands" in the acquisition of habit', *catching and comprehending movements through environments*, including in the uses of equipment. Of course, he is well aware that for many of his readers such an argument 'will appear absurd' (Merleau-Ponty, 2002 [1962], p. 167) because it challenges standard rationalist assumptions in the philosophical tradition, but still he insists that 'the phenomenon of habit is just what prompts us to revise our notion of "understand" and our notion of the body'.

More recently, social theorist John Tomlinson (2007, pp. 107–111), in the context of developing an analysis of speed in modern living, has offered an interesting 'excursus' on keyboards that helps to update Merleau-Ponty's reflections on the knowledge in the hands of the typist. Quite rightly, Tomlinson (2007, p. 108) contends that 'our habitual way of accessing and communicating via keyboards and keypads...has generally been ignored' (quite wrongly) by those working in media studies, with contemporary practices of keyboard use, 'which do obviously involve the body, particularly the hands and the sense of touch', tending to be overlooked.[14] Although he contrasts 'the typical deftness' (Tomlinson, 2007, p. 109) of computer keyboard uses with the more 'muscular' manipulations of a mechanical typewriter, and although he does not cite Merleau-Ponty's phenomenology of perception in his excursus, Tomlinson's reference to 'acquired habits and sensory-bodily rhythms' has a distinctly Merleau-Pontyan tone and indicates that he is both familiar with and sympathetic to the philosopher's arguments.

I will be returning specifically, in the concluding chapter of my book, to the movement and touch of the hands in habitual uses of computer keyboards and other hardware associated with new media. At this stage, though, to supplement Tomlinson's discussion of acquired habits of the hand in contemporary keyboard use and to update further Merleau-Ponty's example of the typewriter, I want to mention a particular aspect of some work done by media theorist Mark Nunes (2006). At one point in his book on everyday spaces of the computer, Nunes (2006, p. 41) draws attention to the nowadays taken-for-granted and unremarkable matter of 'knowing the proper speed to "double click" a mouse'. Indeed, he sees this practical, embodied knowledge as part of a broader range of routine 'point-and-click' (Nunes, 2006, p. 39) skills or competences, enabling the deft manoeuvring of a mouse device that usually sits and runs around on a mat beside the keyboard, as the user finds ways about on the computer screen.[15]

A final example that I want to take here from Merleau-Ponty is one which involves the manipulation of another instrument with keys. This is the practice of playing a musical instrument, the organ, which actually calls for knowledge in the feet as well as in the hands of the performer's comprehending body, since the traditional organ has pedals to operate as well as stops to pull and a keyboard for skilled fingers to press. It seems that Merleau-Ponty's main purpose, in introducing this example of organ playing into his account, is to make a crucial point about *the adaptability or generative capacity of the performer's bodily and sensuous understanding*. He writes:

> An experienced organist is capable of playing an organ which he does not know... compared with...the instrument he is used to playing. He needs only an hour's practice to be ready to perform his programme.... During the short rehearsal preceding the concert, he...sits on the seat, works the pedals, pulls out the stops, gets the measure of the instrument with his body, incorporates...the relevant directions and dimensions, settles into the organ as one settles into a house. (Merleau-Ponty, 2002 [1962], pp. 167–168)

Merleau-Ponty (2002 [1962], p. 169) is quite clear in his view that habitual practices are caught up with the formation of 'stable dispositional tendencies', but his example of the organist (who settles into using an instrument which is not the one routinely played) serves to show that along with stability embodied dispositions also have a degree of flexibility and a certain improvisational quality.[16]

Based on extensive previous experience of musical performance, the organ player is able to adapt to the instrument's slightly different layout, getting the measure of it in Merleau-Ponty's terms. However, in making this adaptation, the organist 'does not learn objective spatial positions for each stop and pedal...he does not...draw up a plan' (Merleau-Ponty, 2002 [1962], p. 168). No formal measurements are taken, and this is not a case of the player preparing a prior mental diagram to guide bodily movements in the concert. Rather, during the rehearsal period, there is an incorporation process or a merging of body and instrument in practice, as subject-object distinctions are dissolved.

In comparing the process of finding ways about at the keyboard with that of settling into a house, Merleau-Ponty also suggests the strong connection between matters of orientation and habitation, which will continue to be a key theme of my book in the chapters ahead. Of course, these matters have to do with more than the knowledge in the hands (and sometimes in the feet) of keyboard users, or with the readiness-to-hand of hammers (and canes) as bodily auxiliaries, on which I have been focusing in this section. The meaningfulness of precognitive familiarity with inhabited worlds has to do more generally with the development of generative abilities 'to know and find your way around' (Carman, 2008, p. 19) environments at different geographical scales. For instance, the laptop keyboard that I am currently writing these words on, with which I have a familiarity born of habit, is situated in a room that I also know how to get around with ease. In turn, that room is part of a larger domestic space which I can move about in and, even in the dark in the middle of the night, negotiate without too much difficulty. Stepping out of the front door and into the street, I am familiar with those parts of my local area which I routinely walk or run through, and I know intimately the commute to my workplace, which these days is done on the train. At each of those scales, then, from that of my laptop keyboard to that of a regional rail network, *the body inhabits or grasps spaces.*

A brief link to the next chapter

Having discussed aspects of phenomenological philosophy and phenomenological geography in this and the preceding chapter, highlighting issues to do
with embodiment, movement and the making of places, I go on in the next
chapter to report the findings of a qualitative research project that Monika
Metykova and I collaborated on some years ago, in which we were looking
to investigate precisely these issues in our study of the experiences of young,
trans-European migrants. There is something of a shift in style coming up,
though, in the transition from what has been primarily a theoretical or conceptual discussion into a chapter with a strong empirical focus. The brief link
I want to offer here, between Merleau-Ponty's phenomenology of perception
and the research that Monika and I carried out, has to do with a basic difficulty
faced by any researchers who are interested in exploring empirically a precognitive familiarity with inhabited worlds. *If that familiarity born of habit is bound
up with practical behaviour and embodied know-how, how might the precognitive
be brought to discursive consciousness?* A possible answer to this question and a
way of trying to solve the problem would be to adopt what John Urry (2007,
pp. 39–40; see also Büscher et al., 2011) thought of as new 'mobile' methods of research, which include 'travelling with people' as they get around and
observing their routine activities (indeed, it could be argued that there are eth-
nographers in the anthropological tradition who have been employing such
on-the-move-participant-observational methods for quite a while now). However, the research that is featured in the following chapter relied instead upon
in-depth conversational interviews, of a sort that have been more common
in qualitative investigations within media and cultural studies. Its distinctive
twist, then, is provided by the emphasis that Monika and I put on the experiences of migrants in the period soon after their transnational physical relocations. Could these be special social circumstances in which people are able
to speak, at least to some extent, about elements of their practical knowing
and their senses of place, so as 'to articulate what was previously just lived out'
(Taylor, 2005, p. 32)?

Notes

1. A fuller quote is: 'I perceive with my body...my body and my senses are precisely that
    familiarity with the world born of habit' (Merleau-Ponty, 2002 [1962], p. 277). This helps
    to indicate Maurice Merleau-Ponty's concern with embodied knowledge, which will be at
    the centre of my discussion of his work later in the chapter.

2. As noted in my acknowledgements, this chapter has its origins in a plenary paper that was presented at a conference for audience researchers in the field of media studies. It is probably fair to say that for many such researchers, I am still known for having written that book on audiences all those years ago, which is why I have chosen to offer a critique of it here.

3. I would accept that in the past I have bought into this kind of analytical framework myself. Indeed, I might even have made a small contribution to its establishment, as one of the consultant authors employed by the UK's Open University (OU) in the 1990s to work on a course chaired by Stuart Hall (see Moores, 1997). This undergraduate course operated with a circuit-of-culture model that included moments of production, representation and consumption (identity and regulation too). Subsequently, quite a few introductory books written for undergraduates in media studies featured a broadly similar model and set of organising concepts (for example, Gripsrud, 2002; Taylor & Willis, 1999; Williams, 2003), as did a later OU course on understanding media (see especially Evans & Hesmondhalgh, 2005; Gillespie, 2005).

4. Although I would want to take issue with aspects of the agenda for so-called media studies 2.0 (see Gauntlett, 2007a, 2015, pp. 17–25; Merrin, 2014), I think David Gauntlett (2015, p. 19) is absolutely right to say that it is unacceptable to treat 'new digital media… as an "add on" (to be dealt with in…a…segment tacked on to a media studies…book or degree)'. So whilst I do not regard his and William Merrin's 2.0 versions of the field, or, for that matter, Gauntlett's earlier advocacy of web studies (Gauntlett, 2000), as the answer, I am at least partly in agreement with him about the nature of the problem that is now facing media studies. I should add, since I am discussing Gauntlett's work, that I do regard his thesis on making and connecting (Gauntlett, 2011) to be a valuable contribution to non-media-centric media studies (see also Gauntlett, 2015, pp. 30–33), given his concern there with creative practices across a range of areas 'from DIY and knitting to YouTube and Web 2.0' (as he puts it in the book's subtitle), and I wholeheartedly welcome his view, expressed in a previous book on creativity, that 'some spheres of media studies could do with a substantial injection of social context' (Gauntlett, 2007b, p. 192).

5. There have been valuable previous attempts, mainly in the context of media and communication studies in North America, to blur the division between mass and interpersonal communications and to develop a notion of mediated interpersonal communication (see, for example, contributions to Gumpert & Cathcart, 1986).

6. To avoid any possible confusion, I must emphasise that when referring to media uses I am not calling for a return to what was known as the uses and gratifications paradigm in audience research (see especially Blumler & Katz, 1974). Furthermore, my preference for that term is not intended to suggest that the concepts of production and consumption are somehow redundant. They clearly still have an analytical value, including in the study of some communications that are associated with new media technologies. However, I am proposing that they should no longer be among the key points of departure for the field of media studies as a whole academic area.

7. Nick Couldry (2006, p. 13), a former postgraduate student of David Morley's, makes a related call for media studies that are 'media-oriented, but not media-centred', and, interestingly for me, some of Couldry's recent work (see especially Couldry, 2010, 2012) has been influenced by practice theory. I am a little puzzled, therefore, by his dismissal of a

non-representational approach (see Couldry, 2012, p. 31) as being 'deeply unhelpful for studying media'. On this, he and I clearly disagree. Indeed, Couldry's dismissal seems to me to be based on something of a misunderstanding, since near to the start of his latest, co-authored book (see Couldry & Hepp, 2017, p. 2) there is the claim that Nigel Thrift's writings are 'looking…for forms of connection…that bypass "meaning" altogether'. As I hope will be clear in my own book here, a non-representational approach is not looking to bypass matters of meaning. On the contrary, contemporary non-representational theorists like Thrift in geography and Tim Ingold in anthropology (and before them, Merleau-Ponty in philosophy) have sought to expand conceptions of the meaningful.

8. Valentin Volosinov's materialist critique of Saussurean structural linguistics (Volosinov, 1986 [1973]), written in the Soviet Union in the 1920s, is still, in my view, one of the strongest cases ever put against structuralism, and yet his social semiotics never had the degree of influence that was enjoyed by a Saussurean tradition imported into media studies in the 1970s and 1980s, chiefly via the early writings of Roland Barthes. For an interesting recent appropriation of Volosinov's work, though, see Hannah Rockwell (2011), whose theory of communication combines his philosophy of language with Merleau-Ponty's philosophy of the body.

9. An important point made in my introductory chapter, which I feel the need to reiterate here, is that I am not wanting to rule out considerations of language, the cognitive and the symbolic. I wrote there of how meaning emerges out of habitual practices or movements, requiring an exploration of non- or more-than-representational meanings, but it is also crucial to regard language as habitual practice (as one type of habitual practice among many others).

10. It is significant that Don Ihde (1990, pp. 27–28) includes there, alongside phenomenology in his discussion of work by 'family' members, the writings of Karl Marx as well as those of American pragmatist philosopher John Dewey. In particular, the reference to Marx as a theorist of practice is an important one, I feel, because the brand of Marxism that informed the critical paradigm of media and cultural studies was too often inflected by structuralism, with Louis Althusser's thesis on ideology-as-representation (and on ideology's interpellation of individuals as subjects) being the most obvious example (see Althusser, 1984 [1971]). So in his much-cited essay on ideology and ideological state apparatuses, Althusser (1984 [1971], pp. 43–44) does write at one point of 'material practices' and 'material rituals', but he goes on to argue that 'there is no practice except by and in…ideology', which appears, to me at least, to be a clear assertion of the primacy of representation rather than the primacy of practice. Interestingly, literary and cultural theorist Terry Eagleton (2016, p. 61), who was once swayed by Althusserian arguments, has recently described Marx as 'a somatic materialist whose starting point is active, sensuous, practical human life', which seems to confirm Ihde's view. Indeed, Eagleton's new discussion of materialism is introduced as 'a book about the body' (Eagleton, 2016, p. viii), and he even goes so far as to claim that the early Marx was engaged in a 'phenomenology of capitalism' (Eagleton, 2016, p. 76).

11. More recently, philosopher Raymond Tallis (2003, 2010) has written at great length on the subject of hands (and fingers, especially the index finger). He refers to the 'knowing hand' (Tallis, 2003, pp. 29–30), which has an 'exquisite knowledge of the size, shape, surface, texture, density…etc. of the object it manipulates'. Along similar lines, architect

Juhani Pallasmaa (2009), in a book on what he calls the thinking hand, explores related notions of 'embodied wisdom' and sensory thought, while sociologist Richard Sennett (2009, pp. 149–153), who regards his own work as being part of a second wave of pragmatism, discusses the grip and touch of the 'intelligent hand'.

12. For a media-related example of technology that withdraws in use, see William Blattner (2006, p. 51), who writes of listening to music through his stereo speakers: 'As I turn on the music in my living room…I do not encounter the speakers at all. The speakers… recede from my experience. What stands out…is the music.' As he goes on to discuss, a technology tends to stand out as an object only in circumstances of malfunction or 'breakdown' (see Blattner, 2006, pp. 56–59), or, I would add, perhaps in the initial period of unfamiliar use.

13. That possibility of knowing how to type (in the actual bodily effort of typing) without being able to give a verbal description of the layout of the keys, if, say, the machine was physically removed and out of sight, serves to highlight a distinction that Anthony Giddens (1984, p. 7) has identified as one between practical consciousness and discursive consciousness, or 'between what is…simply done…and…what can be said'. In such circumstances, when the technology was taken away, perhaps only the activity (bodily effort) of air typing would have enabled the user to come close to identifying the positions of the letters and other symbols. Furthermore, I find it interesting that Giddens (1984, p. 6) refers to *practical consciousness* as 'that characteristic of the human agent or subject to which structuralism has been particularly blind'. Significantly, too, he notes that the division between these two types of consciousness is not completely 'rigid and impermeable' (Giddens, 1984, p. 7), and this is important for what follows in my next chapter.

14. On this oversight, see also Tony Bennett (2005, p. 93), who observes that most research perspectives on 'media-audience relationships' have been concerned with 'the content of media messages' and with 'audience…interpretation' (he cites Hall on encoding and decoding as an example): 'But they do suggest a view of audiences as essentially disembodied, as if their relations to the media take place without…eyes, ears…and fingers being particularly involved.' According to Bennett (2005, p. 93), it is now necessary to regard 'what we do as audiences as being…embodied practices'. Similarly, in the context of literary studies, Karin Littau (2006, p. 11) is critical of the way in which 'contemporary… theories of reading have systematically marginalized…or ignored…the body of the reader'. Much as I have suggested with regard to media uses more generally in the opening section of my chapter, Littau (2006, p. 37) argues that 'reading is not primarily an act of interpretation', and she concludes her review of theories of reading by expressing serious doubts about those perspectives which 'affirm the cognitive and are thus aligned with the rational at the cost of the passional…affirm interpretation over feeling, mind over body' (Littau, 2006, p. 155).

15. I can still recall the occasion, some time back in the late 1980s, when I first attempted to manipulate a mouse on its mat, and I certainly did not have it, in Merleau-Ponty's terms, well in hand. Quite the contrary. An acquaintance had insisted that I have a go at playing a basic computer game on his new machine. After reluctantly agreeing to do so, I found that my hand was incapable of manoeuvring the device in a way required to move the cursor successfully in the game context. Laughter followed, and it was mostly at my

expense! The serious point of this anecdote, though, is that the bodily acquisition of habit is far from immediate, even in cases of so-called intuitive design. Of course, before long, once I began to use a computer regularly in my office at work, knowing the proper speed to push and click a mouse became a taken-for-granted skill, but there was still a process of acquisition to be gone through.

16. Pierre Bourdieu's concept of *habitus* is another attempt to get at these dispositions that are, in his words, both 'durable' (Bourdieu, 1977, p. 72) and 'transposable'. He writes of 'regularities' (Bourdieu, 1977, p. 78), then, but also of a 'generative principle' that is at work.

References

Althusser, L. (1984 [1971]), 'Ideology and Ideological State Apparatuses (Notes Towards an Investigation)', in *Essays on Ideology*, London: Verso.

Bennett, T. (2005), 'The Media Sensorium: Cultural Technologies, the Senses and Society', in Gillespie, M. (ed.) *Media Audiences*, Maidenhead: Open University Press.

Blattner, W. (2006), *Heidegger's* Being and Time: *A Reader's Guide*, London: Continuum.

Blumler, J. & Katz, E. (eds.) (1974), *The Uses of Mass Communications: Current Perspectives on Gratifications Research*, Beverley Hills, CA: Sage.

Bourdieu, P. (1977), *Outline of a Theory of Practice*, Cambridge: Cambridge University Press.

Bourdieu, P. (1984), *Distinction: A Social Critique of the Judgement of Taste*, London: Routledge and Kegan Paul.

Büscher, M., Urry, J. & Witchger, K. (eds.) (2011), *Mobile Methods*, London: Routledge.

Carman, T. (2008), *Merleau-Ponty*, London: Routledge.

Couldry, N. (2006), *Listening Beyond the Echoes: Media, Ethics and Agency in an Uncertain World*, Boulder, CO: Paradigm.

Couldry, N. (2010), 'Theorising Media as Practice', in Bräuchler, B. & Postill, J. (eds.) *Theorising Media and Practice*, Oxford: Berghahn.

Couldry, N. (2012), *Media, Society, World: Social Theory and Digital Media Practice*, Cambridge: Polity.

Couldry, N. & Hepp, A. (2017), *The Mediated Construction of Reality*, Cambridge: Polity.

de Certeau, M. (1984), *The Practice of Everyday Life*, Berkeley, CA: University of California Press.

Eagleton, T. (2016), *Materialism*, New Haven, CT: Yale University Press.

Evans, J. & Hesmondhalgh, D. (eds.) (2005), *Understanding Media: Inside Celebrity*, Maidenhead: Open University Press.

Fielding, G. & Hartley, P. (1987), 'The Telephone: A Neglected Medium', in Cashdan, A. & Jordin, M. (eds.) *Studies in Communication*, Oxford: Blackwell.

Gauntlett, D. (ed.) (2000), *Web.Studies: Rewiring Media Studies for the Digital Age*, London: Arnold.

Gauntlett, D. (2007a), 'Media Studies 2.0' (available at http://www.theory.org.uk).

Gauntlett, D. (2007b), *Creative Explorations: New Approaches to Identities and Audiences*, London: Routledge.

Gauntlett, D. (2011), *Making is Connecting: The Social Meaning of Creativity, From DIY and Knitting to YouTube and Web 2.0*, Cambridge: Polity.

Gauntlett, D. (2015), *Making Media Studies: The Creativity Turn in Media and Communications Studies*, New York: Peter Lang.

Giddens, A. (1979), *Central Problems in Social Theory: Action, Structure and Contradiction in Social Analysis*, Berkeley, CA: University of California Press.

Giddens, A. (1984), *The Constitution of Society: Outline of the Theory of Structuration*, Cambridge: Polity.

Gillespie, M. (ed.) (2005), *Media Audiences*, Maidenhead: Open University Press.

Goggin, G. (2006), *Cell Phone Culture: Mobile Technology in Everyday Life*, London: Routledge.

Goggin, G. (ed.) (2008), *Mobile Phone Cultures*, London: Routledge.

Gripsrud, J. (2002), *Understanding Media Culture*, London: Arnold.

Gumpert, G. & Cathcart, R. (eds.) (1986), *Inter/Media: Interpersonal Communication in a Media World*, third edition, New York: Oxford University Press.

Hall, S. (1973), 'Encoding and Decoding in the Television Discourse', CCCS Stencilled Paper no. 7, Centre for Contemporary Cultural Studies, University of Birmingham.

Hall, S. (1982), 'The Rediscovery of "Ideology": Return of the Repressed in Media Studies', in Gurevitch, M., Bennett, T., Curran, J. & Woollacott, J. (eds.) *Culture, Society and the Media*, London: Methuen.

Heidegger, M. (1962), *Being and Time*, Oxford: Blackwell.

Hopper, R. (1992), *Telephone Conversation*, Bloomington, IN: Indiana University Press.

Ihde, D. (1990), *Technology and the Lifeworld: From Garden to Earth*, Bloomington, IN: Indiana University Press.

Ihde, D. (2007), *Listening and Voice: Phenomenologies of Sound*, second edition, Albany, NY: State University of New York Press.

Katz, J. (2006), *Magic in the Air: Mobile Communication and the Transformation of Social Life*, New Brunswick, NJ: Transaction.

Katz, J. & Aakhus, M. (eds.) (2002), *Perpetual Contact: Mobile Communication, Private Talk, Public Performance*, Cambridge: Cambridge University Press.

Ling, R. (2004), *The Mobile Connection: The Cell Phone's Impact on Society*, Amsterdam: Elsevier.

Ling, R. & Donner, J. (2009), *Mobile Communication*, Cambridge: Polity.

Littau, K. (2006), *Theories of Reading: Books, Bodies and Bibliomania*, Cambridge: Polity.

Merleau-Ponty, M. (2002 [1962]), *Phenomenology of Perception*, London: Routledge.

Merleau-Ponty, M. (2004 [1964]), 'Merleau-Ponty's Prospectus of His Work', in Baldwin, T. (ed.) *Maurice Merleau-Ponty: Basic Writings*, London: Routledge.

Merrin, W. (2014), *Media Studies 2.0*, London: Routledge.

Moores, S. (1988), '"The Box on the Dresser": Memories of Early Radio and Everyday Life', *Media, Culture and Society*, vol. 10, no. 1, pp. 23–40.

Moores, S. (1990), 'Texts, Readers and Contexts of Reading: Developments in the Study of Media Audiences', *Media, Culture and Society*, vol. 12, no. 1, pp. 9–29.

Moores, S. (1993a), *Interpreting Audiences: The Ethnography of Media Consumption*, London: Sage.

Moores, S. (1993b), 'Satellite TV as Cultural Sign: Consumption, Embedding and Articulation', *Media, Culture and Society*, vol. 15, no. 4, pp. 621–639.

Moores, S. (1996), *Satellite Television and Everyday Life: Articulating Technology*, Luton: John
Libbey Media.

Moores, S. (1997), 'Broadcasting and Its Audiences', in Mackay, H. (ed.) *Consumption and
Everyday Life*, London: Sage.

Moores, S. (2005), *Media/Theory: Thinking about Media and Communications*, London: Routledge.

Moores, S. (2012), *Media, Place and Mobility*, Basingstoke: Palgrave Macmillan.

Morley, D. (2007), *Media, Modernity and Technology: The Geography of the New*, London: Routledge.

Morley, D. (2009), 'For a Materialist, Non-Media-Centric Media Studies', *Television and New
Media*, vol. 10, no. 1, pp. 114–116.

Moyal, A. (1992), 'The Gendered Use of the Telephone: An Australian Case Study', *Media,
Culture and Society*, vol. 14, no. 1, pp. 51–72.

Nunes, M. (2006), *Cyberspaces of Everyday Life*, Minneapolis, MN: University of Minnesota
Press.

Pallasmaa, J. (2009), *The Thinking Hand: Existential and Embodied Wisdom in Architecture*,
Chichester: Wiley.

Rakow, L. (1992), *Gender on the Line: Women, the Telephone and Community Life*, Urbana, IL:
University of Illinois Press.

Rockwell, H. (2011), *The Life of Voices: Bodies, Subjects and Dialogue*, New York: Routledge.

Sennett, R. (2009), *The Craftsman*, London: Penguin.

Silverstone, R. (1990), 'Television and Everyday Life: Towards an Anthropology of the Television Audience', in Ferguson, M. (ed.) *Public Communication: The New Imperatives – Future
Directions for Media Research*, London: Sage.

Tallis, R. (2003), *The Hand: A Philosophical Inquiry into Human Being*, Edinburgh: Edinburgh
University Press.

Tallis, R. (2010), *Michelangelo's Finger: An Exploration of Everyday Transcendence*, London:
Atlantic Books.

Taylor, C. (2005), 'Merleau-Ponty and the Epistemological Picture', in Carman, T. & Hansen,
M. (eds.) *The Cambridge Companion to Merleau-Ponty*, New York: Cambridge University
Press.

Taylor, L. & Willis, A. (1999), *Media Studies: Texts, Institutions and Audiences*, Oxford: Blackwell.

Thrift, N. (2004), 'Summoning Life', in Cloke, P., Crang, P. & Goodwin, M. (eds.) *Envisioning
Human Geographies*, London: Arnold.

Thrift, N. (2007), *Non-Representational Theory: Space/Politics/Affect*, London: Routledge.

Todes, S. (2001), *Body and World*, Cambridge, MA: MIT Press.

Tomlinson, J. (2007), *The Culture of Speed: The Coming of Immediacy*, London: Sage.

Urry, J. (2007), *Mobilities*, Cambridge: Polity.

Volosinov, V. (1986 [1973]), *Marxism and the Philosophy of Language*, Cambridge, MA: Harvard
University Press.

Williams, K. (2003), *Understanding Media Theory*, London: Arnold.

· 5 ·

ON THE ENVIRONMENTAL EXPERIENCES OF TRANS-EUROPEAN MIGRANTS

Knowing How to Get Around
(with Monika Metykova)

Meet Petra, one of the 20 young, trans-European migrants interviewed in the course of our collaborative research project on matters of *environmental experience, place and migration*. This Hungarian woman had been living in London for 18 months when the interview with her was recorded in 2007, having moved there from Budapest, and at that time she was working as a nanny.

Petra spoke of how, initially, she found London to be a strange and alienating urban environment. There were several reasons for this, which she set out as follows:

> I'd learned some English at home but not so much.... At the beginning, I was even scared to travel on my own.... In fact, the transport was very strange for me...I was literally feeling unwell on the underground...an enclosed space.... The fact...you had to look in a different direction when you stepped off the pavement as well...once I was almost run over by a car because I looked in the wrong direction.

This feeling of being an outsider was compounded by an uncomfortable situation at work. Before finding employment as a nanny (with a Belgian family living near Queensway), Petra had been washing dishes in the kitchen of a cafe, following her arrival in the English capital city in 2005. She explained that her boss and one of the other workers 'treated me with disdain, and it was very hard to come to terms with'.

After a year and a half, though, Petra was able to talk of her growing familiarity with those parts of London that she frequented on foot and on public transport, and, in relation to her developed patterns of movement and her *knowing how to get around*, she was also able to reflect on her emerging emotional ties to the city:

> It's no longer like 'Oh my God, I want to go from here to here. How do I do that?' I know how to do that. I know how to get around.... It was really nice because my parents visited me...nice that I could show them this and that. I travelled with them on the underground and my dad told me he was so proud that I could cope in this huge city...that he would be lost.... It's such a good feeling.... There were difficult times at the beginning, but now...it's good.... To some extent, I consider myself a Londoner.

Alongside the formation of that attachment to her new city, Petra was becoming increasingly aware, too, of the feelings she had for Budapest. Indeed, that established attachment to her former city was brought into focus precisely by her physical absence from the Hungarian capital. In the interview, she told a story about going to book a flight, 'in the Malev Airlines office' in London, for a trip back to Hungary: 'The office was full of photos of Budapest, and there was an English guy telling me to come and have nostalgic moments over the pictures any time.' On returning to Budapest for the first time after moving to live in Britain, Petra's heart was, in her words, 'pounding, pounding, pounding' as she crossed the River Danube, and while staying there she visited several 'places that are related to...memories', including the restaurant where her farewell party had been held.

Those photographic images on display in the airlines office allowed Petra to travel imaginatively while making arrangements for a physical journey and, more generally, media of communication were helping her to maintain contact with people (mainly friends and family) and happenings in Hungary. For example, she spoke of an older friend 'I call every Sunday' on the telephone: 'In the summer he had a heart attack...so I call him on a weekly basis.' Petra also commented on how she and her two Hungarian flatmates in London would regularly go online to 'check the net for home news', adding that: 'We *are always at home in home news*.'[1]

This has been just a short, opening account, relating to the environmental experiences of only one of our interviewees, but it serves to highlight four key themes that run through the empirical material generated by the project. The first of these themes, then, is the trans-European migrants' *initial impressions on arrival in Britain*. A second theme is *the gradual emergence of senses of place* in new physical locations. The third is migrants' *reflections on previously taken-for-granted, established senses of place*, and a fourth is the feeling of reach that comes from *making use of transnational transportation and media networks*. In this chapter, we will be returning to each of these key themes at greater length, referring to far more of the interview data. Before doing so, however, it is important for us to explain a little about why the research was conceived in the way that it was, and how, in practical terms, it was carried out.

For a phenomenology of place and migration

At the close of the preceding chapter, it was suggested that a notable feature of this research project is its emphasis on the experiences of migrants in the period soon after their transnational physical relocations (when previous routines are likely to have been disrupted and when new quotidian habits or everyday patterns of movement are in the process of being acquired), with such a project having the potential to bring elements of the precognitive to discursive consciousness, or, as Maurice Merleau-Ponty (2002 [1962], p. xv) might have put it, the possibility of slackening 'the intentional threads which attach us to the world', thereby bringing them 'to…notice'.[2] Of particular interest to us, at least partly because of our own earlier, personal experiences of transnational physical migrations, was that aspect of the precognitive and the affective which is most closely related to place-making practices or to the constitution of senses of place. We felt that an opportunity for *the empirical exploration of familiar, taken-for-granted practices and attachments* might actually be afforded by a qualitative study of migration, and saw phenomenology (in its philosophical and geographical forms) providing the most appropriate analytical framework for such a study, given its concerns with corporeal knowledge, movement and dwelling.

Another reason for doing this research on experiences of *trans-European migration*, associated as much with our political leanings as it was with an academic interest in the making of place or in matters of orientation and habitation, was a deep frustration with the character of public discussions in Britain at that time about movements of people from the then-new European Union member states in Eastern Europe, following a significant enlargement of the union in 2004. These discussions, including in the print media and broadcasting, tended to be dominated by expressions of anxiety about the number of migrants arriving and the perceived negative consequences for national or

regional economies and cultures in Britain, with the voices of migrants themselves rarely being heard there.[3] So it was in this specific social-historical and
political context that we planned the research, in part with the positive aim
of paying serious attention to the everyday-life circumstances of some of those
who had made the move across a continent.

Conversational interviews with the 20 young people who feature in our
study were recorded and transcribed during 2006 and 2007. All of the interviewees were in the 18–34 age range, within which, at least according to the
official worker-registration scheme that was in operation, the vast majority of
post-2004 migrants from Eastern Europe had been. At the time of the conversations, the migrants interviewed were based in London, Newcastle or Edinburgh, and these interviews were held in cafe, bar or household settings, with
their average length being well over an hour and a half. Some interviewees
spoke in Hungarian, Czech or Slovak (languages that are known to Monika)
and their words were later translated into English, whilst other conversations
were conducted in English from the outset.

One further point that needs to be stressed in the context of this brief
methodological outline, ahead of our return to the interview data and the
four themes highlighted above in the portrait of Petra, is the way in which
we explicitly designed the research so as not to centre the trans-European
migrants' media uses. Those uses, which were principally uses of new, digital
media technologies, were certainly of considerable interest to us, as we hope
to demonstrate below in discussing the fourth and final key theme here. However, very much in the spirit of *a non-media-centric perspective*, which is advocated at various stages elsewhere in this book, it was important for us to try
to understand how routine media use, including these interviewees' electronically mediated mobilities (see especially Urry, 2000, 2007), came to have a
particular significance in relation to a range of other practices or movements.

'I couldn't grasp it':
Initial impressions on arrival in Britain

Petra's initial environmental experiences on arrival in London can be conceptualised within the terms of phenomenological geography as ones of 'existential outsideness' (Relph, 2008 [1976], p. 51). She had 'a sense of strangeness
and alienation…often felt by newcomers' (Seamon & Sowers, 2008, p. 45),
and there are many similar accounts of *not belonging* (Relph, 2008 [1976],
p. 51) in the project's empirical material.

For example, there is the case of Simona, a Lithuanian woman from Vilnius who also came to live in London. Although she had grown up in the Lithuanian capital and made the journey to London fully expecting to find a city that was much larger than Vilnius, she was still overwhelmed on arrival by the scale and pace of urban living that she encountered: 'My first impression was "it's huge"…something more than I expected…the huge amount of people…so busy…. *I couldn't grasp it*…it was like…"Oh my God, can I stay here?"' A further example is that of Agnes, a Hungarian woman who, like Petra, had left Budapest. In her case, the move was to Newcastle in the North East of England, where she was employed by a computer company with offices on the outskirts of that city. Agnes explained that:

> I was driving from the very beginning because…bus transport there is awful, so I had to buy a car…driving on the other side, sitting in the car on the other side. I didn't know where I was, a big challenge…. For a long time, when I knew I'd have to drive somewhere, I had a stomach ache…studying the map for half an hour and then, once I arrived, half an hour of catching my breath.

Just as Petra, as a pedestrian, talked of her trouble with the way in which 'you had to look in a different direction when you stepped off the pavement', so Agnes was initially uncomfortable with 'driving on the other side' of the road in a new national context and being seated at the wheel in a different location within the car. That discomfort, which is evident in her references to getting a stomach ache and having to catch her breath, had to do precisely with a lack of familiarity (her *not knowing how to get around*) in strange physical settings. Merleau-Ponty (2002 [1962], p. 165), in his account of the acquisition of habit, writes at one point of 'the habit of driving a car', in which that transport technology becomes an extension of the human body in the practice of driving, but the experience described by Agnes, who had previously driven in Hungary, shows how this habitual practice may be disrupted, at least temporarily, when there are significant changes in the driver's environmental conditions.[4]

When Petra set out the reasons for her first feelings of outsideness, as reported in the introductory account with which we opened this chapter, she mentioned language use, too, as a difficulty for her, despite having 'learned some English at home'. Interestingly, this was an issue raised by several other interviewees, and even by some who had previously considered themselves to be proficient speakers of English. For instance, Marcin, a Polish man who moved to Edinburgh and was working as a cleaner at a hospital in the Scottish capital, recalled how, as a newcomer to the city, the locals 'didn't understand me…and…I thought my English was so pure'. In a similar fashion, Marta, a Czech woman who was living in Newcastle with an English partner, made the following remarks:

> Although I'd studied English at…university, it was quite a shock…because…really, the practical life in English is so different from what you actually learned…. It's sometimes small things like phrases. I do feel…a foreigner because I'm treated as such… based on my accent…in shops and when I meet people.

In fact, bringing together the apparently quite different examples discussed so far in this section, it might be argued that learning to negotiate what Marta called 'the practical life in English' is rather like, and is often bound up with, having to find one's way in a new urban environment. As sociologist Margaret Archer (2000, p. 135) has insisted, following a Merleau-Pontyan line, language acquisition is best understood as being 'of a piece with acquiring other kinds of practical conduct'. Becoming a skilled, habitual language user, then, is also to do with orientation (and with habitation, insideness or belonging).

We must conclude this section, though, by acknowledging that not all the interviewees had the same experiences of outsideness on their arrival in Britain. Notable exceptions were the few who had previously spent periods of time abroad. For instance, Ilija, a Slovenian man from Ljubljana who was working as a researcher in a university science department in London, had experience of staying in large cities in Japan and the USA. When asked about his emotional response at the point of his migration to the English capital, he replied: 'I spent…time in Tokyo and I visited New York before and…I really like…never-ending streets…. I really enjoy such an environment.' Katerina, a Czech woman who was working (again like Petra) as a nanny, had also been abroad on other occasions before accepting her position with a family in London. Formerly, Katerina had been employed on a cruise liner in the Caribbean and, most significantly, she had already worked for a while as an 'au pair' in London as a teenager.[5] Describing how she felt when arriving back there years later, she exclaimed: 'Yippee! I mean I knew what I was getting into…the first couple of weeks was just seeing my favourite places like Covent Garden…real bliss!'

'I don't need a map':
The gradual emergence of senses of place

As we reported earlier in the chapter, Petra experienced a growing familiarity with, and feeling for, the parts of London that she travelled through on a regular basis. In Yi-Fu Tuan's words (see Tuan, 1977, p. 199), what was strange town gradually became place for her, and this involved some of what David Seamon (2015 [1979], p. 33) identifies as the 'movements in the outdoor environment' that are typically associated with a local making of place. There are many other examples in the interview data of how such movements, including practices of driving, cycling and walking, served to facilitate at-homeness in a new city, and we turn to these examples in the current section.

Agnes, who declared that 'I didn't know where I was…studying the map for half an hour' before venturing out on the streets of Newcastle in her car, went on to explain how her anxieties about driving there 'disappeared…after about half a year' as she 'became a routine driver, discovering the city in small steps'. Similarly, Boris, a Slovak man employed as a delivery driver by a catering company in Central London, reflected on his own period of adjustment in gradually becoming a routine road user in that area. When asked about the difficulties of getting around busy city streets by car, in initially unfamiliar surroundings, he ended his reply by claiming that 'if you work in one area for two years then you find your way, even blindfolded'. A further interviewee, Marius from Kaunas in Lithuania, offered the following comment on his experiences of driving in different parts of the English capital: 'One year and…*I don't need a map*. A little bit hard in the north and east…but…west and centre I know very well.'

Honza, a Czech man who worked in London for a commercial television station, talked of his knowing how to get around as having been accomplished mainly by means of routine running (for leisure) and cycling (for his daily commute). Putney, the local area where he lived is by the side of the River Thames and he enjoyed taking exercise there along the river paths: 'I know all the bends…. I'm glad that I found such a place…that's my London home.' He also recalled how, after first arriving in the city:

> I rode my bike the whole summer. I was the happiest person in London…. I jump on the bike. I am at work in 40 minutes. I meander through the traffic, quarrel with the taxi drivers and so on.

Meanwhile, for Darek and Magda, a Polish couple living in Edinburgh, walking had been a key familiarising practice. So when speaking about their favourite sites in and around that city, they referred to various locations visited on foot. Darek, a cleaner, spoke about the Grassmarket area of Edinburgh's Old Town: 'I like walking there very early in the morning…when the street is empty.' Similarly, Magda, a care worker with the elderly, mentioned the outer suburb of Cramond by the Firth of Forth, where 'there's a small island…you can walk to when the sea isn't in'.

In the case of fellow Edinburgh-based Pole, Marcin, as for Honza in London, a regular commute to work was significant in helping to shape a sense of place, and this involved a combination of walking and using public transport: 'On my way to work every day, I meet the same people, just knowing each other by sight. The lady goes the same time in the same direction… we're catching the bus in exactly the same place.' What Marcin pointed to here, then, was the meshing of morning time-space routines in a public, urban setting, which is one element of what Seamon (2015 [1979]) would conceptualise as a larger place choreography, or what Nigel Thrift (2009, p. 92) has similarly described as a rhythmic 'spatial dance' of 'bodies and things'.

Along with those different sorts of outdoor movement, our empirical material also features certain instances of indoor movement (as well as moments of stillness or rest) that were clearly important in place-making processes. For example, Ilija came to experience at-homeness in the old library building at his university, remarking on its 'special smell' and its wooden floors that were 'squeaky' underfoot.[6] In the private setting of his rented apartment, too, he felt 'at home…in the bathroom', where he had got into the habit or ritual of taking 'a long bath' at the end of each day, initially because the shower was broken. For Krzysztof, a Polish man from Wroclaw living in London, it was a second-hand armchair, and the view that he had from it, which provided a valued resting place within the domestic sphere:

> I love my room…. I've got a…high tree in front of my window…. There was a squat evicted from down the road and they got this beautiful, massive chair to my room. I put it opposite my window and I can see this tree in our garden.

Finally in this section, we return to Simona, who had been overwhelmed by the scale and pace of life in London after she arrived from Lithuania. What helped her to settle into the first room that she rented was something she brought with her on the budget-airline flight from Vilnius. She described this emotionally significant possession as a piece of netting, onto which she had clipped postcards and pictures of her friends, and she hung it on her wall as soon as she moved in: 'It's always in the room where I'm living.' Indeed, in

anticipation of our discussion of media uses later in the chapter, it is interesting to note that this was not the only net with pictures which she had in her
London room. Simona was also engaged in online interactions with several
Lithuanian friends, who, like her, had left Vilnius to live abroad, sharing stories and digital photographs 'from our travels'.[7]

'I didn't realise how attached I am': Reflections on previously taken-for-granted, established senses of place

Having concentrated in the previous section on the constitution of senses
of place in the migrants' new physical locations, our focus now shifts onto
a realisation, which many of our interviewees reported, of the strength of
affective attachments or emotional bindings to previously inhabited material
environments in Eastern Europe. As was the case for Petra, reflections on such
established, unselfconscious senses of place became possible precisely because
of a physical move away from inhabited spaces, throwing into relief the
taken-for-grantedness of lifeworlds and thereby enabling migrants to speak, at
least to some degree, about what geographer Anne Buttimer (1976, p. 281)
once called *precognitive givens*.

To begin with here, let us stay with Simona's story, since she gave a powerful account of her feelings on occasional trips made back to Lithuania:

> When I go back there I really feel like at home…walking the streets of Vilnius….
> Yeah, it's different because I no longer live there, but…you feel it's your own town….
> So many things happened there, in particular places…. I walk there…where I used
> to hang out…this happened there, there it was that, the atmosphere…the mood….
> These streets carry…meaning…for me…. I never realised that before I left, *I didn't
> realise how attached I am*.

This meaning became evident mainly as a consequence of the distance that
Simona now had ('because I no longer live there'), but it is also significant
that her realisation of attachment was brought to notice in the very act of
'walking the streets of Vilnius' again, as memories of social happenings and
their associated moods were evoked.[8]

A similar example can be found in the interview with Honza, who
described going back to visit the city in the Czech Republic, Hradec Kralove,
where he had grown up: 'When I arrive in Hradec, I simply know every corner,

every street and every pub…. When I walk…I'm at home…. I've never felt like this anywhere else.' In the case of his compatriot, Marta, a trip to Brno from Newcastle resulted in a comparison being made between her old and new cities, bringing to her attention some previously taken-for-granted features of the urban landscape she had known:

> The last time I was in Brno…what struck me was how quiet it was…. I hadn't realised that until that moment…walking through the city…. No music coming out of shops…fewer people…. This is what I miss…I really like the peacefulness.

Another Czech woman, Pavla, who was working as a waitress in London, reflected on how: 'I increasingly miss the Czech language…. I miss…films, television, books in Czech.' A sense of place involving familiarity with her native tongue was apparent to Pavla only after leaving the country in which she had been routinely immersed in that language. In relation to this matter of talk, text and nationality, she had something else to say that was also of interest to us, remarking on 'English…stereotypes' regarding her accent: 'They tell me that the Poles are all moving here…. I tell them, "I'm not a Pole, I'm a Czech." Since I moved to London, it makes me angry when someone tells me I'm Polish.' Those comments serve as a helpful, cautionary reminder that our broad use of the term Eastern Europe in this research project risked obscuring strongly felt national differences.

To complete this section of the chapter, four more illustrations from the empirical material should suffice, in order to confirm a general point we are making here about the potential for migrants to reflect on previously taken-for-granted, established senses of place. The first two of these echo statements that we have reported earlier. So, like Petra, who spoke of how hard her heart was pounding on returning to Budapest, Zsuzsanna, a fellow Hungarian living in London, described a particularly poignant moment as she arrived back on a visit to her home country (on realising the unanticipated strength of her affective attachment): 'I was crying…when the plane landed…. I just started crying.' In addition, as when Simona declared that she 'didn't realise how attached' she was to Vilnius, Darek in Edinburgh offered this reflection:

> I love our culture in Poland…. Now, when I live here, I see that…. When you have something every day you don't appreciate it, but when you have it only a few times, when you move to another country and you don't have contact with it like before, you…miss it…. I think for many people it works like that.

However, it did not work quite 'like that' for his partner Magda. Asked about her own emotions on making return trips to Poland, she replied: 'I feel like I belonged...before, but I don't belong...now.... I have my friends, my family...but after a couple of days I feel like I want to be back here.' Similarly, for Katerina, one of the Czech women whose experiences we have already touched on, reflections on the life she had left behind led her to conclude that: 'If I was to put them on a piece of paper, there would probably be more things that I like connected with a Western European way of life rather than an Eastern European one.'

'We are always at home in home news': Making use of transnational transportation and media networks

In thinking about the distinctive characteristics of the contemporary trans-European migrations that we investigated, it is necessary to take into account the relative physical nearness of Britain and Eastern Europe, in comparison with the distances involved in travelling between, say, Europe and North America or South Asia. Of course, moving thousands of miles across a continent was still a major relocation that could lead to a disturbance of lifeworlds, and yet many cities in Eastern Europe were only a few hours away by air (allowing for the realistic possibility of return visits for short periods, or even return moves to the migrants' countries of origin).[9] In addition, media uses, and especially the uses of digital media technologies, brought a new dimension to 'proximal experience' (Scannell, 1996, p. 89; see also Urry, 2002) that altered or modified, in certain respects, the dynamics of transnational physical migration, helping to give these trans-European mobilities a further element of historical specificity.

Our purpose in putting together, quite explicitly in this section, a discussion of *transport and media technologies* (and see Morley, 2011) is to emphasise the migrants' experiences of *reach* (Buttimer, 1980), which were related in complex ways to their senses of place. One indication of such experiential complexity, as we will try to show here, was the potential for particular media environments (sometimes associated with physical settings in Eastern Europe) to become meaningful places (see Tuan, 2004) when they were returned to repeatedly, as was the case with the Hungarian news sites accessed routinely from London by Petra and her flatmates.

Consider the example of Krzysztof's feeling of reach. He commented on how: 'Gatwick Airport is very convenient and...from the time I leave...to the time I enter my mother's house it takes about five hours.'[10] However, the experiential closeness of Wroclaw was not only to do with occasional plane journeys. Krzysztof also maintained a familiarity of a kind with that Polish city by regularly engaging in virtual travel. For 'at least half an hour a day' on the internet, then, he visited a site on which numerous digital photographs of his former city were being displayed by locals, at a time when it was going through a period of rapid urban regeneration:

> There's a...website called *skyscrapercity*.... People take pictures and put them on... and...I actually know more about what's going on in the city than my mum.... I ask her 'did you see this building?'

Krzysztof's inhabiting of that online setting resembled Petra's at-homeness with what she called 'home news', and there are several other stories in the empirical material of migrants using the internet in this way. For instance, a Slovak man named Julius, who was working as a computer programmer in London, revealed how, 'in winter, when the Danube was frozen', he had regularly watched live webcam images of the river, while sitting at his desk during coffee breaks in the office, and, on the day of his interview, Ilija talked in a matter-of-fact way of having just viewed a 'Slovenian news programme... last night's TV news...via internet'. These imaginative and virtual mobilities appeared to be experienced as quite ordinary features of day-to-day living.

Indeed, more generally, interviewees spoke about the ways in which their uses of new media, including for the purpose of mediated interpersonal communications with family members in Eastern Europe, were intricately woven into the quotidian fabric. For example, in Agnes's case, online contact with her mother in Hungary was maintained whilst at work in Newcastle: 'She's got email at work too, so we exchange emails during the day and phone each other from time to time.' Meanwhile, for Marcin in Edinburgh, 'coming home from the job' each working day was associated with a ritual of checking his email inbox for any new messages from Poland: 'I try to be in touch regularly with my family. I've got a younger sister. We have a close relationship.'

On those occasions when Marcin made visits back to Poland, he took Scottish food and drink to give as small gifts ('shortbread and whisky...for my family and friends'), and there are numerous other examples in our interview data of *the transnational physical movement of objects* (see Urry, 2007, p. 47) of different sorts. For instance, Ildiko, a Hungarian woman who lived in Newcastle, where she was working in marketing, had managed to move her most valued house-plants across Europe when she migrated: 'I cut them down...and put them...in a shoe box.' Similarly, Zsuzsanna, rather like Simona with her piece of netting, had transported various 'small...belongings with which I try to make it more personal here...all sorts of souvenirs...anything that is connected to some memories', and when Boris's girlfriend came to visit him in London she would bring Slovak biscuits and 'loads and loads of sausages' to make goulash 'with the smell of your homeland'. In the case of Marius, who, unusually amongst our interviewees, chose to make occasional return visits on the road rather than by air, 'good money' was earned by ferrying Lithuanian migrants' heavy luggage and parcels either way between London and Kaunas in his car.

To conclude this section, we turn again to the trans-European migrants' media uses, or, more precisely, to their non-uses of certain media technologies and services (because the electronically mediated links with Eastern Europe, to which we have referred above, were sometimes accompanied by a discon-nection from British news and popular entertainment). Indeed, most of the young migrants who were interviewed in the project did not possess a televi-sion set, preferring new media with a greater capacity for dialogical interac-tion and typically with a greater portability too. Simona was one of those, and she admitted that she was not particularly interested in engaging with news about the city, or even the local area of it, that she had moved to: 'My parents call me up and tell me what's going on in London, actually.... "Have you heard about this shooting?" "No." "There was something in Lewisham." "No." I'm this kind of a person.' A further example of disconnection was provided by Zsuzsanna, who related the following story of her conversation with a group of British college students:

> Someone said something about *Big Brother*, and I didn't know what it was about so I asked...and everyone stared at me...as if I lived on another planet.... 'Oh my God... you don't know about it?'... It was really embarrassing.

In a similar way, when Julius had first moved to live and work in London, he experienced an exclusion from some of the conversations that went on between colleagues in his office: 'Friends at work would talk...about a pro-gramme, and...you are completely left out because...you're not following it.' In fact, in Julius's case, it was this uncomfortable feeling of being 'left out' of office talk which led him to purchase a tuner card so that he could access live broadcasting via his laptop, thereby helping him to integrate into work culture.

A brief link to the next chapter

One of the key arguments of the current chapter, made with reference to findings from a qualitative empirical investigation of transnational migration, has been that formations of place are bound up with what philosopher Charles Taylor (2006, p. 212) calls 'a kind of "knowing how"…our ordinary ability to get around'. As Petra put it when she spoke of an emerging sense of place, on finding her way about in a new city and national context: 'I know how to get around.' Today, of course, such getting around is typically done across a mix of overlapping physical and media settings, and it is possible to feel at home (or to be estranged and alienated) in both of those sorts of environment. In the previous chapter, these matters of orientation and habitation were discussed in relation to Merleau-Ponty's philosophy of the knowledgeable body, and in the next chapter that discussion will be extended still further in a detailed critical engagement with Tim Ingold's anthropology (see especially Ingold, 2000, 2007, 2011, 2015). Among contemporary theorists in the humanities and social sciences who are advocating a non-representational approach, he has done perhaps more than any other to highlight the significance of 'everyday skills of orientation' (Ingold, 2000, p. 219).

Notes

1. It is interesting to compare this identification made by Petra and her compatriots (as recently arrived migrants) with the responses of some established London Turks, as reported by Asu Aksoy and Kevin Robins (2003), to the live television from Turkey that was available to them via satellite in their domestic spaces. These viewers were unable to watch Turkish news 'from the inside' (Aksoy & Robins, 2003, p. 103), because the 'conditions no longer exist for feeling at home' in that media environment. In addition, it is interesting for us that whilst Aksoy and Robins were not drawing on the literature of phenomenological geography they do effectively employ notions of *insideness and at-homeness* there, which we would associate with books by Edward Relph (2008 [1976]) and David Seamon (2015 [1979]).

2. Of course, there was already a good deal of published work in media and cultural studies on migration and diaspora (see, for example, Bailey et al., 2007; Karim, 2003; King & Wood, 2001; Qureshi & Moores, 1999), and yet there is still very little that concentrates, as we did in this project, on migrant experiences in the period immediately following transnational physical relocations. However, see Maggie O'Neill's innovative research on refugees and asylum seekers (O'Neill, 2007), which is rather different from ours in methodological terms but which does refer to the sensuous knowing of then-recently arrived migrants.

3. It has to be said that by the time of the 2016 referendum debate that led to a so-called Brexit vote (a vote for Britain to leave the European Union), the character of these public discussions had hardly moved on and the voices of migrants from Eastern Europe are still rarely heard today.

4. As discussed in the previous chapter, with reference to Maurice Merleau-Ponty's example of the 'experienced organist' (Merleau-Ponty, 2002 [1962], p. 167), the knowledgeable or comprehending body has an adaptability and a generative capacity that usually enables it to adjust over time to altered circumstances. Still, whereas Merleau-Ponty's organ player required 'only an hour's practice to be ready to perform his programme' (Merleau-Ponty, 2002 [1962], p. 168), it took Agnes, as we will report later, rather longer to get used to driving in Newcastle.

5. A fascinating anthropological ethnography of Slovak au pairs living in the London area, published shortly after we wrote the articles on which this chapter is based, is Zuzana Búriková and Daniel Miller (2010).

6. These remarks are significant in emphasising the multi-sensual character of dwelling or habitation. Ilija's embodied perception of that library evidently incorporated senses of hearing and touch as well as smell (and we assume there must have been a visual dimension too, since he went there to read).

7. Given Simona's reference to the 'travels' of this group of friends, we wonder whether, for at least a few of the migrants featured in our project, the move to Britain might have turned out to resemble, retrospectively, what John Urry (2007, p. 10) once termed the 'discovery travel of...young people on their "overseas experience"'.

8. A few years ago, a respected older colleague in our field offered the comment, in the context of giving his critical feedback on our writing, that this project's findings seemed to lack an element of surprise which he considered to be desirable in qualitative empirical investigations. Indeed, many years before, one of the pioneers of ethnographic research in cultural studies, Paul Willis (1980, p. 90), had pointed to 'a profoundly important methodological possibility...that of being "surprised", of reaching knowledge not prefigured in one's starting paradigm'. It is worth noting a couple of things in response to this. Firstly, whilst it is true that our empirical material appears to fit quite neatly with the phenomenological philosophy and geography which, in large part, framed the study (with what Willis might call our starting paradigm), perhaps the surprise on show here is that which was expressed by those young, trans-European migrants, who had not previously realised the strength of their attachments or bindings to material environments. Secondly, although our research, carried out by way of conversational interviews, would not be considered by anthropologists or sociologists to be fully ethnographic, since it did not also incorporate participant-observational techniques, it nevertheless dealt with matters of interest to Willis (2000) in a later, valuable discussion of the 'ethnographic imagination'. In fact, although he does not employ the term non-representational theory, Willis's approach is in some respects remarkably close to Nigel Thrift's. For instance, Willis (2000, pp. 14–23) challenges ideas from within 'the language paradigm' (about there being 'no meaning outside language') that came into cultural studies from 'varieties of structuralism', arguing that they 'cannot help us very much to understand...the sensuousness of cultural practices, including the sensuous use of objects', and his conceptual vocabulary includes terms such

as 'embodiment', 'practical knowledge', 'moving around' and 'sensuous meaningfulness'. Willis (2000, p. 22) acknowledges the significance of speech as social practice, but insists that 'we need to see social life as containing many different kinds of meaningfulness, incarnate in different practices and forms, layered and overlapping'. He makes it clear, too, that his approach has grown out of a left-culturalist or cultural-materialist strand of cultural studies. So as far back as the 1970s, Willis (1977, p. 175) had criticised structuralist-Marxist perspectives that saw 'no cracks in the billiard ball smoothness of…the…reproductive functions of ideology'.

9. It strikes us that an under-researched area in cultural studies is the experiential dimension of return transnational migrations. How does it feel, then, to go back to live in a country that was once left behind? For example, what degrees of insideness and outsideness or familiarity and estrangement (possibly even loss) might be felt following such return moves?

10. In a similar fashion, Ilija, referring to the 'cheap flights to Ljubljana' that were available to him from London, stated that: 'No one would mind if I leave work at two on Friday, catch a flight at five or six and come back on Sunday night…. I realised…that's possible.'

References

Aksoy, A. & Robins, K. (2003), 'Banal Transnationalism: The Difference that Television Makes', in Karim, K. (ed.) *The Media of Diaspora*, London: Routledge.

Archer, M. (2000), *Being Human: The Problem of Agency*, Cambridge: Cambridge University Press.

Bailey, O., Georgiou, M. & Harindranath, R. (eds.) (2007), *Transnational Lives and the Media: Re-Imagining Diaspora*, Basingstoke: Palgrave Macmillan.

Búriková, Z. & Miller, D. (2010), *Au Pair*, Cambridge: Polity.

Buttimer, A. (1976), 'Grasping the Dynamism of Lifeworld', *Annals of the Association of American Geographers*, vol. 66, no. 2, pp. 277–292.

Buttimer, A. (1980), 'Home, Reach and the Sense of Place', in Buttimer, A. & Seamon, D. (eds.) *The Human Experience of Space and Place*, London: Croom Helm.

Ingold, T. (2000), *The Perception of the Environment: Essays on Livelihood, Dwelling and Skill*, London: Routledge.

Ingold, T. (2007), *Lines: A Brief History*, London: Routledge.

Ingold, T. (2011), *Being Alive: Essays on Movement, Knowledge and Description*, London: Routledge.

Ingold, T. (2015), *The Life of Lines*, London: Routledge.

Karim, K. (ed.) (2003), *The Media of Diaspora*, London: Routledge.

King, R. & Wood, N. (eds.) (2001), *Media and Migration: Constructions of Mobility and Difference*, London: Routledge.

Merleau-Ponty, M. (2002 [1962]), *Phenomenology of Perception*, London: Routledge.

Morley, D. (2011), 'Communications and Transport: The Mobility of Information, People and Commodities', *Media, Culture and Society*, vol. 33, no. 5, pp. 743–759.

O'Neill, M. (2007), 'Re-Imagining Diaspora Through Ethno-Mimesis: Humiliation, Human Dignity and Belonging', in Bailey, O., Georgiou, M. & Harindranath, R. (eds.) *Transnational Lives and the Media: Re-Imagining Diaspora*, Basingstoke: Palgrave Macmillan.

Qureshi, K. & Moores, S. (1999), 'Identity Remix: Tradition and Translation in the Lives of Young Pakistani Scots', *European Journal of Cultural Studies*, vol. 2, no. 3, pp. 311–330.

Relph, E. (2008 [1976]), *Place and Placelessness*, London: Pion.

Scannell, P. (1996), *Radio, Television and Modern Life: A Phenomenological Approach*, Oxford: Blackwell.

Seamon, D. (2015 [1979]), *A Geography of the Lifeworld: Movement, Rest and Encounter*, London: Routledge.

Seamon, D. & Sowers, J. (2008), '*Place and Placelessness* (1976): Edward Relph', in Hubbard, P., Kitchin, R. & Valentine, G. (eds.) *Key Texts in Human Geography*, London: Sage.

Taylor, C. (2006), 'Engaged Agency and Background in Heidegger', in Guignon, C. (ed.) *The Cambridge Companion to Heidegger*, second edition, New York: Cambridge University Press.

Thrift, N. (2009), 'Space: The Fundamental Stuff of Geography', in Clifford, N., Holloway, S., Rice, S. & Valentine, G. (eds.) *Key Concepts in Geography*, second edition, London: Sage.

Tuan, Y. (1977), *Space and Place: The Perspective of Experience*, Minneapolis, MN: University of Minnesota Press.

Tuan, Y. (2004), 'Sense of Place: Its Relationship to Self and Time', in Mels, T. (ed.) *Reanimating Places: A Geography of Rhythms*, Aldershot: Ashgate.

Urry, J. (2000), *Sociology Beyond Societies: Mobilities for the Twenty-First Century*, London: Routledge.

Urry, J. (2002), 'Mobility and Proximity', *Sociology*, vol. 36, no. 2, pp. 255–274.

Urry, J. (2007), *Mobilities*, Cambridge: Polity.

Willis, P. (1977), *Learning to Labour: How Working Class Kids Get Working Class Jobs*, Aldershot: Saxon House.

Willis, P. (1980), 'Notes on Method', in Hall, S., Hobson, D., Lowe, A. & Willis, P. (eds.) *Culture, Media, Language: Working Papers in Cultural Studies, 1972–79*, London: Hutchinson.

Willis, P. (2000), *The Ethnographic Imagination*, Cambridge: Polity.

· 6 ·

WE FIND OUR WAY ABOUT

Everyday Media Use and Inhabitant Knowledge

A passing remark

My starting point for this chapter is a passing remark of Paddy Scannell's about broadcasting (see Scannell, 1996, pp. 7–8), which has long intrigued me: 'Programme output…has a…known and familiar character…we find our way about in it.'[1] The reference that he makes there to *finding ways about* in the programme output of radio and television suggests two important things to me, which, taken together, can help to extend understandings of how listeners and viewers engage with broadcasting, and may also contribute more generally to a reconceptualising of relationships between media and their users in everyday lives. His linked assertion that programme output has a *known and familiar* character begs a crucial question, too, which I will come to shortly.

Scannell's notion of finding ways about is significant, firstly, because it suggests that radio and television provide spaces or, better, time-spaces of movement for audience members. Of course, he is not the only theorist to indicate that media have an environmental quality or that everyday media use involves a moving around. As should be clear by now from previous chapters of my book, Joshua Meyrowitz (1985) has referred to media settings or environments, and John Urry's social theory of mobilities (see, for example, Urry, 2000, 2007) employs concepts of imaginative, virtual and communicative travel, along-side ideas about the corporeal travel of people and the physical movement of objects. A defining feature of Scannell's approach, though, is his commitment to investigating the institutional formations of broadcasting as 'a daily service' (Scannell, 1996, p. 149) of programme output. On the basis of detailed histor-ical research into the early years of radio in Britain (Scannell & Cardiff, 1991), he argues that the creation of such a service required the discovery of tech-niques of serial production and fixed scheduling, as well as the appropriation of ordinary, sociable styles of talk-in-interaction and the associated development of modes of address which were suitable for household audiences (see also, for example, Scannell, 1988, 1991, 2000, 2014). These methodical, reproducible techniques and distinctive communicative styles enabled programme output to become merged with other time-spaces of movement in day-to-day living, so that broadcasting could be experienced by listeners and viewers in its dai-liness, as a routine entitlement or as 'a domestic utility...always on tap...a continuous uninterrupted flow' (Scannell, 1988, p. 24).

Secondly, and most significantly, in those words of Scannell's that I have borrowed for the main title of my chapter, an implicit association is being made between the uses of broadcasting's daily service and what Tim Ingold (2000, p. 219) calls *everyday skills of orientation and wayfinding*. In an attempt to make this association explicit, I want to open up an exploration of how people find their way about media settings just as they know, in the very course of their bodily movements, how to get around, say, a room, a building, a street, a neighbourhood or a city. Additionally, it is important to acknowl-edge that finding ways about is fundamental for dwelling (a key theme of my book, which I have been seeking to establish through my engagements with phenomenology in earlier chapters and which I am now looking to pursue by paying particular, close attention to Ingold's anthropological writings). As Ingold (2007, p. 89) expresses it: 'It is...through the practices of wayfaring that beings inhabit the world.'[2]

Within media studies, meaningful relations between media and their audiences or users have typically been conceptualised, at least since the 1970s in the critical paradigm, as matters of symbolic representation and cognitive interpretation. However, in what follows, my focus will be on those of orienta-tion and habitation, which have been largely neglected in media analysis.[3] For me, then, Scannell's passing remark points to precisely this sort of focus, indi-cating the possibility of developing what might be named *non-representational theories of everyday media use*, where the emphasis would be put on habitual practices and on precognitive familiarity with environments. I want, therefore, to take Scannell's notion of finding ways about in this new theoretical direction for media studies, while considering media uses alongside a number of other, ordinary activities of getting around.[4]

Let me turn now to the question that arises for me when Scannell (1996, p. 8) asserts that the programme output of radio and television comes to be experienced as known and familiar. Exactly what kind of knowledge is alluded to here? I would argue that it is a form of what Ingold (2007, p. 89) terms *inhabitant knowledge*. Inhabitants, he contends, 'know as they go, as they journey through the world along paths of travel' (Ingold, 2011, p. 154). This is an 'alongly integrated' (Ingold, 2007, p. 89) knowledge, to which he has returned again and again in his work (see Ingold, 2000, 2007, 2011, 2015a). Still, as I will try to show in due course, later in the chapter, Ingold's anthropology does not arrive ready-made for the purposes of media analysis. He rarely mentions contemporary media of communication, and, in any case, the account of cultural change that he offers, with its overly pessimistic view of 'modern metropolitan societies' (Ingold, 2007, p. 75), does not easily lend itself to an understanding of *media uses as practices of wayfaring today*. Nevertheless, I want to accept the open, generous invitation that is issued by Ingold (2007, p. 170) in the final paragraph of his remarkable first book on 'lines' (the second is Ingold, 2015a), in which he states that: 'I have left plentiful loose ends for others to follow and to take in ways they wish.' Ultimately, I suspect that the direction in which I wish to take his work will not be one that he could approve of, but it is with the aim of convincing my fellow media theorists and researchers of the value of Ingold's non-representational approach that I enter into a critical encounter with his writings in the pages ahead.

A dwelling perspective

As Ingold (2011, p. 4) explains, his 'current explorations in the comparative anthropology of the line' grew out of an earlier but overlapping (because he has 'not ceased thinking about' it) phase of his research, in which he had become 'preoccupied with the notion of dwelling'. It might be helpful, then, as a basis for understanding the relationship between lines of movement and processes of dwelling that is important for him (and also for me, in my proposal for non-media-centric media studies with a non-representational theoretical emphasis), if I discuss in some detail, in this section of my chapter, Ingold's development of *a dwelling perspective* for his academic discipline.[5]

I will begin here by reproducing a short passage in which Ingold (2000, p. 153) provides the following definition:

> By this I mean a perspective that treats the immersion of the organism-person in an environment or lifeworld as an inescapable condition of existence. From this perspective, the world continually comes into being around the inhabitant, and its manifold constituents take on significance through their incorporation into a regular pattern of life activity.

He goes on to contrast the notion of dwelling with what he calls 'the building perspective', which has, he asserts, 'been rather more usual…in…anthropology' (Ingold, 2000, p. 153), and from which it is assumed that people must first '"construct" the world, in consciousness, before they can act in it'. Furthermore, from this other, commonly found building perspective, to which a dwelling perspective is firmly opposed, it tends to be assumed that the human construction of a world 'in the mind' (Ingold, 2000, p. 178) is a specifically 'cultural construction' involving the imposition of frameworks of meaning on reality (a reality which is often 'envisioned…as an external…nature'), and therefore that there is a clear 'separation between the perceiver and the world' or between culture and nature. As I argued in the introductory chapter of my book, such models of social or cultural construction, which foreground the cognitive and the symbolic, are also commonly found in the literature of media studies, and so, at least in part, I am interested in Ingold's development of a dwelling perspective for anthropology because of the potential that it has to help shift thinking in my own field towards what he terms 'a new ecology' (Ingold, 2000, p. 173).

In this ecology, for Ingold (2000, p. 168), there is no separation between perceiver and world, no clear divide in which mental picturing and cultural-representational systems must necessarily intervene in giving meaning to the real, but rather there is in phenomenological terms 'a being-in-the-world' or, as he puts it in the passage that I quoted above, an immersion: 'In short… the world becomes a meaningful place for people through being lived in…far from being inscribed upon the bedrock of…reality, meaning is immanent in… people's practical engagement with their lived-in environments.' Indeed, with direct reference to Maurice Merleau-Ponty's phenomenology of perception (Merleau-Ponty, 2002 [1962]), Ingold (2000, p. 169) proceeds to emphasise the point that immersion in, incorporation of and practical engagement with environments requires 'an embodied presence…the body is…the subject of perception'.[6]

One of Ingold's early statements of a dwelling perspective (and of the associated *critique of cultural constructionism*) appeared in the context of his intervention in a live debate with fellow anthropologists (later published in Ingold, 1996a), and it was this debating forum which facilitated what is perhaps the strongest statement of his position in that phase of his evolving research (see Ingold, 1996b). There, he set out the general contrast between ideas of dwelling and building or engagement and construction that I have just been discussing. However, in turning to this intervention of Ingold's, I will focus on two particular features of the argument made there, so as to push further my commentary on the notion of dwelling with which he is working.

The first of these points has to do with what Ingold (1996b, pp. 112–113) considers to be a taken-for-granted assumption made by the cultural constructionists, namely 'that non-human worlds are not culturally constructed', since 'cultural construction…is supposed to be uniquely human, a fundamental aspect of the human condition as opposed to that of the animal'. So the building perspective sets up an opposition between humanity and animality as well as between culture and nature, and at the root of those divisions is the idea that language or symbolic representation provides the human and cultural dimension. This leads Ingold (1996b, p. 113) to pose the question: 'What, then, can we say about animal worlds?' Indeed, years later (see Ingold, 2011, pp. 76–77), he asks again, in a slightly longer form: 'Are we really meant to believe…that all meaning is symbolic, and therefore that…non-human animals…inhabit meaningless worlds?' Of course, the answer he gives to his own question is that it would be quite wrong to believe this.

Whilst Ingold (1996b, pp. 115–118) does accept that humans differ from other animals in at least one important respect, he concludes his intervention in the debate mentioned above by challenging what he calls 'the dichotomy between the human and the animal', stating that:

> There is no fundamental difference here…. We perceive the world by moving around in it and exploring its possibilities…just as…non-human animals can…through… their dwelling in the world…. It is in the…capacity to construct imagined worlds that humans surely differ from other animal species, and in this…language and culture are…implicated. But…let me remind you that such imagining is not a necessary prelude to our contact with reality…rather an epilogue…. We do not have to think the world in order to live in it, but we do have to live in the world in order to think it.

This insistence that it is necessary *to live in the world in order to think it* (and not the other way round) is right at the heart of a dwelling perspective. It echoes Merleau-Ponty's claim that the world is 'the homeland of our thoughts' (Merleau-Ponty, 2002 [1962], p. 28; see also Ingold, 2000, p. 186). Referring back to a phrase that I used with reference to Nigel Thrift's geography in my opening, introductory chapter, I would say that what Ingold is challenging here is not just the dichotomy between the human and the animal but also, more broadly, the centrality of representations to life. He was a non-representational (Thrift, 1996, 2007) or a more-than-representational (Lorimer, 2005) theorist long before he identified explicitly with such a label (Ingold, 2015b), and, when talking of a dwelling perspective, what he was seeking to assert was precisely the primacy of practice or movement.

Another specific point that I wish to pick out from Ingold's intervention has to do with the distinction which he draws (based loosely on Heidegger, 1993 [1971], p. 348; and see Ingold, 2000, p. 185) between *a house and a home*:

> So how does a house become a home? Not, I argue, by assimilating its physical features to a…representational blueprint for the organization of domestic space, but rather by incorporating those features…walls, doors, windows…furnishings and so on…into…day-to-day activities. Thus it is the very engagement of persons with the objects of their domestic surroundings…that turns the house into a home. (Ingold, 1996b, p. 116)

Once again, as with his questions about animal worlds and whether all meaning is symbolic, this example of the house being turned into a home through the routine practical engagements of dwelling is a theme that he returns to years later, when writing of his own day-to-day movements in domestic surroundings: 'Any ordinary day sees me wandering around between the sitting room, dining room, kitchen, bathroom, bedroom, study and so on' (Ingold, 2011, p. 146). Alongside that indoor wandering, Ingold also lists his habitual practices of travelling to and from work, the shops and other sites of social interaction, as well as his children's journeys to and from school. He then uses these experiences in domestic and public settings to illustrate his argument that *places are entwined threads or knots*: 'A house…is a place where the lines of its residents are tightly knotted…but these lines are no more contained within the house than are threads contained within a knot…they trail beyond it' (Ingold, 2011, p. 149). Indeed, such trailing lines get 'caught up with other lines in other places' (Ingold, 2011, p. 149) like a university campus or a school yard, and together these entanglements make up what he calls a 'meshwork' or a 'mesh of lines'.

Here, it starts to become more evident how Ingold's preoccupation with the notion of dwelling flows into the current phase of his research as a 'linealogist' or a 'student of lines' (Ingold, 2015a, p. 53), and, in the introduction to his first book on lines, he deals directly with matters of place in relation to movement, asserting that: 'Life on the spot surely cannot yield an experience of place...life is lived...along paths...and paths are lines of a sort' (Ingold, 2007, p. 2). To constitute places, according to Ingold and co-researcher Jo Lee (see Lee & Ingold, 2006, pp. 76–78), with whom he worked on a study of walking practices in the North East of Scotland, is precisely to move 'to, from and around them', so that through 'the interweaving of routes...place is made'.[7]

Of course, attentive readers of my book will realise that there are echoes of previous theorisations of place in these statements. In particular, the reference to an interweaving of routes offers me a strong reminder of David Seamon's geography of the lifeworld (Seamon, 2015 [1979]), with the attention that it paid to place choreographies, and Ingold's account of how a house becomes a home (to my eye) looks remarkably similar to Yi-Fu Tuan's notes on the pieces of furniture that mark 'pauses...along a complex path of movement...followed day after day' (Tuan, 1977, pp. 180–182), so that this 'path and the pauses along it constitute a...place'. My purpose, in bringing to notice these similarities with the earlier writings of Seamon and Tuan, is to emphasise once more the unfortunately 'undervalued' (Cresswell, 2012, p. 99) character of phenomenological geography as a 'precursor to' (Cresswell, 2006, p. 31) contemporary non-representational approaches in the humanities and social sciences.[8]

Movement is the inhabitant's way of knowing

Next, I want to stay with Ingold's relating of the notion of dwelling to lines and movement, but to consider it with reference to matters of knowledge (and especially his concept of inhabitant knowledge, which appears in my chapter's subtitle). My point of departure here is an important set of reflections that he offers on maps and on 'what it means to know one's whereabouts' (Ingold, 2000, p. 219). Given its significance for him, which is clearly demonstrated by the fact that he keeps returning to much the same issues in parts of his later writings, it seems appropriate to quote Ingold's words at length (in slightly edited form):

Everyone has probably had the experience...of feeling lost.... Yet for most of the time we know where we are.... Ordinary life would be well-nigh impossible if we did not. It remains a challenge, however, to account for everyday skills of orientation and wayfinding.... For the...stranger...in unfamiliar country, 'being here' or 'going there' generally entails the ability to identify one's...position with a certain...geographic location, defined by the intersection of particular coordinates on the map. But a person who has grown up in a country...knows...in what direction to go, without having to consult an artefactual map.... According to a view that has found wide support...there is no difference in principle between them...the native inhabitant's map is held not in the hand but in the head...in the form of a comprehensive...representation...or 'cognitive' map.... I...argue, to the contrary, that there is no such map.... It is...the ability to situate one's current position within the historical context of journeys previously made...journeys to, from and around places...that distinguishes the countryman from the stranger. Ordinary wayfinding, then, more closely resembles storytelling. (Ingold, 2000, p. 219)

I will be coming back to that resemblance between journeys and stories which is hinted at in the last, intriguing sentence in this passage, because I regard it as having particular relevance for non-media-centric, non-representational media studies. To begin with, though, it is necessary to unpack Ingold's comments on maps, both those that are held in strangers' hands and those that are often assumed to be lodged in inhabitants' heads, and in doing so I draw on some of his subsequent discussions of *knowledge and movement*.

What is referred to in that extract as an artefactual map, and is described elsewhere by Ingold (2007, p. 88) as 'a cartographic map', is produced by surveyors who take 'observations...from a number of fixed points' in an attempt to assemble 'a complete picture', which appears as a sort of view from a great height. The classificatory knowledge of the surveyor can therefore be thought of as 'upwardly integrated' (Ingold, 2007, p. 89) or as 'vertically integrated' (Ingold, 2011, p. 160). Meanwhile, proponents of the idea of a cognitive map believe 'that we are all surveyors in our everyday lives' (Ingold, 2007, p. 88), obtaining data 'from multiple points of observation that are then passed to the mind...from which it assembles a...representation of the world'. However, for Ingold, such in-the-head maps do not exist. This is because 'the ways of knowing of inhabitants go along...not up' (Ingold, 2007, p. 89), so that 'for the inhabitants of the lifeworld, knowledge is not vertically but alongly integrated' (Ingold, 2011, p. 160). As philosopher Charles Taylor (1993, pp. 55–56) put it a few years before, their 'practical ability...to get around...a certain environment...without hesitation...unfolds in time and space', involving an 'inarticulate familiarity', whereas maps 'by their very nature, abstract from lived time and space'.

Inhabitant knowledge is a bodily knowledge in movement. As Ingold (2011, p. 154) puts it: 'Inhabitants…know…as they journey through the world…movement is…the inhabitant's way of knowing'. Indeed, further emphasising his critique of the notion of cognitive maps, as well as his distinction between upwardly or vertically integrated and *alongly integrated knowledge*, he later insists that for inhabitants, thoroughly immersed in and practically engaged with their environments or surroundings, 'movement is…not merely a means of getting from point to point in order to collect the raw data…for subsequent modelling in the mind…moving is knowing' (Ingold, 2015a, p. 47).

Let me return now to that resemblance between *journeys and stories* which Ingold hinted at in his reflections on orientation and wayfinding. When he remarks that finding ways about an environment resembles storytelling, and when he proceeds to refer to 'narratives' (Ingold, 2000, p. 237) of movement, his argument owes something to one which had been advanced earlier by theorist of practice Michel de Certeau (1984, p. 110), who wrote metaphorically of the 'unfolding…stories' that pedestrians compose as they move through urban settings. In de Certeau's account of walking in the city, pedestrian practices are understood as the writing 'of an "urban text"' (de Certeau, 1984, p. 93), which transforms the 'planned city' (de Certeau, 1984, p. 110) into a 'mobile city'.[9]

In addition, if finding ways about has been compared in that manner with storytelling, Ingold asks whether journey-story relations might be approached from the opposite direction. *Can involvement in stories (including the hearing or reading of a narrative) helpfully be understood as moving through a world?* In his view it can, since 'the storyline goes along' (Ingold, 2007, p. 90). For Ingold (2011, pp. 160–161), then, 'the epitome of alongly integrated knowledge is the story…in the story, as in life, it is in…movement…that knowledge is integrated'. Indeed, another name that he gives to this type of knowing-while-going is 'storied knowledge' (Ingold, 2011, p. 159).

I very much welcome this perspective on narrative as a going along (see also Iser, 1978), which can be contrasted with what I see as the upwardly or vertically integrated, classificatory knowledge of stories that has tended to be produced by structuralist analyses of narratives.[10] Still, for reasons that will become evident shortly, Ingold's examples of how the storyline goes along, in, say, practices of *reading as wayfaring*, are far from contemporary. For instance, he notes that:

> Commentators from the Middle Ages…would time and again compare reading to wayfaring, and…the page to an inhabited landscape. Just as to travel is to remember the path, or to tell a story is to remember how it goes, so to read, in this fashion, was to retrace a trail through the text.… The reader, in short, would inhabit the world of the page, proceeding from word to word as the storyteller proceeds from topic to topic…there is no difference, in principle, between the handwritten manuscript and the story voiced in speech. (Ingold, 2007, p. 91)

Why should it be necessary, though, for Ingold to go quite so far back, in order to come up with an example of how involvement in a story could be understood as getting around and thereby inhabiting an environment? Recalling a specific aspect of Scannell's work on radio and television (see Scannell, 1996, pp. 156–159), I do wonder whether a broadcast soap opera or 'continuous serial' (Geraghty, 1981) might also be thought of, borrowing Ingold's term, as *an inhabited landscape* for its regular followers. While such programmes are often denigrated for their supposed low quality, Scannell (1996, p. 156) actually regards soap operas as being 'among the most remarkable things that broadcasting does'. These stories, some of which have been running several times a week for several decades, provide listeners and viewers with routine 'access to…fictional worlds' (Scannell, 1996, p. 159), of a kind that 'corresponds closely to the forms of access one has to the people in one's own everyday world'. The continuous-serial narrative unfolds, then, at the same rate as the lifetimes or biographical journeys of those listeners and viewers, in 'a perpetual "now"' (Scannell, 1996, p. 157) and with 'no perceptible ending'.

Furthermore, regular followers are able to draw on their knowledge of the serials' pasts (in Ingold's words, this would be the historical context of journeys previously made) so as to speculate on possible narrative futures.[11] The expert listener or viewer acquires, over time, what Ingold (2015a, p. 48) calls, in writing of the experienced walker, 'a greater sensitivity to cues in the environment and a greater capacity to respond to those cues with judgement'. My guess, however, is that Ingold, who has nothing at all to say about radio and television (let alone soap operas) in his reflections on journeys and stories, would be reluctant to accept the parallel that I am drawing here between his non-representational approach in anthropology and Scannell's 'phenomenology of radio and television' (Scannell, 1995), and I want to explain why it is that I am confident in this assumption.

Staying with stories for a little while longer, let me go back to that statement of Ingold's on reading as wayfaring which I have reproduced. Remember that in the last few of those words I extracted, he insists there is no difference in principle between the handwritten manuscript and the story voiced in speech. The way in which Ingold (2007, pp. 91–92) goes on from there is indicative of his generally pessimistic take on cultural change and modernity:

> There is however...a fundamental difference between the line that is written or voiced and that of a modern typed or printed composition.... Writing as conceived in the modern project is not a practice of inscription...the lines of the plot are not traced by the reader as he moves through the text.... These lines are connectors. To read them...is to study a plan rather than to follow a trail. Unlike his medieval predecessor...an inhabitant of the page...entangled in its inked traces...the modern reader surveys the page as if from a great height.... In doing so he occupies the page.... But he does not inhabit it.

According to this account, then, the technologies of the typewriter and, later, the word processor are part of a wider series of historical shifts in which 'the line became straight' (Ingold, 2007, p. 152). Ingold (2007, p. 144), with an implicit reference to Merleau-Ponty's philosophy, acknowledges that 'typing is a manual operation...like organ playing, which can...involve the feet as well', yet his contention is that in contrast to the gestural hand movements of the scribe: 'The hands of skilled typists dance on...the keyboard, not on... the page.' It seems that using a manual typewriter or, worse still for Ingold (2007, p. 144), a computer (since 'modern electronic keyboards have removed even...the...heaviness of the graphic marks on the page' in relation to 'the force of the impact on the keys') is considered by him to be somehow less human than using traditional pen-and-ink instruments.[12]

It is noticeable that when discussing a modern typed or printed composition in the way that he has done above, Ingold is associating it with an artefactual or cartographic map. I detect this in his notion that the contemporary reader is studying a plan rather than following a trail, surveying the page as if from a great height. In thinking of the lines of the plot as connectors, he is also making a further association, in this case with the transportation networks of modern metropolitan societies. Indeed, his overall assessment of modernity identifies changes in each of the three 'related fields of...mapping...textuality...and...travel, where wayfaring is replaced by...transport' (Ingold, 2007, p. 75). Having dealt with Ingold's views on maps and texts in this section, I focus in the next on his reflections on travel and especially that distinction which he mentions between *wayfaring and transport*. My particular way in to dealing with this theme of travel, though, will be via some fleeting but fascinating comments that he offers on what could be termed the *lines of internet use*.

An interesting question

As noted near to the start of my current chapter, Ingold, across the range of his writings on dwelling and lines, rarely mentions contemporary media of communication (and as noted in the previous section, he has nothing to say about the programme output of broadcasting, in which, as Scannell puts it, audience members find ways about). However, in the small print of the end-notes at the back of one of his volumes of collected essays (see Ingold, 2011, p. 249), he provides an unexpected and intriguing set of comments on the character of *movement through the internet*, which fascinate me partly because of his references there to the difference between a meshwork and a network or between the trail-following activities of wayfarers and what he thinks of as point-to-point, destination-oriented transportation:

> To me, as a relatively inexperienced user, navigating the internet is a matter of acti-
> vating a sequence of links that take me, almost instantaneously, from site to site.
> Each link is a connector, and the web itself is a network of interconnected sites.
> Travel through cyberspace thus resembles transport. Experienced users, however, tell
> me that...they follow trails like wayfarers, with no particular destination in mind.
> For them, the web may seem more like a mesh than a net. How, precisely, we should
> understand 'movement' through the internet is an interesting question, but it is...
> most certainly beyond my own competence...to address it further here.

I absolutely agree with Ingold that this is *an interesting question*. This is because answering it promises to open up a much wider consideration of media uses as practices of wayfaring. It is therefore disappointing for me that he moves on quite so quickly, having posed the question, citing his own inability to address it.

Undoubtedly, Ingold's failure to attempt an answer could be taken as an instance of refreshing academic honesty (and I have to admit that it would be beyond my competence to address issues of, for example, reindeer herding in northern Finland, about which he knows a lot as a consequence of anthropo-logical fieldwork conducted there many years ago). Even so, my feeling is that he is rather too dismissive of a sort of everyday media use which may cause trouble for his pessimistic version of cultural history. If it turns out that the internet is, after all, at least in the lives of its experienced users, more like a mesh than a net, involving practices of wayfaring, his narrative of modernity and technology begins to lose its way.[13]

When Ingold gives specific examples of travel-as-wayfaring today, these sometimes come from reports of research done by other anthropologists, relating to contexts that he would presumably regard as being beyond, though not entirely untouched by, modern metropolitan societies. Such examples feature vehicular movement that is powered by non-human animals or by the wind, and where they occasionally feature a technology such as 'a motor-bike... or snowmobile' (Ingold, 2007, p. 78), or even 'the car', the drivers of those vehicles are not in modern urban settings.[14] For instance, Ingold (2007, p. 78) notes that: 'In the Australian Western Desert Aboriginal people have turned the car into an organ of wayfaring...in the bush...cars are driven gesturally.' In most cases, though, his references to wayfaring are to the movements of human animals on foot (in urban as well as non-urban environments) and it is telling that his more recent fieldwork, on which I touched briefly a few pages ago, was a collaborative ethnography of walking (Lee & Ingold, 2006), just as de Certeau's earlier account of the 'wandering lines' (de Certeau, 1984, p. xviii) of a mobile city focused on acts of 'pedestrian enunciation' (de Certeau, 1984, p. 99) rather than on, say, practices of driving in the city (see Thrift, 2004).

Indeed, the problem that I raised with Ingold's assessment of the uses of a typewriter or computer keyboard is paralleled by a difficulty that Thrift has with de Certeau's walking-in-the-city thesis. Thrift (2004, p. 75) is puzzled, then, by the absence of the car in de Certeau's arguments about the uses of urban environments, suggesting that this theorist 'takes the practice of walking...as a sign of the human' and thereby neglects driving because it is implicitly regarded as less embodied and sensuous than moving around on foot. However, for Thrift (2004, pp. 80–81), driving and 'passengering' are 'both profoundly embodied and sensuous experiences', and, he adds, 'drivers experience cars as extensions of their bodies' (echoing Merleau-Ponty, 2002 [1962], p. 165). Of course, it is important to realise that there are serious frictions between the place-making activities of pedestrians and car drivers in cities, yet driving, like walking, is 'a means of habitation, a dwelling' (Amin & Thrift, 2002, p. 101), and the use of in-car audio media can contribute to this at-homeness on the road or 'automobile habitation' (see Bull, 2001).

Ingold's selection of examples with which to illustrate travel-as-wayfaring has to be understood in the light of his contrasting conceptualisation of travel-as-transport. Transportation, for him, is not to 'go along...to thread one's way through the world' (Ingold, 2007, p. 79) as the wayfarer does, but to be moved instead 'from point to point across its surface'. He views transport as the mode of travel that characterises modern metropolitan societies and he distinguishes 'the network as a set of interconnected points from the meshwork as an interweaving of lines' (Ingold, 2011, p. 64). So, for instance, Ingold (2011, p. 152) writes of 'transport systems that span the globe', such as the system of international air travel, as having 'converted travel…into…an experience of…enforced immobility and sensory deprivation', to the extent that: 'The traveller who departs from one location and arrives at another is, in between, nowhere at all' (Ingold, 2007, p. 84).[15]

Whilst Ingold's case is eloquently argued, I find his perspective on travel-as-transport, which is part of a broader, negative assessment of cultural change and modernity, to be unnecessarily dark. It is true that there are occasional flashes of optimism in his writing, as when he refers to 'the sheer irrepressibility of life' (Ingold, 2011, p. 125) in contemporary social circumstances, or when he asserts confidently that: 'Life will not be contained' (Ingold, 2007, p. 103). Nevertheless, *there remain some major problems for me with many of Ingold's assumptions about people's uses of modern technologies and texts.* To be sure, I have no desire to deny that there are containing, classifying elements of modern social organisation, and neither do I wish to adopt the more unbridled optimism of de Certeau (1984, p. 40), whose tendency was to flag up positively the 'clever tricks of the "weak"' at almost every opportunity. Rather, as ever in cultural analysis, the task is to find a viable path running somewhere between such overly negative and positive judgements of contemporary living (between those poles of pessimism and optimism).

To conclude my critical encounter with Ingold's impressive range of writings on dwelling and lines, I want to propose that despite the difficulties with his work identified in this chapter his rich conceptual vocabulary (inhabitant or alongly integrated knowledge, practices of wayfaring, meshwork, and so on) might now be applied productively in areas of everyday activity and experience to which he has paid little or no attention. Of course, given my own academic background in media studies, I am thinking mainly, but by no means exclusively, of practices of media use in day-to-day living. Scannell's passing remark on finding ways about in the programme output of radio and television, which was where I started out from, clearly resonates with Ingold's interest in matters of orientation. I have also tried to show how these two theorists, operating in separate fields, share similar concerns with storytelling and narrative as a meaningful going along or moving through (and see Tuan, 2004, p. 52). For new media researchers, too, Ingold's interesting question about the character of movement through the internet is potentially a very fruitful one, even if he fails to answer it.

A brief link to the next chapter

A further shift in style follows in the next chapter, which is a three-way conversation that involves me in discussion with two fellow advocates of non-media-centric media studies, Zlatan Krajina and David Morley. In our conversation across academic generations, we each talk initially about our particular routes into the field of media studies at different moments in its development, before going on to explore our overlapping empirical research interests and our broadly shared theoretical, methodological and pedagogical concerns. For the most part, this is a discussion in which we confirm our joint commitment to a form of media studies that is about far more than just the study of media, and in which there is a renewed call for a recovery of the field's early spirit of interdisciplinary adventure, but a certain difference of emphasis emerges there too. This is most evident, to me at least, in the final section of the chapter to come, where Morley and I are engaged in a friendly exchange about issues of representation, power and embodiment, and where I explicitly advocate non-media-centric media studies that are informed by non-representational theories of practice (returning to Ingold's work, as well as to that of Thrift, Merleau-Ponty and others).

Notes

1. The term programme output, for Paddy Scannell (1996, p. 7), refers both to 'particular programmes' and to 'the totality of output'. Finding ways about 'in it' (Scannell, 1996, p. 8) is not quite as 'untroubled' as it once was, given a substantial increase in the number of shows and channels that are now available. Nevertheless, over time, listeners and viewers can still become accustomed to negotiating such programme output, even if most of it will inevitably go unheard and unwatched by any individual audience member.
2. In Tim Ingold's later work, he tends to use the word wayfaring rather than wayfinding, and, as should become clear towards the end of my current chapter, that concept of wayfaring, which refers to 'lineal movement along paths of travel' (Ingold, 2011, p. 149), gets employed in opposition to his particular notion of 'transport', defined as 'lateral movement across a surface'.
3. I say largely neglected because there are a few notable exceptions. For example, at the margins of media studies, see books (all of them quite different) by Vivian Sobchack (2004), Michael Bull (2007) and Jason Farman (2012), which I regard as part of an emerging yet dispersed tradition of analysis that has begun to take seriously matters of movement and dwelling.
4. Geographer Paul Adams (2005, pp. 16–17), in the context of his writing on communications in 'physical and virtual spaces', offers a brief but valuable discussion of interrelated

movements through different sorts of environment, which overlaps with the concerns of my current chapter. For instance, he comments that: 'Navigation skills learned in physical spaces help children get around in virtual spaces and vice versa' (Adams, 2005, p. 17). My difficulty, though, is with his choice of the term navigation, since it is typically associated with the use of maps. Following Ingold, I prefer to talk of inhabitants' everyday skills of orientation and wayfinding (described in my opening, introductory chapter as a *feeling-a-way-along-and-through*).

5. Among the main theoretical influences cited by Ingold (2000, pp. 162–170), whilst outlining his development of a dwelling perspective for anthropology, are Martin Heidegger's phenomenological philosophy (see especially Heidegger, 1993 [1971]), Pierre Bourdieu's social theory of practice (especially Bourdieu, 1977) and James Gibson's ecological psychology (especially Gibson, 1979).

6. Another anthropologist who has drawn on Maurice Merleau-Ponty's philosophy, and on phenomenology more broadly, is Michael Jackson (1995, 1996), employing the label 'phenomenological anthropology'.

7. In that research project, Jo Lee and Tim Ingold (2006, p. 83) declared their interest in the '"webs of significance"…comprised of trails that are trodden on the ground, not spun in the symbolic ether, as people make their way about', understanding people's 'oft-repeated walks' (Lee & Ingold, 2006, p. 77) as forming '"thick lines" of…meaningful place-making'. Their reference to webs of significance that are apparently spun in the symbolic ether is directed critically at cultural anthropologist Clifford Geertz (see Geertz, 1973), and the accompanying references to meaningful trails or lines that are trodden relate to Ingold's slightly earlier concern with formations of culture 'on the ground' (Ingold, 2004) and with a world 'perceived through the feet'.

8. Indeed, even cultural geographer Tim Cresswell (2006, pp. 26–32), who has been one of phenomenological geography's most vocal defenders over recent years, somewhat puzzlingly positions the work of David Seamon and Yi-Fu Tuan within a perspective that he labels 'a sedentarist metaphysics', from which mobility is seen as a 'threat to the… existence of place'. Now, whilst I have accepted in a previous chapter that this was pretty much Edward Relph's view of the mobilities of modern communications, in his arguments about place and placelessness (Relph, 2008 [1976]), and whilst I have also accepted that Seamon was wrong to adopt this view in those parts of his lifeworld study where he considered technologies of mass communication, I cannot accept Cresswell's suggestion that mobility simply 'plays second fiddle' (Cresswell, 2006, p. 30) in writings from the 1970s by Seamon (2015 [1979]) and Tuan (1977). Rather, for both of them, as I have shown, dwelling and the making of place depend upon everyday movements along paths of travel. There may be moments of rest (pauses on the path), but the quotidian cultures that they describe are clearly far from sedentary.

9. This account begins with a striking juxtaposition, in which de Certeau (1984, p. 92) writes first of his view from a New York City skyscraper, 'looking down like a god', as if at a map, before going on to describe the 'ordinary practitioners of the city' (de Certeau, 1984, p. 93), below at 'ground level' (de Certeau, 1984, p. 97), whose footsteps constitute 'a process of appropriation of the topographical system on the part of the pedestrian'.

10. For a classic example of such map-like representations of stories, see Umberto Eco's analysis of a range of James Bond novels written by Ian Fleming in the 1950s and 1960s, which were later adapted as popular films (Eco, 1981 [1966]). It is true that Eco (1981 [1966], p. 156) identifies a series of narrative 'moves' there, but his main concern is not so much with movement or with the journeying experiences of peripatetic readers as it is with charting what he calls an 'invariable...set scheme', in which the same 'elements are always present in every novel'.

11. Christine Geraghty (1981, pp. 16–18), in her pioneering analysis of time and narrative in continuous serials, reflects on the importance of this 'use of the past'. Relatedly, she also emphasises the importance, both for storytelling in a serial and for regular followers, of a form of talk that is known, often pejoratively, as 'gossip' (see Geraghty, 1981, pp. 22–25). So the gossip engaged in by a serial's characters 'constitutes a commentary' (Geraghty, 1981, p. 22) that reveals 'different moral positions' (Geraghty, 1981, p. 24), whilst experienced audience members (often in interaction with one another) can themselves become highly skilled commentators, since, as Geraghty (1981, p. 25) puts it (positioning herself with regular followers as an insider or inhabitant), 'our years of watching/listening make us experts'. Of course, I am not denying that cognition and interpretation are in play here, but the judgements and projections made by regular followers are based primarily on their feeling-a-way-along-and-through a story, in the context of following 'a path of movement along a way of life' (Ingold, 2011, p. 4).

12. Ingold (2013, pp. 121–124) returns to precisely this theme later in his work, pointing to what he regards as 'the problem of the regression of the hand' with reference to the typewriter and other machines associated with 'technological progression'. He asserts that: 'The very movement by which the hand tells, when it holds a pen, is annihilated when it strikes the keyboard...correspondence of gesture and inscription...is broken' (Ingold, 2013, p. 122). Furthermore, his stark conclusion is that whilst a hand is 'still anatomically human' (Ingold, 2013, p. 123) today, it 'has lost something of its humanity'. My own preference, though, is for Merleau-Ponty's approach to the human-thing interactions and incorporations of keyboard use, because this philosopher's work does not display the same negative judgements of how hands dance on keys. By the final chapter of my book, where I reflect more fully on the mobile, generative ways of the hand that is at home in negotiating contemporary media technologies and environments, it becomes increasingly evident that I reject Ingold's regression-of-the-hand thesis.

13. If that does turn out to be the case, it might also call for a rethinking of some terms employed elsewhere in my book, such as the idea of a network society (Castells, 1996) and even a very widely used, popular word like internet, which, pushing Ingold's terminology a bit, could perhaps be better conceptualised, in routine use, as an *intermesh*. Of course, I realise there will be those who see all this talk about wayfaring and meshwork as being rather too romantic to be applied in the analysis of online communications or in media research more generally, and I am aware that some of my colleagues in media studies are presently heading in a quite different direction. This other way forward involves taking a keen interest in 'data-based processes that operate, as it were, behind the scenes of social interaction' (Couldry & Hepp, 2017, pp. 10–11). 'A large proportion of...data is produced automatically', write Nick Couldry and Andreas Hepp (2017, p. 125), 'relying on

processes of aggregation and algorithmic calculation', and these authors worry over the consequences of automated data-processing for experiences of day-to-day living. Indeed, Couldry and Hepp (2017, pp. 5–8) characterise their approach as a 'materialist phenomenology of the social world' because they pay particular attention to 'material infrastructures through which, and on the basis of which, communications today take place'. Whilst acknowledging the continuing importance of agency in contemporary social life, they are concerned about what they regard as 'a tendency towards a new type of social order distinctive to…datafication' (Couldry & Hepp, 2017, p. 214). For me, though, their version of phenomenological analysis presents too dark a vision of technological and cultural change, just as Ingold's 'linealogy' (Ingold, 2015a, p. 53) ends up doing. As must be clear from the arguments I have been advancing in my book, I would not be opposed to the notion of a materialist phenomenology. Still, my principal focus remains on bodily orientations or the materiality of body-environment entanglements (that is, more on daily rhythms of being than on algorithms, even if I accept that the two can now be related).

14. Ingold's reference to wind-powered travel foreshadows a later claim that there is an 'affiliation between lines and the weather' (Ingold, 2015a, p. 53), or that 'in becoming a linealogist, it is necessary to become something of a meteorologist as well', although he looks to go beyond 'the reductions of…scientific meteorology' in his reflections on the weather and 'atmosphere'.

15. This sounds similar to Marc Augé's problematic position on spaces of transit as non-places (Augé, 2009 [1995]), or to Relph's pronouncements on placelessness, technology and mass culture (Relph, 2008 [1976]).

References

Adams, P. (2005), *The Boundless Self: Communication in Physical and Virtual Spaces*, Syracuse, NY: Syracuse University Press.

Amin, A. & Thrift, N. (2002), *Cities: Reimagining the Urban*, Cambridge: Polity.

Augé, M. (2009 [1995]), *Non-Places*, London: Verso.

Bourdieu, P. (1977), *Outline of a Theory of Practice*, Cambridge: Cambridge University Press.

Bull, M. (2001), 'Soundscapes of the Car: A Critical Study of Automobile Habitation', in Miller, D. (ed.) *Car Cultures*, Oxford: Berg.

Bull, M. (2007), *Sound Moves: iPod Culture and Urban Experience*, London: Routledge.

Castells, M. (1996), *The Rise of the Network Society*, Malden, MA: Blackwell.

Couldry, N. & Hepp, A. (2017), *The Mediated Construction of Reality*, Cambridge: Polity.

Cresswell, T. (2006), *On the Move: Mobility in the Modern Western World*, New York: Routledge.

Cresswell, T. (2012), 'Non-Representational Theory and Me: Notes of an Interested Sceptic', *Environment and Planning D: Society and Space*, vol. 30, no. 1, pp. 96–105.

de Certeau, M. (1984), *The Practice of Everyday Life*, Berkeley, CA: University of California Press.

Eco, U. (1981 [1966]), 'Narrative Structures in Fleming', in *The Role of the Reader: Explorations in the Semiotics of Texts*, London: Hutchinson.

Farman, J. (2012), *Mobile Interface Theory: Embodied Space and Locative Media*, London: Routledge.

Geertz, C. (1973), *The Interpretation of Cultures: Selected Essays*, New York: Basic Books.

Geraghty, C. (1981), 'The Continuous Serial: A Definition', in Dyer, R., Geraghty, C., Jordan, M., Lovell, T., Paterson, R. & Stewart, J., *Coronation Street*, London: British Film Institute.

Gibson, J. (1979), *The Ecological Approach to Visual Perception*, Boston, MA: Houghton Mifflin.

Heidegger, M. (1993 [1971]), 'Building Dwelling Thinking', in Krell, D. (ed.) *Martin Heidegger: Basic Writings*, London: Routledge.

Ingold, T. (ed.) (1996a), *Key Debates in Anthropology*, London: Routledge.

Ingold, T. (1996b), 'Human Worlds are Culturally Constructed: Against the Motion (1)', in Ingold, T. (ed.) *Key Debates in Anthropology*, London: Routledge.

Ingold, T. (2000), *The Perception of the Environment: Essays on Livelihood, Dwelling and Skill*, London: Routledge.

Ingold, T. (2004), 'Culture on the Ground: The World Perceived Through the Feet', *Journal of Material Culture*, vol. 9, no. 3, pp. 315–340.

Ingold, T. (2007), *Lines: A Brief History*, London: Routledge.

Ingold, T. (2011), *Being Alive: Essays on Movement, Knowledge and Description*, London: Routledge.

Ingold, T. (2013), *Making: Anthropology, Archaeology, Art and Architecture*, London: Routledge.

Ingold, T. (2015a), *The Life of Lines*, London: Routledge.

Ingold, T. (2015b), 'Foreword', in Vannini, P. (ed.) *Non-Representational Methodologies: Envisioning Research*, New York: Routledge.

Iser, W. (1978), *The Act of Reading: A Theory of Aesthetic Response*, Baltimore, MD: Johns Hopkins University Press.

Jackson, M. (1995), *At Home in the World*, Durham, NC: Duke University Press.

Jackson, M. (ed.) (1996), *Things as They Are: New Directions in Phenomenological Anthropology*, Bloomington, IN: Indiana University Press.

Lee, J. & Ingold, T. (2006), 'Fieldwork on Foot: Perceiving, Routing, Socializing', in Coleman, S. & Collins, P. (eds.) *Locating the Field: Space, Place and Context in Anthropology*, Oxford: Berg.

Lorimer, H. (2005), 'Cultural Geography: The Busyness of Being "More-Than-Representational"', *Progress in Human Geography*, vol. 29, no. 1, pp. 83–94.

Merleau-Ponty, M. (2002 [1962]), *Phenomenology of Perception*, London: Routledge.

Meyrowitz, J. (1985), *No Sense of Place: The Impact of Electronic Media on Social Behavior*, New York: Oxford University Press.

Relph, E. (2008 [1976]), *Place and Placelessness*, London: Pion.

Scannell, P. (1988), 'Radio Times: The Temporal Arrangements of Broadcasting in the Modern World', in Drummond, P. & Paterson, R. (eds.) *Television and Its Audience: International Research Perspectives*, London: British Film Institute.

Scannell, P. (1991), 'Introduction: The Relevance of Talk', in Scannell, P. (ed.) *Broadcast Talk*, London: Sage.

Scannell, P. (1995), 'For a Phenomenology of Radio and Television', *Journal of Communication*, vol. 45, no. 3, pp. 4–19.

Scannell, P. (1996), *Radio, Television and Modern Life: A Phenomenological Approach*, Oxford: Blackwell.

Scannell, P. (2000), 'For-Anyone-as-Someone Structures', *Media, Culture and Society*, vol. 22, no. 1, pp. 5–24.

Scannell, P. (2014), *Television and the Meaning of Live: An Enquiry into the Human Situation*, Cambridge: Polity.

Scannell, P. & Cardiff, D. (1991), *A Social History of British Broadcasting: 1922–1939, Serving the Nation*, Oxford: Blackwell.

Seamon, D. (2015 [1979]), *A Geography of the Lifeworld: Movement, Rest and Encounter*, London: Routledge.

Sobchack, V. (2004), *Carnal Thoughts: Embodiment and Moving Image Culture*, Berkeley, CA: University of California Press.

Taylor, C. (1993), 'To Follow a Rule...', in Calhoun, C., LiPuma, E. & Postone, M. (eds.) *Bourdieu: Critical Perspectives*, Cambridge: Polity.

Thrift, N. (1996), *Spatial Formations*, London: Sage.

Thrift, N. (2004), 'Driving in the City', *Theory, Culture and Society*, vol. 21, nos. 4/5, pp. 41–59.

Thrift, N. (2007), *Non-Representational Theory: Space/Politics/Affect*, London: Routledge.

Tuan, Y. (1977), *Space and Place: The Perspective of Experience*, Minneapolis, MN: University of Minnesota Press.

Tuan, Y. (2004), 'Sense of Place: Its Relationship to Self and Time', in Mels, T. (ed.) *Reanimating Places: A Geography of Rhythms*, Aldershot: Ashgate.

Urry, J. (2000), *Sociology Beyond Societies: Mobilities for the Twenty-First Century*, London: Routledge.

Urry, J. (2007), *Mobilities*, Cambridge: Polity.

NON-MEDIA-CENTRIC MEDIA STUDIES

A Cross-Generational Conversation
(with Zlatan Krajina and David Morley)

As explained in the acknowledgements near the beginning of this book, the present chapter is based on a live conversation with Zlatan Krajina (ZK) and David Morley (DM), which we conducted in front of an audience of staff and students at the University of Zagreb in Croatia. What appears here is a reshaped version of the transcript of our discussion at that event, where the talk between us revolved around the notion of *non-media-centric* media studies.[1]

Ways in and through

ZK: I'd like to start by inviting David and Shaun to reflect on their respective ways into media studies, and by asking them to say just a little at this stage about how they came to argue explicitly for a non-media-centric perspective (see Moores, 2012, pp. 103–110; Morley, 2007, 2009). First, David, could you explain what helped to shape your initial interest in media and also something about the development of your research over the years, which has led you to state that it's now necessary *to de-centre the media in our analytical framework* (Morley, 2007, p. 200), in order to see better how media and everyday life are interwoven?

DM: Well, I was very much a child of the television generation. Media, and television in particular, were initially important to me in that everyday sense. It had to do with what my family did in the evenings as I was growing up. My father sat in the same armchair every evening and watched television, while my mother came in and out of the room, bringing things like sandwiches and tea. That was a crucial part of how my home life was organised. Also, when I was going to university in the 1960s to study economics, whilst I was hanging about waiting to start doing that at the LSE (London School of Economics and Political Science), I met some people who were doing a subject called sociology. Amongst other things, they were studying the ideas of a guy called Marshall McLuhan (see especially McLuhan, 1994 [1964]). I'd never heard of him before, but at the time he sounded very funky to me. I thought to myself, you know, this is much more interesting than demand and supply curves! So I decided to study this stuff about media, which I found very engaging. Of course, later on I lost interest in McLuhan because of his *technological determinism*, though it's interesting that all these years later, in some writings on new media, there's a kind of born-again McLuhanism (with which I'm not much enchanted).

Anyway, when I got into researching these matters more seriously, and after I'd found my way to the Centre for Contemporary Cultural Studies (CCCS) at Birmingham University in the 1970s, something rather odd happened. I became known internationally in media studies for having researched audience reactions to a television programme, *Nationwide*, which was deliberately chosen for analysis because of its ordinary, everyday triviality and which nobody outside of Britain had seen (Morley, 1980; see also Morley & Brunsdon, 1999). What I was interested in there, though, was the role of media in the maintenance of social order (and particularly the role of everyday television in the construction of common sense), in relation to larger matters of ideology and hegemony. Even back then, I wasn't centrally interested in the media as such. When I applied to Goldsmiths, where I've been working for a long time now, I applied for a job in what was described as television studies.[2] When asked in the interview why I wanted to lecture about television, I said I actually thought that the idea you might study television in isolation was a bit strange. At CCCS, I'd been interested in television and its audiences as a way of focusing, empirically, *the question of cultural power and its limits*, as a way of working with Stuart Hall's encoding/decoding model (Hall, 1973), allowing us to explore, from a Gramscian perspective, the contours of hegemony within Britain in that period. The media stuff was of interest to me primarily as a way of focusing and exemplifying that debate.

What happened to me then was that having investigated which types of people accept or reject the ideological messages relayed to them by the television set, I realised that I was doing this in an inappropriate way. I used to go to schools and colleges where my friends and contacts could get me a group of students who'd discuss a video recording of a programme with me, but I'd be asking them to interpret the things they'd watched in quite a formal setting. That's not how people usually watch television. So what I had to do next was to go and study television viewing in the places where television is typically viewed, in people's homes, and I did that in some households in London (Morley, 1986). I carefully chose the households for my sample. I had families from different class backgrounds and I thought I'd be doing a study of class patterns of watching television, but it didn't quite work out like that. What the data showed me is that I had to pay much more attention to questions of gender. The differences in gendered patterns of domestic television viewing ended up being far more important in that research than the divisions between social classes. So although I set off to do one thing, I ended up doing quite another and, in this process, I also came to realise that the context of domestic consumption was a key issue for me.[3]

Having realised that, I then had to start *thinking more generally about the domestic environment itself* and the ways in which the social relations of households (including the links between house and world) are bound up with the uses of a range of technologies (see, for example, Morley & Silverstone, 1990; Silverstone & Morley, 1990). Partly, this took me back to Raymond Williams' concept of *mobile privatisation* (Williams, 1974, p. 26), to his account of a modern lifestyle that's got to do with precisely the sort of suburban viewing practices I'd known as a child.[4] Around that time, too, I came across the work of writers like Mary Beth Haralovich (1988) and Lynn Spigel (1992) from the USA. They were arguing that if you're going to understand post-war American culture, what you have to understand it as is precisely a combination of particular forms of television and particular forms of suburban living. It's both of these things together, what we might call the virtual and the material dimensions, and that's partly where my interest in broader questions of cultural geography (and in the material settings of television viewing or other uses of technology) comes from (see, for instance, Morley, 1991, 1992, 1996, 2000, 2003, 2007, 2010, 2011, 2017; Morley & Robins, 1995). Questions about media are important, then, but they only seem to me to be really significant if they're set in *a far wider frame*, rather than focusing just on media forms and technologies themselves.

ZK: Thanks David. Now, Shaun, you were among the first generation of students to be enrolled on a degree programme in media studies, and you went on to become a lecturer in this field soon after you graduated. Could you tell some bits of your own story of coming into media studies, saying a few things, too, about continuities and shifts in your work over time?

SM: Yes, I was part of the academic generation that followed Dave's. As you've just mentioned, I was among the first students to take a degree course in media studies, when I started out as an undergraduate at the Polytechnic of Central London (PCL), now the University of Westminster, back in the early 1980s. A few years before, the School of Communication at PCL had set up the only degree in Britain with that specific title, although it's important to remember that there was also a small number of undergraduate degree courses in communication or cultural studies, which contained elements of media studies, and which emerged during roughly the same period in other polytechnics (including what's now the University of Sunderland, where I work these days). My lecturers at PCL were mostly the editors of what was then a new academic journal, *Media, Culture and Society*. One of them was Paddy Scannell, a social historian and theorist of broadcasting (see especially Scannell, 1996, 2014; Scannell & Cardiff, 1991), whose classes I found inspiring, and it was Paddy who supervised my final-year dissertation, a study of broadcasting's entry into households in the 1920s and 1930s, which was subsequently published as an article in the journal (Moores, 1988). This was a study based mainly on a series of oral history interviews that I'd recorded in my home town in the North West of England, with elderly people who offered their memories of radio's arrival.

What I focused on in that historical research was a process in which the medium of radio gradually got domesticated as the domestic sphere was mediated by broadcasting, a shift from the radio set being a novel, obtrusive gadget through to its becoming a taken-for-granted part of the furniture. What I found, though, was that in order to understand radio's entry and incorporation into household cultures, it was necessary to consider all sorts of other things as well, like patterns of working-class labour and leisure, gendered practices and relationships in families, the organisation of people's daily routines and the design of their domestic spaces. So, without realising it and without having the words to express it, I think I was already starting to do a kind of non-media-centric media studies whilst I was still an undergraduate student, because the work I did then was centrally about *everyday practices and experiences*. It ended up as a study of everyday social relations and of how these relations were being performed and experienced around (and through) what had been, in the 1920s and 1930s, a new media technology.

Similarly, in the qualitative research that I went on to do in the early 1990s, on the consumption of satellite television in a city in South Wales, what interested me primarily were social relationships of class, gender and generation, in and across particular households and urban or suburban residential neighbourhoods, along with the varied identifications that my interviewees were making with image spaces at national and transnational levels (Moores, 1993a, 1996).[5] By the way, it was Dave who'd suggested to me, after reading my historical work on radio, that I might want to look at the arrival of satellite television as a new technology in people's everyday lives, and of course he'd been involved in the pioneering non-media-centric work that he's just spoken about, investigating practices of family television viewing and, with Roger Silverstone and others at Brunel University, carrying out some detailed ethnographic investigations of the household uses of information and communication technologies.

Now, there's another part of the story to tell here, because, as well as developing my empirical research on media in everyday lives, I was also trying to figure out how to teach media studies as a young lecturer. After my degree course, and this is probably because the field itself was still so young, I quickly found myself lecturing. Initially, this was on the communication studies programme at what in those days was the Polytechnic of Wales, and then later at Queen Margaret College, Edinburgh.[6] In fact, even though I was awarded a British Academy scholarship to go on and study for an MA, I never got to be a full-time postgraduate student, and I only obtained my PhD many years later for a collection of published work (Moores, 2000). Anyhow, in the 1980s, as a student and subsequently to inform my teaching, I spent a lot of time reading what seemed to me to be the main theoretical literature of the day in my field. This was predominantly a mix of Western Marxist perspectives on ideology and hegemony with approaches to representation and interpretation that had their roots in structuralism and semiotics, along with certain psychoanalytical conceptions of subjectivity and the symbolic order or Foucauldian perspectives on discourse and power.[7] I taught about all this stuff and I referred to it in my writing, for example, in the first book that I wrote (Moores, 1993b). I never felt wholly comfortable with it, though, and in retrospect I can see that this is because most of it, maybe with the exception of some of Antonio Gramsci's work (see Gramsci, 1971), doesn't actually help us much in coming to terms with the practical and experiential dimensions of the everyday, which is where my research interests have always been.

Of course, it's true that there was also, alongside the European, 20th-Century Marxist and structuralist traditions, a more British, left-culturalist or cultural-materialist tradition that fed into media and cultural studies. Like Dave, I had an interest in Williams' writings, including his notes on mobile privatisation (see Moores, 1993c), which, I came to feel, allowed more room for an exploration of the practical, the everyday and the ordinary. I developed a broader interest, too, in engaging with Anthony Giddens' social theories of structuration and modernity (Giddens, 1984, 1990; Moores, 1995, 2005), and with Erving Goffman's sociology of what he came to call the interaction order (Goffman, 1983; Moores, 1999). Still, it's only in recent years, since I've been engaging with a range of *phenomenological approaches in the humanities and social sciences* (and following Scannell's phenomenological turn), that it feels as though I've eventually found a literature which is enabling me to get to grips with everyday practices and experiences (see, for example, Moores, 2006, 2008, 2009, 2012, 2014, 2015). I could say a bit, later in our discussion, about my current interest in phenomenology, but what about your story, Zlatan? Your more recent way into media studies was via the MA in media and communications at Goldsmiths, wasn't it? Then you went on to become a PhD student in that department with Dave as your supervisor, and I first met you at your viva where I was the external examiner!

ZK: Actually, it's probably best to start the story a bit further back. Before my postgraduate studies, I'd worked in Croatian public broadcasting as a producer and presenter of news and documentary programmes, and I'd also been an undergraduate student here, in the Faculty of Political Science at the University of Zagreb, where I've now returned to work as a lecturer. The classes that I took on media, though, whilst I was an undergraduate, had to do mainly with issues of freedom of the press on the one hand and with abstract communication science models on the other. Many of the concepts and perspectives that are quite commonplace in media and cultural studies elsewhere were largely unknown in this part of Europe, and there was little access to key books in those fields.

As you said Shaun, I came to London as a student on the MA in media and communications at Goldsmiths (having received a scholarship), and things felt very new there at first, like there were these two different academic worlds on either side of the same continent. I was reading a lot of media and cultural studies literature, trying to bring myself up to speed on the course. Among the many interesting things that were being taught by staff in the Department of Media and Communications, there were David's classes on media audiences and media geographies, and I was encouraged to take classes in other departments too. For example, I came across some work in urban studies, which was highly relevant to the media-related issues that I was beginning to be concerned with.

Looking back on my four years at Goldsmiths, having done my PhD there as well, I can make sense of it now as *a sort of training in non-media-centric media studies*. My thesis, which is being published in revised form as a monograph (Krajina, 2014; and see Krajina, 2013), was based on qualitative empirical research that I did, both in London and in Zadar in Croatia, on people's encounters with public screens in everyday urban living. The book includes four specific case studies that came out of this research project. One is about relations to street advertising, another considers screen advertisements in an underground train system, and two further case studies focus on encounters with installation art and with media facade architecture. My research, which was challenging to design and carry out, involved investigating passing interactions with these various types of screen (in ordinary situations like taking a stroll, rushing to work or waiting for public transport), understanding such interactions as particular social and spatial practices. For instance, there was the practice of looking-at-screens as a way of avoiding eye contact with strangers moving in the opposite direction, or the practice of routinely glancing at a screen image in order to imagine oneself in a nicer place. I was even fascinated by some people's not-noticing-screens as a feature of their routine, habitual activity. So public screens are technologies that form an increasingly important part of contemporary urban environments. They've become pieces of street furniture. What's central for me, though, is everyday practice, everyday movement or *the way in which people are negotiating the mediated city*.[8] Since returning to Zagreb, my teaching at the university has been on such matters of media in urban settings, as well as on audience research more generally.

Geographies, mobilities and experiences

ZK: Let's hear some more from both of you now, about this non-media-centric perspective and how it might look in action. David, you've been insisting recently (and you hinted at this earlier in our discussion) that it's crucial to pay attention to the material as well as the virtual dimensions of communication. Maybe it'd be helpful if you could explain that point in greater detail?

DM: Okay, well to explain it backwards in a way, in the 1990s Kevin Robins and I were talking about the emergence and transformation of what we called electronic landscapes (Morley & Robins, 1995), and we were making the case that media researchers and cultural geographers should be paying more attention to such issues. For me, though, the problem is that nowadays academics working in media and communication studies too often focus only on the virtual dimension. That's why I've been suggesting a return to the more classical notion of communications that was developed by Karl Marx and Friedrich Engels in the 19th Century, which involved a broader understanding of communications as the movement of information, people and commodities (see especially Morley, 2009, 2011, 2017). This definition is very rich as a starting point for investigations in our field. So what I'm interested in doing is not replacing the study of material geographies with the study of electronic landscapes or virtual geographies. Rather, it's the changing relations between them that are significant, and the ways in which one is now overlaid on the other. To pick out just the virtual and to focus on that doesn't make any sense to me.

A little while back, many commentators were arguing that the recent political transformations in Egypt (and throughout the Arab world) could be understood as a Facebook revolution. When you get to Cairo, though, and you ask people what actually happened, it turns out that the use of social media played a relatively small part in the events, and only for a small proportion of the people taking part. Other more banal, face-to-face modes of communication, such as the gossip networks of the taxi drivers based in Tahrir Square, played a more important role, and this is the kind of thing that interests me when we're thinking about *how material geographies and virtual geographies get articulated.*

Let's take some other examples. Cyber industries are actually one of the most geographically concentrated industries in the world, in terms of physical location. If you're setting up an internet company in London, say, you've really got to be in Shoreditch if you're going to be on the ball, and you've even got to be in a particular part of Shoreditch, in what's known as Tech City. It's very concentrated. Cyberspace has its own geography too. The densities of internet connections per square kilometre, across the world, vary dramatically. Where you are in social and material space makes a huge difference to your degree of access to these new virtual geographies.

In a way, this goes back to what Arjun Appadurai (1996, pp. 33–36) was getting at when he wrote about connections between ethnoscapes, mediascapes, technoscapes and so on.[9] Still, what needs thinking about is *the question of precisely who is how mobile* in relation to which material and virtual geographies. Who has access to what, and with what consequences for everyday experiences of movement? It's important for us to avoid any kind of generalised, romanticised nomadology, like the idea that we're all mobile now and in much the same way. It's necessary to attend to different degrees and types of mobility (also to different types of immobility), in both the material and the virtual realms (see, for example, Cresswell, 2010; Hannam et al., 2006; Massey, 1994).

Another thing is that here we are in the so-called digital world, talking about convergence, about multi-platform delivery systems and so on, but if you turn to the much neglected field of transport studies, you'll see that in physical transportation there's been a multi-platform delivery system since the innovation of the container box in the 1950s (Morley, 2010, 2011, 2017). If anything is the emblem of our era of globalisation, it's this container box, and you don't even see that because it's so ordinary, so absorbed into the everyday. Years ago, back in the 1930s, psychologist Rudolf Arnheim (quoted in Rath, 1985, p. 199) talked about how television should be understood 'as a means of transport'. Evidently, he was speaking metaphorically, but his idea helps to make the connection between electronically mediated communications and physical transportation systems. So, yes, my current interest is in how it might be possible to put together a non-media-centric perspective on communications, which can do justice both to its material and its virtual dimensions. As part of this project, *it's crucial to restore the wrongly broken link between media studies and transport studies* (see also Carey, 1989; Packer & Robertson, 2006).

SM: I'm with you on the need for research that addresses different sorts of mobility and that links media studies into a wider consideration of movement (of patterned mobilities). Directly in response to what Zlatan was asking, about how non-media-centric media studies might look in action, I'd like to explain just a bit about a research project that I was involved in a few years ago, working with Monika Metykova (Moores & Metykova, 2009, 2010).

Monika and I were investigating what we called the environmental experiences of trans-European migrants, and that notion of environmental experience is one that we borrowed from phenomenological geography. Those migrants were young people from Eastern Europe who'd moved to live and work in Britain following an expansion of the European Union. Monika conducted lengthy conversational interviews with 20 of these young people, who were based at that time in London, Newcastle or Edinburgh. We were interested, of course, in their everyday practices of media use, including what John Urry (2007, p. 47) would have called their imaginative, virtual and communicative travellings, because it was partly through this media use that an ongoing (often experientially instantaneous) contact could be maintained with the countries they'd left, which helped to give their migrant experiences a certain historical and cultural specificity. At the same time, though, we were interested in their various corporeal mobilities, their routine urban practices of walking, driving, cycling and travelling by bus or train, as well as their more occasional use of budget-airline routes to fly back to visit friends and family members in Eastern Europe. Our empirical research threw up some data, too, on the closely associated transnational mobilities of material goods such as packs of biscuits or sausages and bottles of whisky! In Dave's terms, we were concerned with *the interwoven movements of information, people and commodities*.

I think of that research as a concrete example of non-media-centric media studies, because the main focus for us was on matters of migration and, even more centrally, on senses of place. When people move across a continent, there's often a profound disturbance of their routines, and we found that this can enable them to reflect on previously taken-for-granted attachments, but we were also trying to find out how, in the period immediately following these young people's transnational physical migrations, they were gradually forming new senses of place in initially unfamiliar surroundings. Our phenomenological approach led us to see place as a practical accomplishment, as something more than just location. So we were looking at the migrants' ordinary activities of getting around as place-making practices, whether that was finding ways about on foot in a local urban neighbourhood, or on the roads of a city in a car, or on public transport systems or else on the internet. Our non-media-centric perspective was important, I believe, because we were able to highlight some significant interconnections between several kinds of travel, and in a way that more media-centred media studies would, quite frankly, be likely to miss.

There's a common misconception that media studies are simply about studying media (see Moores, 2005, p. 3), but I've been arguing that they're about much more than this, that it's always necessary to situate media and their uses in relation to a range of other technologies and activities. When I came across Dave's notion of non-media-centric media studies, it seemed to me to crystallise this sort of view very well. It seemed to be a helpful name for the things that some of us have been up to for a while now. For instance, back in the late 1980s, Janice Radway (1988), who's best known in media and cultural studies for her pioneering work on romantic-fiction readers (see Radway, 1984), wrote an interesting piece in which she advocated a move beyond audience or reception research, to explore, in a full-blown community ethnography, what she referred to as *habits and practices of everyday life* (Radway, 1988, p. 366). Although her proposal for a collaborative investigation of the everyday was overambitious (indeed, that proposed research project never came to fruition), I do think that she was absolutely right to call for things to be broadened out so as not to isolate the media-user link.[10] It also strikes me that Joke Hermes' innovative work in the 1990s, on the routine contexts of magazine reading (Hermes, 1995), could be made sense of retrospectively as part of this non-media-centric research strand, and it's an early example of work in our field which has drawn on phenomenology, specifically on the phenomenological sociology of Alfred Schutz. More recently, Nick Couldry (2010, 2012), who's another of Dave's former PhD students from Goldsmiths, has argued against media-centrism and has been advocating a focus on practices. Anyhow, Dave rightly stresses *a need to understand the particularities of media*, their distinctive affordances (like the potential that electronic and digital media offer for new experiences of simultaneity or of liveness at a distance), but crucially he's made the case, too, for de-centring media in our investigations and explanations of contemporary social life, and of course he's currently interested in re-broadening the definition of communications.

DM: Non-media-centric media studies is a form of words that Shaun and I, amongst others, have adopted, and I think it usefully indicates where our work came from, although, like Shaun, I didn't always think of it like that. I can now trace that thread back a long way in my own research, but I couldn't have said years ago that this is what I was doing. It's only now, looking back, that I can see more clearly what I was doing and am then able to say, programmatically, what it is that I feel we should be doing and how to take this research perspective forward.

SM: Talking about how we might move things forward, I'm also with you on what you've written recently about the field of media studies needing to take more seriously its *interdisciplinary roots* (Morley, 2009, p. 115). When I was an undergraduate in media studies, my lecturers came from different backgrounds in the humanities and social sciences, and when you were sent to the library you were sent to the four corners of it.[11] In the early 1980s, there wasn't really an established canon of key writings in media studies, which students were required to read. I don't want to get too nostalgic about this, but I wonder if something our students miss out on these days is the spirit of interdisciplinary adventure that I felt all those years ago at PCL, even though I try hard to get my own postgraduate students at Sunderland, at MA and PhD levels, to read well beyond what are usually considered to be the boundaries of media studies. I'd suggest that in general our field feels more insular now, and of course that's partly a consequence of the success of media studies in establishing a territory for itself in the university system, with its own specialist literature (its own section of shelves in the library). For me, though, *media studies are at their strongest when they're looking outwards* and in dialogue with what's going on in other fields or disciplines, in geography, philosophy, sociology, anthropology and so on.

DM: Just going back to what Shaun's been saying about everyday experience, and to what I've said about articulations of the material and the virtual, I think one of the best things that's happening at the moment is the way in which sociologists and anthropologists are increasingly contributing to our understanding of media uses, and uses of technology more generally, in quite varied social settings. For instance, sociologist Don Slater (2013) gives us a marvellous example from West Africa.[12] It's an example concerning new media technologies in the different conditions of two villages there. One of these villages got lots of funding for a purpose-built computer centre, but it was at a location where it didn't fit in with what people tended to do and where they tended to go. In another village, though, there was an aid worker who'd left behind, when he went home, an almost clapped out laptop. Its connection was dodgy and yet it worked a bit. He'd handed it on to a friend of his who ran a cafe, and this cafe was next to a bus stop that lots of people passed through. Guess what? The old laptop, because it connected with people's everyday practices, the everyday paths of movement that took them by the cafe, where they were already accustomed to having a chat, made much more of a difference in the context of their everyday lives than the shiny new computer centre. So this is to add something more about the importance of the everyday.

Of course, it's necessary to remember, too, how difficult it may sometimes be to study everyday cultures (that which is simply taken for granted). Georges Perec (1999) argued that a problem with studying the everyday is that you can't see it, so you have to force yourself to see almost stupidly, to force yourself to take notice of things you'd ordinarily find to be invisible, precisely because of their ordinariness, such as those ubiquitous container boxes that I mentioned earlier. This might also be a way in which we can better understand the significance of media-and-their-uses-in-context.

ZK: On the basis of my own work on encounters with public screens, I can certainly confirm that point about *the difficulty of studying everyday cultures*. Initially, when I went out to try to observe what people were doing as they pass beside screens in a city context, I was struck by just how little overtly researchable activity there was. I nearly gave up at that early stage! Next, I asked selected people to carry small voice recorders with them, so that they could speak into them about what they noticed as they were moving around. One of my research participants, who was a professional working in London, took a trip on the underground (which is thought of by advertisers to be a captive space, covered with various screens and promotional messages), and he actually returned a silent tape. In a subsequent interview, he stated that he didn't usually pay much attention to public screens. This is exactly the problem that David has pointed to, of *investigating the invisibility of the ordinary*, and yet the silent tape itself told me something interesting about what wasn't consciously noticed, or, at least, what wasn't discursively noted. A related thing that interested me, though, in my London Underground case study, was a reported feeling of discomfort when someone was walking through a pedestrian tunnel where all the advertising screens had been removed while renovations were being carried out. So what's sometimes unnoticed in everyday life isn't necessarily an insignificant part of the environment. When it's not there for some reason, the absence can become highly visible.

These empirical examples led me to question arguments made by another researcher who's written about media in urban settings, Todd Gitlin (2002). He suggests that contemporary cityscapes are a flashing spectacle to which people surrender, and the assumption there is that the provision of more and newer technologies will necessarily bring people into more communication with media. On the contrary, what I found is that people develop various creative skills of using screens as a background to their movements.[13] For instance, some of the women who participated in my study reported feeling unsafe in a particular part of London, and so they chose to walk a route where screens light up the space and make it feel more lively. They were certainly looking around, then, but they weren't viewing any particular image or were noticing only those that changed. Therefore, assuming that mediated urban environments are simply about media communications seems to me to be wide of the mark. There's much else going on as well, and we need a non-media-centric perspective to appreciate this.

Anyway, I feel fortunate now that I didn't give up on my research, and I'd like to think that I eventually managed to overcome those initial difficulties which I faced when doing the empirical work. Ultimately, the readers of my book will have to make a judgement about that (see Krajina, 2014).

Representation, power and embodiment

ZK: Moving into the final part of our discussion now, having talked about these issues of everyday experience, and about various mobilities and geographies, I'm wondering if you could say something, quite explicitly, about how this non-media-centric perspective relates to what might be thought of as the more traditional questions in media studies, to matters of representation and power, for example?

SM: Perhaps I'd better start with representation, because the phenomenological approaches that I favour these days do involve shifting the emphasis away from those theories of representation which have helped to shape our field. Adapting a term from Nigel Thrift's writings (see especially Thrift, 1996, 2007) in the discipline of geography, I've become increasingly interested in the possibility of developing a type of media studies that's not only non-media-centric but also, at least in terms of its theoretical emphasis, *non-representational*. This would require more attention to be paid (far more than media studies scholars have done in the past) to matters of embodiment and to related issues of orientation and habitation. It'd call for a much greater emphasis on bodily, pre-reflective knowledges or dispositions, on knowing how to find ways about and on the inhabiting of everyday environments. Let me try to explain, as briefly and straightforwardly as I can.

For me, one of the main difficulties facing media studies today is the field's inability to leave behind entirely some of its early structuralist influences. It's true that there probably aren't many academics in media studies who'd still identify with the tradition of structuralism, with old-fashioned structuralist semiotics, but I suspect that most would still subscribe to the view that it's only through language or representation that worlds can be made to mean. This remains one of the key principles in our field, certainly in terms of how the subject of media studies has been taught in universities, and I want to take issue with it.

In particular, there are two problems with this sort of view, and in offering my critique of it I'm drawing especially on Tim Ingold's development of a dwelling perspective (Ingold, 1995, 2000) for anthropology. Firstly, there's an assumption that people are necessarily living out their relationships to an external world through systems of symbols, and, secondly, there's a closely linked assumption that these relationships depend primarily on cognitive processes (on mental representations), which supposedly guide practical action and give meaning to experience. What I want to suggest instead, though, is that it's quite possible for inhabited worlds to be meaningful, as Ingold (2011, p. 77) has put it, *in the absence of symbolic representation*, and also that it's important to see how meanings can emerge from routine practices, through embodied and sensuous engagements with lived-in environments. Actually, these days, Ingold's preference (see Ingold, 2013, pp. 94–96) is to speak of animacy and animate life rather than of embodiment or embodied practice, yet his initial attacks (implicit or explicit) on structuralism and rationalism hold good and they serve to support my targeting of an old difficulty that continues to trouble media studies.

Now, I realise that this might all sound a bit abstract, but what I'm getting at is the need for media studies to take more seriously the significance of ordinary doings and dwellings. For instance, in my current work I'm interested in movements of the hands and fingers in dealings with media and with other routinely used equipment. What I'm thinking of here are manual activities like the sliding and tapping of fingers or digits on various touch-screen devices, their pressing on keyboards and so on, and I've been considering such digital media uses alongside skilled practices like the playing of musical instruments. I've become interested in how media users acquire what sociologist David Sudnow (2001), with reference to piano playing, once called ways of the hand, or, in other words, *the formation through habitual movement of hands at home with media and other technologies.*[14] Maurice Merleau-Ponty (2002 [1962], p. 166) referred to the practical know-how that's involved in this formation as a knowledge in the hands, and he saw how wider bodily understandings are bound up with a basic, everyday meaningfulness. These bodily understandings have to do with knowing where we are and where we're going in environments that are thoroughly familiar to us. Of course, there's always the methodological challenge of researching the kind of things that I'm talking about, which returns us to what Dave and Zlatan were saying a few minutes ago, about the difficulty of studying everyday cultures.

DM: What Shaun was just arguing there, about embodied relations to technologies and our knowing where we are in everyday contexts, makes me think about what I do when I first get up in the morning. Until I can orient myself in space by putting on my glasses and orient myself in time by putting on my wristwatch, I'm not quite the person I normally consider myself to be. For many people, it might now be a question of putting in their contact lenses and picking smartphones up off bedside tables, but the general point here is that the boundaries between us and these technologies are not as clear as you might imagine. Some academics have taken Donna Haraway's idea of the cyborg (see Haraway, 1991) as a futuristic figure, when actually we've been cyborgs for a long while.

ZK: So do these notions of embodiment and orientation mean that we no longer need to study representations, at least in the conventional ways that they've been studied in the past? Is there to be a major shift of focus now?

DM: I'm not so sure that a complete shift of focus, based on the notion that one approach should replace another, would actually be helpful. Shaun mentioned non-representational theory, but there's a slightly different term that he's used in his writing too. It's the idea of *the more-than-representational*, towards which I feel more sympathetic.

SM: It's Hayden Lorimer's term (Lorimer, 2005). He talks of more-than-representational cultural geographies.

DM: I think that an idea of the more-than-representational (or the not-only-representational) probably offers a better way of going beyond matters of representation to these other issues that Shaun's raising, without suggesting that we're leaving the old questions behind entirely. I don't think it's either possible or desirable to leave such matters behind. From my point of view, questions to do with symbolic representation and cognitive processes remain important, even if they're not the whole story.

SM: Well, I agree with you to an extent. I agree that language (cognition too) can't simply be left behind and I want to stress that I'm absolutely not against the study of images, utterances or other performances. What I'm wanting to argue, though, is that the concept of representation has been far too central in media studies, and that we certainly do have to leave behind some of the established assumptions that get made in our field, concerning the relations between language, world and meaning. It's about how we theorise those things.[15]

ZK: Okay, we've spoken about representation, but what about issues of power?

SM: I'm well aware, when I start speaking about movements of the hands and fingers, that there'll be colleagues in our field who'd despair, who'd see all this stuff about bodily knowledge as highly trivial and as a diversion from key issues of power and the political. Still, the phenomenological and non-representational approaches that I'm working with these days don't have to lead us away from a concern with power and social inequality, from a politics of everyday living.

On this point about social difference and power, I'll say just a bit about Pierre Bourdieu's social theory of practice (see, for example, Bourdieu, 1990, 2000), because I find it interesting that long before he became a sociologist Bourdieu began his academic career in France as a philosophy student, and so he'd have been reading, amongst other things, Merleau-Ponty's writings. Much like this phenomenological philosopher, Bourdieu became fascinated by *a bodily immersion in the world that presupposes no representation*. He refers, then, to a practical comprehension (also to a practical sense or practical intentionality), remarking on how the agent engaged in practice typically inhabits a familiar habitat and feels at home there (Bourdieu, 2000, p. 143). In fact, Bourdieu was described by one of his academic collaborators as Merleau-Ponty's sociological heir (see Bourdieu & Wacquant, 1992, p. 20).

Where Bourdieu's social theory differs from Merleau-Ponty's philosophy is in its insistence on linking bodily dispositions to social inequalities, most notably to the divisions of social class. Bourdieu (2000, p. 147) considers what he terms the coincidence between habitus and habitat in particular social and historical circumstances. By the way, you can find a similar, sympathetic yet critical engagement with Merleau-Ponty in some important work that's been done by Iris Marion Young (2005 [1980]), a feminist philosopher and political theorist who's written on gendered bodily movements and inhibitions. Anyhow, this raises what seem to me to be crucial questions about the politics of bodies and worlds, to do with *who feels at home and who feels uncomfortable or out of place in which social situations.*

DM: I agree with you that attending to those matters of inclusion and exclusion is terribly important. My own work has always been concerned in one way or another with cultural power, and the dimension of power that I'm still most interested in has to do with how common sense can present itself as natural, even though, of course, it's continually changing. Identifying the way in which any specific form of common sense excludes certain perceptions or possibilities is of enormous significance, so I think that this continues to be a very rich terrain of critical investigation.[16]

ZK: Speaking of politics, I'd like to ask you a slightly different but related question. In these difficult economic times, how would you defend your brand of critical, non-media-centric media studies when the current pressure in universities is increasingly for courses that have some immediate utility or vocational focus?

DM: I can remember a particular occasion, not so long ago, when exactly this issue came up in the context of my MA teaching. I had a student who, after weeks of attending my lectures, I could see, was getting very, very frustrated, and finally she exploded. She said to me: 'Professor Morley, what's the utility of all this?' I said to her: 'It's not designed to have utility in the sense that you're talking about. It's not training, it's education.' Now, the difficulty is that precisely because students at universities in England have to go into such incredible levels of debt these days, in order to get an education, they're much more likely to pose the kind of question I got from this MA student. They're increasingly pushed towards looking for a utilitarian outcome.

What I'm trying to encourage in my teaching is the ability to do a certain sort of thinking. I don't mind if the students agree or disagree with my conclusions, with where I happen to stand on particular topics. I've always attempted to foster a critical engagement through my teaching, and, in terms of the current economic climate and current educational politics, that remains my position.

A few years back, I had the pleasure of being in Hermann Bausinger's company, and, in conversation, this eminent German professor of ethnology (see, for example, Bausinger, 1990) told me an interesting story about his teaching. He told me that at the end of his courses some of his students (including some of the very good ones) would come up to him and say that they'd worked hard and read all the books he'd asked them to read but that they were still confused. His response was to say yes, but now you're confused at a higher level! I think that's really the best we can hope for, and I don't think we should be in the business of teaching students ready-made answers to questions.

A brief link to the next chapter

The next chapter brings this book to an end (although, for a concluding chapter, it will be a distinctly open-ended one, pointing forwards rather than attempting to close things down). Matters of embodiment, and related issues of orientation and habitation, which were discussed late in the present chapter and which emerged as key themes earlier in the book, will be explored further by paying close attention to those *habits or ways of the hand* (Sudnow, 2001) that are found in the uses of new media technologies but also in practical dealings with other equipment that is not obviously media-related. A non-media-centric perspective is maintained, then, whilst a non-representational theoretical emphasis is pursued. The chapter opens with a basic description of a routinely performed manual activity, of a general sort that is likely to be familiar to most media users today. What might strike the reader as unusual, however, is that this description is of actions so ordinary and taken for granted that they can seem, at first, to be not worth the effort of describing in any detail at all (and certainly not worthy of serious academic reflection).

Notes

1. On the day there was also a subsequent discussion in which the panel took questions from audience members, but because of a word-limit restriction on the original journal article that interchange was not included.
2. David Morley later became Professor of Communications there, and has been based in the Department of Media and Communications at Goldsmiths, University of London for over 25 years.
3. This was a key issue for others, too, including Dorothy Hobson (1980) in her early work on women's uses of radio and television in household settings, which raised crucial issues concerning domestic labour and leisure, and Ann Gray (1987) in her research into women's relationships to the video recorder (see also Gray, 1992), which raised related and equally crucial questions concerning gender and domestic technology.
4. Raymond Williams (1974, p. 26) was interested in broadcasting as 'a social product of... two apparently paradoxical yet deeply connected tendencies of modern...living'. As he put it, the condition of mobile privatisation 'is private...centred on the home' (Williams, 1989, p. 171) and yet, at the same time, 'it...confers...an unexampled mobility...it is not living in a cut-off way'. Although he was opposed to the perspective of technological determinism (and implicitly critical of Marshall McLuhan for that reason), Williams regarded the car as a key technological component of this contemporary lifestyle, and so his concept of mobile privatisation brings together matters of media and travel.
5. The notion of 'image spaces' was borrowed from the work of Kevin Robins (1989; see also Morley & Robins, 1995, pp. 31–32), one of the first academics in Britain to operate across the boundary between human geography and media and communication studies. Identifications with image spaces are always socially differentiated or patterned, depending upon the articulation of such spaces with the everyday-life circumstances of viewers.
6. At the Polytechnic of Wales, where communication studies had been developed by John Fiske (before he left to work in Australia and the USA), the degree course included media and culture strands that were led in the 1980s by Tim O'Sullivan and the late Brian Doyle respectively, whilst at Queen Margaret College, Edinburgh, a communication studies programme with media and cultural studies elements was led through the 1990s by Andrew Tolson, formerly a postgraduate student at CCCS in Birmingham (see Weedon et al., 1980).
7. It is important to point out, however, that most of those associated with media studies at PCL (and certainly Nicholas Garnham, Paddy Scannell and Colin Sparks, who were among the founding editors of *Media, Culture and Society*) would have been suspicious of, say, Althusserian Marxism or Saussurean linguistics. Garnham (1983), for instance, was arguing the case for a theory of cultural materialism, and he co-authored an article with Williams that helped to introduce Pierre Bourdieu's sociology of culture to an English-language readership (see Garnham & Williams, 1986).
8. Zlatan Krajina's methodology, for that study of encounters with public screens, is influenced by the phenomenological geography of David Seamon (2015 [1979]) and Yi-Fu Tuan (1977). So Krajina (2014, pp. 45–46) writes of exploring these encounters 'as part of "everyday environmental experience" in contemporary cities', pursuing the phenomenological geographers' interests in habit and the constitution of senses of place (also

referencing, for example, Moores, 2006, 2007, 2012). Another key influence for him is the media studies literature around the concept of domestication (see contributions to Berker et al., 2006; also Silverstone, 1994, pp. 174–175; Silverstone et al., 1992), which, in the past, has related mainly to research on the household uses of technologies. Krajina (2014, p. 9), however, declares his interest in investigating the process of a 'domestication of screens' by passers-by in the mediated city.

9. For example, Arjun Appadurai was interested in relating physical migration to media of communication. He proposed an analysis of how (on a transnational scale) 'moving groups and individuals' (Appadurai, 1996, p. 33) encounter and interact with moving images and sounds (see also Appadurai & Morley, 2011).

10. Ien Ang (1996) has referred to Radway's perspective here as an instance of 'radical contextualism'. While sympathising with the proposed move towards an ethnography of the everyday, Ang (1996, p. 77) warns that 'the will "to do justice" to…contextualization could easily lead to a sense of paralysis'. The same warning might equally apply, of course, to contemporary calls for non-media-centric media studies, and Ang (1996, p. 78) is right to point out that there are always pragmatic methodological decisions to be made about 'which contextual frameworks to take on board' in any specific research project. Indeed, see Morley (1992, p. 187), who argued for the need to establish 'which elements of the potentially infinite realm of…"context" are going to be relevant to the particular research in hand'.

11. It is worth noting, however, that the majority of them came from an academic background in literary studies (even if this was rarely evident in the interdisciplinary flavour of their teaching). For instance, Scannell's undergraduate course was in English literature at Oxford University, before he took up a teaching post in the late 1960s at the Regent Street Polytechnic in London, later to become PCL (see Scannell, 2007, pp. 198–199).

12. Earlier work of Don Slater's, in collaboration with anthropologist Daniel Miller (Miller & Slater, 2000), was on internet use in Trinidad, and Miller (2011) has since done research there specifically on uses of Facebook.

13. This broad finding of Krajina's might be thought of as a helpful supplement to Erving Goffman's notes on behaviour in public places (Goffman, 1963), which included reflections on pavement or sidewalk interactions in urban settings. Indeed, Krajina (2014, pp. 35–36, 77–78) makes reference to some of this sociologist's work on pedestrian practices and relations in public (see Goffman, 1971).

14. That interest in approaching digital media as manual media is one which was first signalled in the opening chapter of this book and it will be the main concern of the book's final chapter (to follow shortly).

15. As argued earlier in the book, a non- or more-than-representational theory of language would begin by approaching it as very much 'in and of the world' (Wylie, 2007, p. 164), challenging any notion of a system of signs that is somehow 'anterior to, and determinative of' everyday practices, including practices of talk-in-interaction or speech performance.

16. For a recent contribution to debates about the politics of common sense (focusing on articulations of common sense in contemporary British politics), see Stuart Hall and Alan O'Shea (2013).

References

Ang, I. (1996), 'Ethnography and Radical Contextualism in Audience Studies', in *Living Room Wars: Rethinking Media Audiences for a Postmodern World*, London: Routledge.

Appadurai, A. (1996), *Modernity at Large: Cultural Dimensions of Globalization*, Minneapolis, MN: University of Minnesota Press.

Appadurai, A. & Morley, D. (2011), 'Decoding, Diaspora and Disjuncture', *New Formations*, no. 73, pp. 39–51.

Bausinger, H. (1990), *Folk Culture in a World of Technology*, Bloomington, IN: Indiana University Press.

Berker, T., Hartmann, M., Punie, Y. & Ward, K. (eds.) (2006), *Domestication of Media and Technology*, Maidenhead: Open University Press.

Bourdieu, P. (1990), *The Logic of Practice*, Cambridge: Polity.

Bourdieu, P. (2000), *Pascalian Meditations*, Cambridge: Polity.

Bourdieu, P. & Wacquant, L. (1992), *An Invitation to Reflexive Sociology*, Cambridge: Polity.

Carey, J. (1989), *Communication as Culture: Essays on Media and Society*, Boston, MA: Unwin Hyman.

Couldry, N. (2010), 'Theorising Media as Practice', in Bräuchler, B. & Postill, J. (eds.) *Theorising Media and Practice*, Oxford: Berghahn.

Couldry, N. (2012), *Media, Society, World: Social Theory and Digital Media Practice*, Cambridge: Polity.

Cresswell, T. (2010), 'Towards a Politics of Mobility', *Environment and Planning D: Society and Space*, vol. 28, no. 1, pp. 17–31.

Garnham, N. (1983), 'Toward a Theory of Cultural Materialism', *Journal of Communication*, vol. 33, no. 3, pp. 314–329.

Garnham, N. & Williams, R. (1986), 'Pierre Bourdieu and the Sociology of Culture: An Introduction', in Collins, R., Curran, J., Garnham, N., Scannell, P., Schlesinger, P. & Sparks, C. (eds.) *Media, Culture and Society: A Critical Reader*, London: Sage.

Giddens, A. (1984), *The Constitution of Society: Outline of the Theory of Structuration*, Cambridge: Polity.

Giddens, A. (1990), *The Consequences of Modernity*, Cambridge: Polity.

Gitlin, T. (2002), *Media Unlimited: How the Torrent of Images and Sounds Overwhelms Our Lives*, New York: Metropolitan Books.

Goffman, E. (1963), *Behavior in Public Places: Notes on the Social Organization of Gatherings*, New York: Free Press.

Goffman, E. (1971), *Relations in Public: Microstudies of the Public Order*, New York: Basic Books.

Goffman, E. (1983), 'The Interaction Order', *American Sociological Review*, vol. 48, no. 1, pp. 1–17.

Gramsci, A. (1971), *Selections from Prison Notebooks*, London: Lawrence and Wishart.

Gray, A. (1987), 'Behind Closed Doors: Video Recorders in the Home', in Baehr, H. & Dyer, G. (eds.) *Boxed In: Women and Television*, London: Pandora.

Gray, A. (1992), *Video Playtime: The Gendering of a Leisure Technology*, London: Routledge.

Hall, S. (1973), 'Encoding and Decoding in the Television Discourse', CCCS Stencilled Paper no. 7, Centre for Contemporary Cultural Studies, University of Birmingham.

Hall, S. & O'Shea, A. (2013), 'Common-Sense Neoliberalism', in Hall, S., Massey, D. & Rustin, M. (eds.) *After Neoliberalism? The Kilburn Manifesto*, London: Lawrence and Wishart.

Hannam, K., Sheller, M. & Urry, J. (2006), 'Editorial: Mobilities, Immobilities and Moorings', *Mobilities*, vol. 1, no. 1, pp. 1–22.

Haralovich, M.B. (1988), 'Suburban Family Sitcoms and Consumer Product Design: Addressing the Social Subjectivity of Homemakers in the 1950s', in Drummond, P. & Paterson, R. (eds.) *Television and Its Audience: International Research Perspectives*, London: British Film Institute.

Haraway, D. (1991), *Simians, Cyborgs and Women: The Reinvention of Nature*, New York: Routledge.

Hermes, J. (1995), *Reading Women's Magazines: An Analysis of Everyday Media Use*, Cambridge: Polity.

Hobson, D. (1980), 'Housewives and the Mass Media', in Hall, S., Hobson, D., Lowe, A. & Willis, P. (eds.) *Culture, Media, Language: Working Papers in Cultural Studies, 1972–79*, London: Hutchinson.

Ingold, T. (1995), 'Building, Dwelling, Living: How Animals and People Make Themselves at Home in the World', in Strathern, M. (ed.) *Shifting Contexts: Transformations in Anthropological Knowledge*, London: Routledge.

Ingold, T. (2000), *The Perception of the Environment: Essays on Livelihood, Dwelling and Skill*, London: Routledge.

Ingold, T. (2011), *Being Alive: Essays on Movement, Knowledge and Description*, London: Routledge.

Ingold, T. (2013), *Making: Anthropology, Archaeology, Art and Architecture*, London: Routledge.

Krajina, Z. (2013), 'Domesticating the Screen-Scenography: Situational Uses of Screen Images and Technologies in the London Underground', in Berry, C., Harbord, J. & Moore, R. (eds.) *Public Space, Media Space*, Basingstoke: Palgrave Macmillan.

Krajina, Z. (2014), *Negotiating the Mediated City: Everyday Encounters with Public Screens*, New York: Routledge.

Lorimer, H. (2005), 'Cultural Geography: The Busyness of Being "More-Than-Representational"', *Progress in Human Geography*, vol. 29, no. 1, pp. 83–94.

McLuhan, M. (1994 [1964]), *Understanding Media: The Extensions of Man*, Cambridge, MA: MIT Press.

Massey, D. (1994), *Space, Place and Gender*, Cambridge: Polity.

Merleau-Ponty, M. (2002 [1962]), *Phenomenology of Perception*, London: Routledge.

Miller, D. (2011), *Tales from Facebook*, Cambridge: Polity.

Miller, D. & Slater, D. (2000), *The Internet: An Ethnographic Approach*, Oxford: Berg.

Moores, S. (1988), '"The Box on the Dresser": Memories of Early Radio and Everyday Life', *Media, Culture and Society*, vol. 10, no. 1, pp. 23–40.

Moores, S. (1993a), 'Satellite TV as Cultural Sign: Consumption, Embedding and Articulation', *Media, Culture and Society*, vol. 15, no. 4, pp. 621–639.

Moores, S. (1993b), *Interpreting Audiences: The Ethnography of Media Consumption*, London: Sage.

Moores, S. (1993c), 'Television, Geography and "Mobile Privatization"', *European Journal of Communication*, vol. 8, no. 3, pp. 365–379.

Moores, S. (1995), 'Media, Modernity and Lived Experience', *Journal of Communication Inquiry*, vol. 19, no. 1, pp. 5–19.

Moores, S. (1996), *Satellite Television and Everyday Life: Articulating Technology*, Luton: John Libbey Media.

Moores, S. (1999), 'The Mediated "Interaction Order"', in Hearn, J. & Roseneil, S. (eds.) *Consuming Cultures: Power and Resistance*, Basingstoke: Macmillan.

Moores, S. (2000), *Media and Everyday Life in Modern Society*, Edinburgh: Edinburgh University Press.

Moores, S. (2005), *Media/Theory: Thinking about Media and Communications*, London: Routledge.

Moores, S. (2006), 'Media Uses and Everyday Environmental Experiences: A Positive Critique of Phenomenological Geography', *Participations: Journal of Audience and Reception Studies*, vol. 3, no. 2 (available at http://www.participations.org).

Moores, S. (2007), 'Media and Senses of Place: On Situational and Phenomenological Geographies', Media@LSE Electronic Working Paper no. 12, Department of Media and Communications, London School of Economics and Political Science (available at http://www.lse.uk/collections/media@lse).

Moores, S. (2008), 'Conceptualizing Place in a World of Flows', in Hepp, A., Krotz, F., Moores, S. & Winter, C. (eds.) *Connectivity, Networks and Flows: Conceptualizing Contemporary Communications*, Cresskill, NJ: Hampton Press.

Moores, S. (2009), 'That Familiarity with the World Born of Habit: A Phenomenological Approach to the Study of Media Uses in Daily Living', *Interactions: Studies in Communication and Culture*, vol. 1, no. 3, pp. 301–312.

Moores, S. (2012), *Media, Place and Mobility*, Basingstoke: Palgrave Macmillan.

Moores, S. (2014), 'Digital Orientations: "Ways of the Hand" and Practical Knowing in Media Uses and Other Manual Activities', *Mobile Media and Communication*, vol. 2, no. 2, pp. 196–208.

Moores, S. (2015), 'We Find Our Way About: Everyday Media Use and "Inhabitant Knowledge"', *Mobilities*, vol. 10, no. 1, pp. 17–35.

Moores, S. & Metykova, M. (2009), 'Knowing How to Get Around: Place, Migration and Communication', *The Communication Review*, vol. 12, no. 4, pp. 313–326.

Moores, S. & Metykova, M. (2010), '"I Didn't Realize How Attached I Am": On the Environmental Experiences of Trans-European Migrants', *European Journal of Cultural Studies*, vol. 13, no. 2, pp. 171–189.

Morley, D. (1980), *The Nationwide Audience: Structure and Decoding*, London: British Film Institute.

Morley, D. (1986), *Family Television: Cultural Power and Domestic Leisure*, London: Comedia.

Morley, D. (1991), 'Where the Global Meets the Local: Notes from the Sitting Room', *Screen*, vol. 32, no. 1, pp. 1–15.

Morley, D. (1992), *Television, Audiences and Cultural Studies*, London: Routledge.

Morley, D. (1996), 'The Geography of Television: Ethnography, Communications and Community', in Hay, J., Grossberg, L. & Wartella, E. (eds.) *The Audience and Its Landscape*, Boulder, CO: Westview Press.

Morley, D. (2000), *Home Territories: Media, Mobility and Identity*, London: Routledge.

Morley, D. (2003), 'What's "Home" Got to Do with It? Contradictory Dynamics in the Domestication of Technology and the Dislocation of Domesticity', *European Journal of Cultural Studies*, vol. 6, no. 4, pp. 435–458.

Morley, D. (2007), *Media, Modernity and Technology: The Geography of the New*, London: Routledge.

Morley, D. (2009), 'For a Materialist, Non-Media-Centric Media Studies', *Television and New Media*, vol. 10, no. 1, pp. 114–116.

Morley, D. (2010), 'Television as a Means of Transport: Digital Teletechnologies and Transmodal Systems', in Gripsrud, J. (ed.) *Relocating Television: Television in the Digital Context*, London: Routledge.

Morley, D. (2011), 'Communications and Transport: The Mobility of Information, People and Commodities', *Media, Culture and Society*, vol. 33, no. 5, pp. 743–759.

Morley, D. (2017), *Communications and Mobility: The Migrant, the Mobile Phone and the Container Box*, Malden, MA: Wiley-Blackwell.

Morley, D. & Brunsdon, C. (1999), *The* Nationwide *Television Studies*, London: Routledge.

Morley, D. & Robins, K. (1995), *Spaces of Identity: Global Media, Electronic Landscapes and Cultural Boundaries*, London: Routledge.

Morley, D. & Silverstone, R. (1990), 'Domestic Communication: Technologies and Meanings', *Media, Culture and Society*, vol. 12, no. 1, pp. 31–55.

Packer, J. & Robertson, C. (eds.) (2006), *Thinking with James Carey: Essays on Communications, Transportation, History*, New York: Peter Lang.

Perec, G. (1999), *Species of Spaces and Other Pieces*, London: Penguin.

Radway, J. (1984), *Reading the Romance: Women, Patriarchy and Popular Literature*, Chapel Hill, NC: University of North Carolina Press.

Radway, J. (1988), 'Reception Study: Ethnography and the Problems of Dispersed Audiences and Nomadic Subjects', *Cultural Studies*, vol. 2, no. 3, pp. 359–376.

Rath, C. (1985), 'The Invisible Network: Television as an Institution in Everyday Life', in Drummond, P. & Paterson, R. (eds.) *Television in Transition: Papers from the First International Television Studies Conference*, London: British Film Institute.

Robins, K. (1989), 'Reimagined Communities? European Image Spaces, Beyond Fordism', *Cultural Studies*, vol. 3, no. 2, pp. 145–165.

Scannell, P. (1996), *Radio, Television and Modern Life: A Phenomenological Approach*, Oxford: Blackwell.

Scannell, P. (2007), *Media and Communication*, London: Sage.

Scannell, P. (2014), *Television and the Meaning of Live: An Enquiry into the Human Situation*, Cambridge: Polity.

Scannell, P. & Cardiff, D. (1991), *A Social History of British Broadcasting: 1922–1939, Serving the Nation*, Oxford: Blackwell.

Seamon, D. (2015 [1979]), A Geography of the Lifeworld: Movement, Rest and Encounter, London: Routledge.

Silverstone, R. (1994), Television and Everyday Life, London: Routledge.

Silverstone, R., Hirsch, E. & Morley, D. (1992), 'Information and Communication Technologies and the Moral Economy of the Household', in Silverstone, R. & Hirsch, E. (eds.) Consuming Technologies: Media and Information in Domestic Spaces, London: Routledge.

Silverstone, R. & Morley, D. (1990), 'Families and Their Technologies: Two Ethnographic Portraits', in Putnam, T. & Newton, C. (eds.) Household Choices, London: Futures Publications.

Slater, D. (2013), New Media, Development and Globalization: Making Connections in the Global South, Cambridge: Polity Press.

Spigel, L. (1992), Make Room for TV: Television and the Family Ideal in Post-War America, Chicago, IL: University of Chicago Press.

Sudnow, D. (2001), Ways of the Hand: A Rewritten Account, Cambridge, MA: MIT Press.

Thrift, N. (1996), Spatial Formations, London: Sage.

Thrift, N. (2007), Non-Representational Theory: Space/Politics/Affect, London: Routledge.

Tuan, Y. (1977), Space and Place: The Perspective of Experience, Minneapolis, MN: University of Minnesota Press.

Urry, J. (2007), Mobilities, Cambridge: Polity.

Weedon, C., Tolson, A., Mort, F. & Lowe, A. (1980), 'Theories of Language and Subjectivity', in Hall, S., Hobson, D., Lowe, A. & Willis, P. (eds.) Culture, Media, Language: Working Papers in Cultural Studies, 1972–79, London: Hutchinson.

Williams, R. (1974), Television: Technology and Cultural Form, London: Fontana.

Williams, R. (1989), Resources of Hope: Culture, Democracy, Socialism, London: Verso.

Wylie, J. (2007), Landscape, London: Routledge.

Young, I.M. (2005 [1980]), 'Throwing Like a Girl: A Phenomenology of Feminine Body Comportment, Motility and Spatiality', in On Female Body Experience: Throwing Like a Girl and Other Essays, New York: Oxford University Press.

· 8 ·

DIGITAL ORIENTATIONS

Ways of the Hand and Practical Knowing in Media Uses and Other Manual Activities

A hand was developing that was possessed of mobile ways…generative ways of knowing how to be at home in a setting of keys…a hand that had its bearings…a hand at home on the keyboard. (Sudnow, 2001, pp. 51–55)

In non-representational theory what counts as knowledge…is a part of practice. (Thrift, 2007, p. 121)

Opening (a laptop and inbox)

I begin here with a description of something done routinely in the course of my working day, of opening my laptop computer to check my email inbox. Gently applying pressure to the base of the machine with the thumb of my right hand, my left-hand thumb lifts the lid while the other fingers of that hand lie on top. My right-hand index finger then slides from left to right across the touch-pad, moving the cursor until it is located over an area in the middle of the screen marked 'Locked'. There, I tap the left side of the touch-pad to reveal my desktop display on screen, or possibly the document that I was last working on (because I am in the habit of just saving and then closing the lid, when I have to pause for some reason or at the end of a day). The same finger then slides downwards on the touch-pad until the cursor lies over the internet-search symbol that appears on the bar across the bottom of my screen, before tapping again to open my search page. Next, the right-hand index finger slides upwards to position the cursor over a 'Bookmark' link to the web app for my university's email system. Tapping there brings up a page with another link, 'Login to Staff Email'. Sliding and tapping a further time now on the touchpad serves to display the page on which I am required to give my university username and private password. These are then typed in at the appropriate on-screen locations, usually with the pressing movements of my right-hand index finger and two of the fingers of my left hand (but occasionally, say if I am holding a cup of tea or coffee in my right hand, with three of the fingers of my left hand). At one moment during this login process, there is typically a rapid sliding and tapping of the right-hand index finger to shift between the username and password locations, and, at another, my left-hand index finger presses 'Caps Lock' before returning to cancel that command a moment later. After the smallest finger of my right hand then presses the 'Enter' key, I am into my inbox.[1]

Although that opening description is basic, writing it still proved difficult. I had to keep stopping to go online and access my email. Without actually performing the ordered, unfolding series of actions repeatedly, noting carefully the fast movement of my hands, phase by phase, as I was going along, I would not have been able to write those words. This is because the activity is usually performed in an unreflective manner (at least without much thought being given to the practices themselves, and yet I may be thinking about something else, such as a message I need to send to students or the document that I will continue to work on after checking my inbox). The knowledge that I have of my-laptop-in-use, of my position in relation to the touch-pad and keys and of how to find ways about there, but also of the cursor's movements on the screen and the way to get to my inbox, is a sensuous, 'practical knowing... knowledge-in-practice' (Thrift, 2007, pp. 121–122).

My dealings with the computer clearly have a visual dimension, and a less obvious aural dimension too, given the gentle sounds of tapping and key-pressing. Essential for my *practical knowing*, however, are the movements of my fingers or digits, with their feel for, and their at-homeness on, the machine. To borrow David Sudnow's words from a different context (see Sudnow, 2001), what have developed over time are specific ways of the hand, and in the pages ahead I want to explore in greater detail such *mobile, generative ways*, emphasising matters of movement and dwelling, which I consider to be crucial for the study of everyday media use. In doing so, I will be taking in reflections on other manual activities that are apparently unrelated to media uses, making what may seem like detours, mainly into the disciplines of sociology and anthropology. I turn first to Sudnow's remarkable, micro-sociological work on the formation of skilled hands, in which he gives detailed descriptions of his own practices of learning to play jazz on the piano.[2]

A hand at home on the keyboard: Piano lessons for media researchers

Near to the start of Sudnow's book-length story about the development of his jazz-making ways of the hand, he remarks that: 'Anyone who's witnessed or been a beginning pianist…notices substantial initial awkwardness' (Sudnow, 2001, p. 12). This difficulty is evident in the 'manifold hesitations…of… beginners' hands' (Sudnow, 2001, p. 135), in the novice player's 'searching and looking…groping to put each finger in a good spot…trying to get a hold on chords properly…to get from one to the next, playing progressions smoothly' (Sudnow, 2001, pp. 12–13). Writing of his early experiences of learning to play chords and chord progressions on the piano, though, Sudnow (2001, p. 15) recalls how (over the course of several months): 'Looking's work load progressively lightens…the gaze at the keyboard progressively diffuses in function.… As I reached for chords…for recurring patterns of them…I was… developing an embodied way of accomplishing distance.' Indeed, after several years of playing the instrument, he confidently states that 'with eyes closed, I may now sit down at the piano, gain an initial orientation with the merest touch…and then reach out to bring my finger precisely into a spot two feet off to the left' (Sudnow, 2001, p. 16).

In Maurice Merleau-Ponty's terms, Sudnow had got 'the measure of the instrument with his body' (Merleau-Ponty, 2002 [1962], p. 168), and the keyboard space, or the 'relevant directions and dimensions' of his dealings with the piano, had come to be gradually incorporated over time.[3] As Paul Connerton (1989, pp. 92–93) puts it in a short commentary on the earlier version of Sudnow's narrative, and in the context of a much longer discussion of bodily practices and memory, the habitual keyboard player 'has acquired…an incorporated sense of places and distances' and is therefore able 'to execute… moves rapidly and spontaneously as when…you move your hand to your ear… without having to think of…the path between them'.

Still, subsequent difficulties faced by Sudnow, in his learning to play jazz piano, had to do with *acquiring skills of improvisation*. He recalls being puzzled on occasion by the 'interweaving intricacies' (Sudnow, 2001, p. 28) of his piano teacher's hand movements on the keyboard:

> I'd ask 'what was that?' He'd ask 'what was what?'...he'd have a hard time finding what he'd just done. He'd at times remark...'I just improvise and can't tell you how... you'll develop a feel for it.'

What this exchange between learner and teacher helps to confirm, of course, is that it can be hard to translate habitually performed practices (in this case, mobile, generative ways of the hand) into words, and yet Sudnow (2001, p. xix) seeks to draw an intriguing parallel between language use and piano playing, asserting that there is 'much in common between ordinary speaking and musical improvisation' and regarding his study as a potential 'preface for the phenomenological description of articulated gestures of all sorts, talking included'.

Interestingly, given Sudnow's reference there to speech or talk as articulated gesture, he goes on to reveal that the founding figure in conversation analysis, Harvey Sacks (1995), had been 'a close friend and then teaching colleague' (Sudnow, 2001, p. 132), and he acknowledges the contribution of Sacks by adding that 'whatever acumen I have for appreciating the possibility of order in the tiniest details was substantially nourished by my long association with him'. Indeed, just as Sacks approached conversation as a sequence of turns at talk, so Sudnow (2001, p. 80) insists that: 'Gestural productions... doing finger-talking...or...when I move...my mouth to speak...must be serialized...in a progressively unfolding way.' His piano playing, then, required 'unfoldingly handled moves' (Sudnow, 2001, p. 66). So a common emphasis there, across the seemingly rather different micro-sociological analyses offered by Sacks and Sudnow, is on seriality and *the practical accomplishment of order*, whether that is in the inter-corporeal interactions of human dialogue or the human-thing interactions involved in playing a musical instrument.[4]

Returning to the exchange between Sudnow and his piano teacher, which I reproduced above in edited form, it is important to note that developing a feel for improvisation was, for the learner, a lengthy and often frustrating process of figuring out new ways to go with his fingers in the temporally unfolding activity of playing. However, he reports that after a while there began to emerge 'up-a-little-down-a-little ways, rocking ways and every-other-finger ways... skipping ways, hopping ways, rippling ways...and more' (Sudnow, 2001, p. 59). His hands were increasingly becoming 'wayfully oriented' (Sudnow, 2001, p. 69), until eventually, as he puts it, 'the hand knew its ways' (Sudnow, 2001,

p. 114). It had its *bearings* (Sudnow, 2001, p. 51) or orientations, and was capable of 'flowing utterance' (Connerton, 1989, p. 92). He reached a stage at which, in his words: 'I don't think at all about where I'm going. My hands make it up as they go along' (Sudnow, 2001, p. 125).

As well as making an unlikely yet convincing link between the gestural production of ordinary talk and the 'extraordinary domain of action' (Sudnow, 2001, p. 2) that is jazz improvisation, Sudnow proceeded to draw a further surprising parallel. No doubt with an eye to Merleau-Ponty's phenomenological philosophy, and especially to an example of Merleau-Ponty's which I discussed in a previous chapter, Sudnow related piano playing to the bodily practices of typing, also approaching the latter as human-thing (more specifically, human-keyboard) interactions involving the formation of skilled hands that know their ways or have their bearings.

Just as the beginning pianist experiences substantial initial awkwardness, so it is the case that: 'The beginning typist may find himself spelling every word as he types, thinking of the spellings as a step-by-step search' (Sudnow, 2001, p. 136). However, in the case of the experienced typist and, by extension, the experienced computer-keyboard user, 'hands behave spellingly' (Sudnow, 2001, p. 136). Once again, in Sudnow's terms, 'looking's work load progressively lightens' (Sudnow, 2001, p. 15) and, in reaching for the correct keys without hesitation, the user has developed an embodied way of accomplishing distance. Fingers move at speed in the flow of the typing, just as Sudnow's digits came to behave jazzfully on the piano keyboard.

Equally, whilst I would accept that jazz-piano improvisation is indeed a rare skill acquired over a lengthy period, I see no reason why yet further parallels cannot be drawn, between piano playing or typing, either on outmoded typewriters or on modern computers, and various other uses of technology, including certain sorts of contemporary media use that are now widely regarded as quite ordinary domains of action. For example, it is possible to argue, too, that the rapidly moving, knowledgeable thumbs of the experienced text-message sender have come to behave spellingly, even if the spellings that appear on mobile screens are not always those found in a dictionary. John Tomlinson (2007, p. 108), then, refers (from the outsider perspective of a middle-aged academic, which I share) to the 'remarkable dexterities that young people seem to possess in text messaging'. I am certainly not trying to suggest that sending a text message and playing jazz on the piano are on a par with each other in terms of the manual dexterity required, but both are clearly skilled activities involving non-cognitive, habitual movements or ways of the hand.

Considered overall, Sudnow's book is of interest to me for two main, closely related reasons. Firstly, following in the footsteps of Merleau-Ponty's philosophical reflections on embodiment and the acquisition of habit, Sudnow offers a uniquely detailed account of the formation of sensuous, in-the-hands knowledge. I have proposed, somewhat playfully, in my subtitle for this chapter's present section, that his work might be thought of as providing *piano lessons for media researchers*. By this, I mean that future investigations of every-day media use would do well to learn from Sudnow's admirable commitment to a descriptive method. Of course, in adopting such a technique, there is the danger that the resulting descriptions could become monotonous for readers (I have to confess that I found reading every word of Sudnow's book to be a challenge for this reason, and perhaps even my own, relatively short opening account of laptop use is an illustration of that danger?), yet in my view the potential gains outweigh the risk. For example, imagine the value of a book-length description and phenomenological analysis, along roughly the same lines as Sudnow's study of piano playing, of the acquired skills and meaningful motilities which are bound up with learning how to use a new, digital media technology.[5]

Secondly, I am interested in Sudnow's account of learning to play jazz on the piano because it points to those matters of movement and dwelling (or orientation and habitation) that I have identified, at several stages earlier in my book, as being of broader significance for studies of day-to-day living. This significance is highlighted by Hubert Dreyfus (2001, p. ix), in a foreword to Sudnow's monograph, where that contemporary philosopher writes of it as 'a phenomenology of how we come to find our way about in the world...of how our bodies gain their grasp of the world' (and also as an investigation of 'giving order to...or...finding order in...our temporally unfolding experience'). Throughout Sudnow's book, then, he characterises his piano playing as the moving through and inhabiting of an environment. With regard to knowl-edgeable movement or orientation, he makes reference to 'the finger's journey' (Sudnow, 2001, p. 63) and to having 'gained handful command over myriad varieties of paths' (Sudnow, 2001, p. 125), and he ends his story by remark-ing on how 'this jazz music is...particular ways of moving from place to place' (Sudnow, 2001, p. 127). He realises, too, that his going along 'in a terrain nexus of hands and keyboard' (Sudnow, 2001, p. 127) is precisely what has enabled him to come to feel 'at home in a setting of keys' (Sudnow, 2001, p. 52), to 'reach for the music' (Dreyfus, 2001, p. x) and gain a grasp of it, and he writes explicitly of pianists' bodily relations to their keyboards as a dwelling (see Sudnow, 2001, p. 134). The keyboard space is inhabited as it gets incorporated.

Furthermore, as part of that *reaching for the music*, as Dreyfus puts it in his foreword, there can also be a feeling of at-homeness and immersion within the musical sounds that are produced, and this is a kind of dwelling or habitation that is potentially open to and shareable with non-playing audience members who are engaged in practices of listening. While these listeners do not have the same knowledge in the hands that the pianist has developed, their corporeal, emotional, with-the-ears involvement in the performance may still be understood as a sort of *journeying along paths*. As they sense the musician's 'wayful series of moves' (Sudnow, 2001, p. 72), they might themselves, in this process, be moved by the jazz.[6]

On sawing through a plank: Responsiveness to environmental conditions and the processional quality of tool use

Sudnow's notions of hands that make it up as they 'go along' (Sudnow, 2001, p. 125) and of having gained handful command over myriad varieties of paths, which were mentioned in the previous section, remind me very much of Tim Ingold's anthropological writings on dwelling and lines (see Ingold, 2000, 2007, 2011, 2015). Indeed, I would argue that Sudnow's knowledge in the hands, in what he terms a terrain nexus of hands and keyboard, is precisely an example of that inhabitant or alongly integrated knowledge which Ingold is so fascinated by. In this comparatively brief section of the chapter, I will therefore make a return to Ingold's work, but, rather than simply revisiting themes that have already been established in the chapter before last, I want to focus on a particular instance of this anthropologist's descriptive and analytical approach, which I have not discussed directly in my book so far.

Consider the following, slightly edited version of a description (similar in style to the one with which I opened this chapter) that is offered by Ingold (2011, pp. 51–52), of the actions associated with his sawing through a plank while making a bookcase:

> Each shelf has to be cut to the right length. Marking the distance along the plank with a tape measure, I use a pencil and set square to draw a...line across it. After these preliminaries I set the plank on a trestle.... The line to be cut slightly overhangs the right

end of the trestle. Then…I place the palm of my left hand on the plank…grasping it around the edge by the fingers. Taking up a saw with my right hand, I wrap my fingers around the handle…all, that is, except the index finger, which is extended along the flat of the handle, enabling me to fine-tune the direction of the blade. Now, as I press down with a rigid arm on the left hand, I engage the teeth of the saw with the edge, at the point where it meets my drawn line, and gently nick the edge with two or three short upstrokes.… Once the slot in the edge is long enough…I can begin to work it with downward strokes. At this point I have to attend…to the alignment of the blade…in order to ensure that the evolving cut proceeds in exactly the right direction. To do this, I have to position my head so that it is directly above the tool.… From this angle…I can see the wood on either side of the cut. The first strokes are crucial, since the further the cut goes, the less room there is for manoeuvre. After a while, however, I can relax my gaze and settle down to a rhythmic…movement with long, smooth and even strokes.

In Ingold's subsequent commentary, he discusses what should now be familiar issues of incorporation and immersion, highlighting the 'synergy of practitioner, tool and material' (Ingold, 2011, p. 56), and in doing so he explores that sensuous, practical knowing which has also been of interest to academic authors such as Merleau-Ponty and Sudnow. However, what I find especially interesting are the things that Ingold has to say about *bodily responsiveness* and about *the processional quality of tool use*. Let me deal with each of these in turn.

Back near to the start of my chapter, when commenting on my laptop use, I noted how accessing an email inbox is typically something that I perform in an unreflective manner, in the sense that little thought is explicitly devoted to its doing. Even so, unreflective practices of this sort must not be understood as unresponsive in character. For Ingold (2011, p. 61), then, 'the skilled handling of tools is…rhythmically responsive to ever-changing environmental conditions'. Crucially, he adds that: 'This…responsiveness…is not the awareness of a mind…aloof from the… hands-on business of work. It is rather immanent in practical, perceptual activity' (Ingold, 2011, p. 61).[7] So in the case of my routine handling of the computer, there is a bodily, rhythmic responsiveness to the depression of the keys beneath the gentle force of my fingers, to the cursor's rapid movements on my screen, and so on.

Intriguingly, Ingold (2011, p. 53) is also concerned to equate the activities of sawing and walking, since in each case, he asserts, one 'step' follows another and anticipates the next in a flowing 'processional…order' (of what Sudnow might have called serialised practices).[8] When sawing through a plank, this procession involves moving through joined-up phases of 'getting ready, setting out, carrying on and finishing off' (Ingold, 2011, p. 53). 'Like going for a walk', he continues (Ingold, 2011, p. 53), 'sawing…has the quality of a journey.' The experienced carpenter is a 'wayfarer who travels from place to place' (Ingold, 2011, p. 59).

From non-media-centric media studies to everyday-life studies?

Media theorists and researchers do not usually spend much time thinking about manual activities such as typing, piano playing and plank sawing. Neither are *movements of the hands and fingers* (or the feet) usually high on the agenda in the field of media studies. Of course, there are several notable examples of previous work, some of it from neighbouring fields, on communications technology, the body and the senses. To mention just a few of these examples, Marshall McLuhan (1994 [1964], p. 90) declared many years ago that 'all technologies are extensions of our physical and nervous systems', and, more recently, human geographer Mark Paterson (2007, pp. 127–145) has written interestingly on digital media as 'technologies of touch' (see also, on touch, Cranny-Francis, 2013) while new media researcher Ingrid Richardson (2008) has reflected on the 'bodily incorporation' of mobile media (see also Richardson & Wilken, 2012).[9] A key purpose of this concluding chapter of my book, though, has been to try to push that kind of work forward in a particular direction, by proposing that investigations of media in everyday contexts might now productively begin by attending to the mobile, generative ways of a hand at home with media and communication technologies, detailing the ordered, processional quality of media use.

As suggested by the interdisciplinary flavour of my discussion, with its apparent detours into phenomenologically inspired sociology (Sudnow, 2001) and social anthropology (Ingold, 2011, pp. 51–62), as well as its references to Nigel Thrift's non-representational geography (Thrift, 2007), any future research within media studies on ways of the hand and practical knowing would necessarily be part of a larger project straddling various fields and disciplines across the humanities and social sciences. This larger project is, therefore, a non-media-centric one (Krajina et al., 2014; Moores, 2012; Morley, 2007), because at its heart is a concern with movement and dwelling rather than any exclusive interest in media-related issues. Nevertheless, for those academics who, like me, are based in media studies, an important contribution that can be made to the wider interdisciplinary effort is to consider what David Morley (2007, p. 1) calls the particularities of media.

In this chapter, then, my emphasis has been on the characteristics that media uses have in common with the routine uses of other equipment. I have been focusing on the manual dexterities (and, more generally, the bodily rhythms and corporeal understandings) that are involved in practices ranging from checking an email inbox to sawing through a plank, and yet, to take these specific examples, the laptop computer and the handsaw clearly have distinctive applications as work tools. Cutting through wood with a computer is probably difficult, and communicating with students and colleagues, or preparing a document, with a saw is not advisable!

What helps to distinguish my laptop from Ingold's saw is *the doubly digital character of contemporary media*. The machine gives me access to numerous media settings that are, borrowing Ingold's terms from another context, 'continually coming into being through the combined action of human and non-human agencies' (Ingold, 2000, p. 155), some of which I adapt to on the basis of extensive previous experience of online environments whilst others are negotiated more regularly and are experienced as thoroughly familiar time-spaces of movement.[10] My inbox is one such time-space of movement. I inhabit it (I know how to get around there), just as my fingers find their way about and have come to feel at home in a setting of touch-pad and keys. Indeed, the crucial point I am making here, which was first aired in the book's introductory chapter, is that there are *digital orientations* of two, closely related types in media uses today. Digital wayfaring (to rearticulate a further term of Ingold's) depends on the habitual movement of knowledgeable human hands and fingers, as the digits press, slide and tap on keys, pads and screens, or as a mouse device is manipulated (see again Nunes, 2006, p. 41).

Rather than ending my book there, though, having come full circle and returned to this point about the doubly digital, I want to go back to something else that I aired, just in passing, in the introductory chapter. All those pages ago, as I was concluding that chapter's section on non-media-centric media studies, I wondered whether *everyday-life studies* may be a better name for the interdisciplinary area that could emerge if media studies academics with a non-media-centric perspective were to join forces with others, elsewhere in the humanities and social sciences, who share concerns with the habits of day-to-day living (and see Moores, 2017). As I noted then, there is already a considerable amount of literature, both classic and contemporary, which could form the foundations for a viable field of investigation to be known as everyday-life studies, and this would be the most suitable location, in my view, for what I have described above as a project with movement and dwelling at its heart.

I indicated, back in the introductory chapter, that two of my favourite recent publications on the everyday and the ordinary are books written by Billy Ehn and Orvar Löfgren (2010) and Ben Highmore (2011). Another firm favourite for me, though, is one by Sarah Pink (2012), the academic whose work in this area feels closest to mine. She is an ethnographic researcher with a background in anthropology, but also with a strong commitment to inter-disciplinary inquiry and a keen interest in bodily, sensory engagements with environments (see Pink, 2009). In fact, her book on everyday practices and places does briefly mention the idea of everyday-life studies (see Pink, 2012, p. 6) and, in her words, she 'draws from...philosophy, anthropology, sociology and geography' (Pink, 2012, p. 2) in attempting to develop a 'phenomenol-ogy of everyday realities and processes of change'. What I particularly admire in Pink's approach there is the way in which she pays serious attention to the uses of new, digital media without privileging everyday media use in rela-tion to a spread of other activities discussed in her book, such as washing the dishes, laundry practices and gardening. Indeed, she does not have to de-centre media in her analytical framework, since, for Pink, they were never central from the outset.

Still, let me say a little about Pink's specific take on new media uses in that book. She does not choose to foreground movements of the hands and fingers in the way that I have done in this chapter (but see, later, Pink et al., 2016), yet her talk of online environments 'that we participate in as we move through' (Pink, 2012, p. 46), and of 'digital ecologies that span online and offline worlds', evidently resonates with my own approach. In addition, she borrows occasionally from Ingold's conceptual vocabulary, in reflecting on the significance of media in everyday lives (see also Pink & Leder Mackley, 2013).

For instance, Pink (2012, pp. 136–137) describes her Facebook page as a '"meshwork"...of stories or narratives that are often previously unrelated... interwoven...on the screen of a computer or mobile device and...lived...by the user of that "home page" as part of everyday life'. These entangled narratives on Pink's Facebook page are also woven into a more complex, extensive mesh-work of movements, and some indication of that complexity is provided in the following account of her passing through a plurality of familiar environments, from place to place, in a way that she seems to experience as quite ordinary:

> Much of what people…do online is increasingly multi-platform, and engages different platforms simultaneously as…for example…where blogs, twitter…and…Facebook…may be synchronised…. Yet it is not only in the online context where we find this multiplicity, but also in the technologies through which it interfaces with our everyday lives. I browse Facebook on the iPad as I sit on the sofa, use my laptop for more keyboard-related activities and then…connect to the public Wi-Fi system to click on a link through my iPhone when I arrive at the municipal library. (Pink, 2012, p. 131)

Her personal account of routine domestic and local-neighbourhood practices serves to document a small fragment of a life 'lived along lines' (Ingold, 2011, p. 4). In this instance, these are on-screen storylines stitched together by the trails of browsing eyes and fingers, and accompanied by the paths and pauses of wandering feet.

Admittedly, Pink's account is of rather mundane quotidian activities, performed partly on a household sofa and later in a public library, and involving the sort of new media technologies and settings that have become a taken-for-granted part of many people's everyday lives in what Ingold calls modern metropolitan societies. However, as I put it in my introductory chapter, and as I have sought to demonstrate throughout this book, it is often the most ordinary features of life (its ongoing practical accomplishments) that turn out to be important for the basic ordering and reproduction of the social. Skilfully moving around and negotiating environments, and thereby constituting place by making oneself at home in everyday worlds (*gaining a grasp* of those worlds, to repeat Dreyfus's helpful metaphor of manual activity), must be central concerns for any future programme of everyday-life studies.

So my preferred take on doing everyday-life studies, like the distinctive version of non-media-centric media studies that I have gradually come to develop over the years, would be informed largely by phenomenological and non-representational approaches. It would proceed from an assertion of the primacy of practice or movement, attending to the sensuous, alongly integrated knowledges of inhabitants. While taking seriously a variety of 'articulated gestures' (Sudnow, 2001, p. xix) in day-to-day living, it would vigorously challenge ideas about the primacy of language or the symbolic, such as those which have had an influence on media studies for far too long. *Which of my readers might now be interested in working towards the institutional establishment of this kind of interdisciplinary area?*

Notes

1. I make absolutely no claims for this being the most efficient way of accessing my email! Rather, it is a description of what I have ordinarily and habitually done (that is, until very recently, when a technician at the university set up my laptop so that the staff email login page is now automatically my first online destination).
2. References to this book which follow here are made specifically to the 'rewritten account' (Sudnow, 2001). Earlier versions, with a different subtitle, were published in 1978 and 1993.
3. It is important to note that David Sudnow (2001, p. 130) cites Maurice Merleau-Ponty's phenomenology of perception (Merleau-Ponty, 2002 [1962]) as a key 'source of...inspiration' for his study of piano playing, commenting that a copy of this philosopher's classic book 'always remains close at hand'.
4. Two other contemporaries of Sudnow's in the discipline of sociology also had an influence on his work (indeed, both were known by Harvey Sacks too, and each had a distinctive interest in the practical accomplishment of order). Erving Goffman had been Sudnow's PhD supervisor: 'Erving first showed me what mundane sociological detail could be' (Sudnow, 2001, p. 132). As I mentioned in this book's preceding chapter, Goffman (1983) developed a sociology of what he named the interaction order. Harold Garfinkel, meanwhile, had a less formal 'personal association' with Sudnow (2001, pp. 131–132), who reports that 'my initial thoughts about ways to study music were influenced by our conversations'. Garfinkel (1984 [1967], p. 11), in defining his own term 'ethnomethodology', saw this approach as an investigation of 'contingent ongoing accomplishments' and of the 'organized artful practices of everyday life'.
5. In fact, a book of this sort already exists and it was written many years ago by Sudnow (1983) himself. There, he gives a remarkable account of his learning how to play video games on early computers (adding to his previous observations on ways of the hand). For example, he writes enthusiastically of how the 'sequencing...potentials of human hands now create sights...these fingers...have a territory for action whose potentials...are electronically enhanced' (Sudnow, 1983, pp. 22–24).
6. For a much fuller consideration of notions of musical motion, which appears in the context of a valuable discussion of how bodies generate meanings in their encounters with worlds, see the penultimate chapter of a book by phenomenologically inspired philosopher Mark Johnson (2007).
7. Elsewhere, with reference to his own experience of having become a proficient cellist, Tim Ingold (2000, pp. 415–416) remarks on how a 'skilled practitioner...is able continually to attune his movements to perturbations in the perceived environment without ever interrupting the flow of action', and he goes on to insist that acquiring skills is not 'an internalisation of collective representations' but an understanding 'in practice...a process...in which learning is inseparable from doing'. Such a view of bodily responsiveness to environments and of learning-through-doing could equally be applied to Sudnow's playing, either of jazz on the piano or games on the computer.
8. As discussed in the chapter before last, walking has been an important theme in Ingold's research and writing (see, for example, Ingold, 2004; Lee & Ingold, 2006).

9. In the preceding chapter, David Morley was (rightly) critical of Marshall McLuhan's technological determinism. However, I believe that McLuhan's work still contains valuable insights, including this particular perspective on technologies as 'extensions of man' (McLuhan, 1994 [1964]), which is not too distant from Merleau-Ponty's view of tools or instruments as bodily auxiliaries.

10. Having marked out my laptop computer from Ingold's handsaw in this manner, though, I must admit that distinguishing the laptop from Sudnow's piano is rather less straightforward. Jazz improvisation does involve the continual coming-into-being of a complex musical environment, precisely through the combined forces of human (knowledgeable hands) and non-human (piano) agencies, and such an acoustic setting is potentially available to audiences, whether those listeners would be physically co-present with the player and instrument or hearing the sounds later by means of electronic or digital reproduction. Clearly, record or CD players have been defined in the past as media of communication, but maybe musical instruments themselves might be approached as media technologies of a sort?

References

Connerton, P. (1989), *How Societies Remember*, Cambridge: Cambridge University Press.

Cranny-Francis, A. (2013), *Technology and Touch: The Biopolitics of Emerging Technologies*, Basingstoke: Palgrave Macmillan.

Dreyfus, H. (2001), 'Foreword', in Sudnow, D., *Ways of the Hand: A Rewritten Account*, Cambridge, MA: MIT Press.

Ehn, B. & Löfgren, O. (2010), *The Secret World of Doing Nothing*, Berkeley, CA: University of California Press.

Garfinkel, H. (1984 [1967]), *Studies in Ethnomethodology*, Cambridge: Polity.

Goffman, E. (1983), 'The Interaction Order', *American Sociological Review*, vol. 48, no. 1, pp. 1–17.

Highmore, B. (2011), *Ordinary Lives: Studies in the Everyday*, London: Routledge.

Ingold, T. (2000), *The Perception of the Environment: Essays on Livelihood, Dwelling and Skill*, London: Routledge.

Ingold, T. (2004), 'Culture on the Ground: The World Perceived Through the Feet', *Journal of Material Culture*, vol. 9, no. 3, pp. 315–340.

Ingold, T. (2007), *Lines: A Brief History*, London: Routledge.

Ingold, T. (2011), *Being Alive: Essays on Movement, Knowledge and Description*, London: Routledge.

Ingold, T. (2015), *The Life of Lines*, London: Routledge.

Johnson, M. (2007), *The Meaning of the Body: Aesthetics of Human Understanding*, Chicago, IL: University of Chicago Press.

Krajina, Z., Moores, S. & Morley, D. (2014), 'Non-Media-Centric Media Studies: A Cross-Generational Conversation', *European Journal of Cultural Studies*, vol. 17, no. 6, pp. 682–700.

Lee, J. & Ingold, T. (2006), 'Fieldwork on Foot: Perceiving, Routing, Socializing', in Coleman, S. & Collins, P. (eds.) *Locating the Field: Space, Place and Context in Anthropology*, Oxford: Berg.

McLuhan, M. (1994 [1964]), *Understanding Media: The Extensions of Man*, Cambridge, MA: MIT Press.

Merleau-Ponty, M. (2002 [1962]), *Phenomenology of Perception*, London: Routledge.

Moores, S. (2012), *Media, Place and Mobility*, Basingstoke: Palgrave Macmillan.

Moores, S. (2017), 'For Everyday-Life Studies', in Adams, P., Cupples, J., Glynn, K., Jansson, A. & Moores, S., *Communications/Media/Geographies*, New York: Routledge.

Morley, D. (2007), *Media, Modernity and Technology: The Geography of the New*, London: Routledge.

Nunes, M. (2006), *Cyberspaces of Everyday Life*, Minneapolis, MN: University of Minnesota Press.

Paterson, M. (2007), *The Senses of Touch: Haptics, Affects and Technologies*, Oxford: Berg.

Pink, S. (2009), *Doing Sensory Ethnography*, London: Sage.

Pink, S. (2012), *Situating Everyday Life: Practices and Places*, London: Sage.

Pink, S. & Leder Mackley, K. (2013), 'Saturated and Situated: Expanding the Meaning of Media in the Routines of Everyday Life', *Media, Culture and Society*, vol. 35, no. 6, pp. 677–691.

Pink, S., Sinanan, J., Hjorth, L. & Horst, H. (2016), 'Tactile Digital Ethnography: Researching Mobile Media Through the Hand', *Mobile Media and Communication*, vol. 4, no. 2, pp. 237–251.

Richardson, I. (2008), 'Pocket Technospaces: The Bodily Incorporation of Mobile Media', in Goggin, G. (ed.) *Mobile Phone Cultures*, London: Routledge.

Richardson, I. & Wilken, R. (2012), 'Parerga of the Third Screen: Mobile Media, Place and Presence', in Wilken, R. & Goggin, G. (eds.) *Mobile Technology and Place*, New York: Routledge.

Sacks, H. (1995), *Lectures on Conversation*, Oxford: Blackwell.

Sudnow, D. (1983), *Pilgrim in the Microworld*, New York: Warner Books.

Sudnow, D. (2001), *Ways of the Hand: A Rewritten Account*, Cambridge, MA: MIT Press.

Thrift, N. (2007), *Non-Representational Theory: Space/Politics/Affect*, London: Routledge.

Tomlinson, J. (2007), *The Culture of Speed: The Coming of Immediacy*, London: Sage.

ABOUT THE AUTHOR

Shaun Moores is Professor of Media and Communications at the Centre for Research in Media and Cultural Studies, University of Sunderland, England, and has been a visiting or associate professor at universities in Italy, Germany and Australia. He is the author of *Interpreting Audiences: The Ethnography of Media Consumption* (1993), *Satellite Television and Everyday Life: Articulating Technology* (1996), *Media and Everyday Life in Modern Society* (2000), *Media/Theory: Thinking about Media and Communications* (2005) and *Media, Place and Mobility* (2012), and a co-author of *Communications/Media/Geographies* (2017). His co-edited books are *The Politics of Domestic Consumption: Critical Readings* (1995) and *Connectivity, Networks and Flows: Conceptualizing Contemporary Communications* (2008), and previous publications also include many articles and chapters in academic journals and edited collections in media, communication and cultural studies.

INDEX

Digital Formations

General Editor: **Steve Jones**

Digital Formations is the best source for critical, well-written books about digital technologies and modern life. Books in the series break new ground by emphasizing multiple methodological and theoretical approaches to deeply probe the formation and reformation of lived experience as it is refracted through digital interaction. Each volume in **Digital Formations** pushes forward our understanding of the intersections, and corresponding implications, between digital technologies and everyday life. The series examines broad issues in realms such as digital culture, electronic commerce, law, politics and governance, gender, the Internet, race, art, health and medicine, and education. The series emphasizes critical studies in the context of emergent and existing digital technologies.

Other recent titles include:

Felicia Wu Song
  Virtual Communities: Bowling Alone, Online Together

Edited by Sharon Kleinman
  The Culture of Efficiency: Technology in Everyday Life

Edward Lee Lamoureux, Steven L. Baron, & Claire Stewart
  Intellectual Property Law and Interactive Media: Free for a Fee

Edited by Adrienne Russell & Nabil Echchaibi
  International Blogging: Identity, Politics and Networked Publics

Edited by Don Heider
  Living Virtually: Researching New Worlds

Edited by Judith Burnett, Peter Senker & Kathy Walker
  The Myths of Technology: Innovation and Inequality

Edited by Knut Lundby
  Digital Storytelling, Mediatized Stories: Self-representations in New Media

Theresa M. Senft
  Camgirls: Celebrity and Community in the Age of Social Networks

Edited by Chris Paterson & David Domingo
  Making Online News: The Ethnography of New Media Production

To order other books in this series please contact our Customer Service Department:
  (800) 770-LANG (within the US)
  (212) 647-7706 (outside the US)
  (212) 647-7707 FAX

To find out more about the series or browse a full list of titles, please visit our website:
  WWW.PETERLANG.COM